CURRENT CRITICAL DEBATES IN THE FIELD OF TRANSSEXUAL STUDIES

Current Critical Debates in the Field of Transsexual Studies introduces new thinking on non-conforming gender representation, addressing transsexuality as a subjective experience that highlights universal dilemmas related to how we conceive identity and exploring universal questions related to gender: its objects, objections, and obstacles. This book seeks to disassemble prejudicial orientations to the challenges and the everydayness of transsexuality and build new understanding and responses to issues including: medical biases, the problem of authenticity, and the agency of the child.

Oren Gozlen leads an examination of three central pressures: transformation of a medical model, the social experience of becoming transgender, and the question of self-representation through popular culture. The chapters reframe several contemporary dilemmas, such as: authenticity, pathology, normativity, creativity, the place of the clinic as a problem of authority, the unpredictability of sexuality, the struggle with limits of knowledge, a demand for intelligibility, and desire for certainty. The contributors consider sociocultural, theoretical, therapeutic, and legal approaches to transsexuality that reveal its inherent instability and fluidity both as concept and as experience. They place transsexuality in tension and transition as a concept, as a subject position, and as a subjectivity.

The book also reflects the way in which political and cultural change affects self and other representations of the transsexual person and their others, asking: how does the subject metabolize the anxieties that relate to these transformations and facilitations? How can the subject respond in contexts of hostility and prohibition? Offering a much-needed interdisciplinary exploration, *Current Critical Debates in the Field of Transsexual Studies* will appeal to psychoanalysts and psychotherapists as well as psychologists and scholars of gender studies, cultural studies and sociology.

Oren Gozlan, PsyD, ABPP, is a clinical psychologist and a psychoanalyst in private practice in Toronto, Canada, and the Gender and Diversity Committee (IPA) Representative for North America, International Psychoanalytical Studies Organization (IPSO). He is a faculty member at the Toronto Institute of Contemporary Psychoanalysis. His book *Transsexuality and the Art of Transitioning: A Lacanian Approach* won the American Academy & Board of Psychoanalysis' annual book prize for books published in 2015.

CURRENT CRITICAL DEBATES IN THE FIELD OF TRANSSEXUAL STUDIES

In Transition

Edited by Oren Gozlan

LONDON AND NEW YORK

First published 2018
by Routledge
2 Park Square, Milton Park, Abingdon, Oxon OX14 4RN

and by Routledge
711 Third Avenue, New York, NY 10017

Routledge is an imprint of the Taylor & Francis Group, an informa business

© 2018 selection and editorial matter, Oren Gozlan; individual chapters, the contributors

The right of the editor to be identified as the author of the editorial material, and of the authors for their individual chapters, has been asserted in accordance with sections 77 and 78 of the Copyright, Designs and Patents Act 1988.

All rights reserved. No part of this book may be reprinted or reproduced or utilized in any form or by any electronic, mechanical, or other means, now known or hereafter invented, including photocopying and recording, or in any information storage or retrieval system, without permission in writing from the publishers.

Trademark notice: Product or corporate names may be trademarks or registered trademarks, and are used only for identification and explanation without intent to infringe.

British Library Cataloguing in Publication Data
A catalogue record for this book is available from the British Library

Library of Congress Cataloging in Publication Data
Title: Current Critical Debates in the Field of Transsexual Studies
ISBN: 9781138481305 was successfully transmitted to the Library of Congress.
Library of Congress Cataloging-in-Publication Data
Names: Gozlan, Oren, editor.
Title: Current critical debates in the field of transsexual studies : in transition / edited by Oren Gozlan.
Description: Abingdon, Oxon ; New York, NY : Routledge, 2018. | Includes bibliographical references and index.
Identifiers: LCCN 2017054545 (print) | LCCN 2017057828 (ebook) | ISBN 9781351058995 (Master) | ISBN 9781351058988 (Web PDF) | ISBN 9781351058971 (ePub) | ISBN 9781351058964 (Mobipocket/Kindle) | ISBN 9781138481305 (hardback : alk. paper) | ISBN 9781138481312 (pbk. : alk. paper)
Subjects: LCSH: Transsexualism. | Gender nonconformity. | Gender identity.Classification: LCC HQ77.9 (ebook) | LCC HQ77.9. C874 2018 (print) | DDC 305.3—dc23
LC record available at https://lccn.loc.gov/2017054545

ISBN: 978-1-138-48130-5 (hbk)
ISBN: 978-1-138-48131-2 (pbk)
ISBN: 978-1-351-05899-5 (ebk)

Typeset in Bembo
by Keystroke, Neville Lodge, Tettenhall, Wolverhampton

CONTENTS

Acknowledgments ix
About the editor and contributors xi

Introduction 1
Oren Gozlan

PART I
Aesthetic tensions 13

1 Revisiting the Friends of the Place Blanche: the transgender
  imaginary through the photographs of Christer Strömholm 15
  David Dorenbaum

2 The two sleeps of Orlando: transsexuality as caesura or cut 36
  Dana Amir

3 Gender transitions and aesthetic possibilities 48
  Dina Georgis

4 Taking (my) time: temporality in transition, queer delays,
  and being (in the) present 59
  Atalia Israeli-Nevo

PART II
Diagnostic phantasies in the (failed) quest for authenticity — 73

5 Psychoanalysis needs a sex change — 75
   Patricia Gherovici

6 Principles for psychoanalytic work with trans clients — 89
   Sheila L. Cavanagh

7 Realities and myths: the gender affirmative model of care for children and youth — 102
   Diane Ehrensaft

8 Transition and childhood: questioning the medical approaches — 115
   Erik Schneider

9 Golden ticket therapy: stigma management among trans men — 131
   Elroi J. Windsor

10 Borders of belonging: challenges in access to anti-oppressive mental healthcare for Indigenous Latino gender-fluid youth — 145
    Silvia Tenenbaum

11 Transgenderism in Iran — 158
    Mehrdad Eftekhar Ardebili

PART III
Cultural montage — 167

12 To return to Schreber: trans literatures as psychoanalysis — 169
    Trish Salah

13 Wronging the right-body narrative: on the universality of gender uncertainty — 181
    Laine Hughes

14 Biopower and the medicalization of gender variance: a Foucauldian analysis of trans subjectivity 194
Kinnon Ross MacKinnon

15 The professional recourse to the adolescent body: the bathroom wars and the limit of thinking in education 208
Aziz Guzel

Index *221*

ACKNOWLEDGMENTS

There are many people who made this project possible. I owe a debt of gratitude to Routledge editor Susannah Frearson, who approached me with the idea of an edited collection, as well as to Routledge editors Kate Hawes and Charles Bath for their assistance and accommodations throughout the project. My ongoing conversations with distinguished professor Deborah Britzman over the years have provided intellectual stimulus. Her name comes up in a number of chapters as her work often bears on the subject of this collection. I owe a debt of gratitude to Dr. Paola Bohorquez, in whose thoughts and invaluable suggestions I find inspiration. I also would like to thank my chief research assistant Vanessa Sluman, as well as Aziz Guzel, for their resourcefulness and tireless help. A special thanks goes to Dr. David Dorenbaum for his support and assistance in obtaining the photographs of Christer Strömholm and much gratitude to Joakim Strömholm for permitting me to include his father's marvelous photos in the collection. Finally, my love and gratitude goes to my wife for her suggestions, editorial assistance, and unwavering support.

ABOUT THE EDITOR AND CONTRIBUTORS

Dana Amir is a clinical psychologist, supervising and training analyst at the Israel psychoanalytic society, faculty member and the head of the interdisciplinary doctoral program in psychoanalysis at Haifa University, poetess, and literature researcher. She is the author of six poetry books and three psychoanalytic books, and the winner of many grants and awards, including four international psychoanalytic prizes.

Mehrdad Eftekhar Ardebili is an associate professor of psychiatry at Iran University of Medical Sciences. He has been working with transsexuals seeking reassignment surgery for several years. He is leading a research team working on transgenderism at the Mental Health Research Center, IUMS,

Sheila L. Cavanagh is an Associate Professor at York University, co-editor of *Somatechnics* journal and outgoing chair of the Canadian Sexuality Studies Association. She edited a special double issue on psychoanalysis in *Transgender Studies Quarterly* (2017) and co-edited *Skin, Culture and Psychoanalysis* (2013). Cavanagh wrote *Queering Bathrooms* (2010) and *Sexing the Teacher* (2007), and is completing a third book on transgender and psychoanalysis.

David Dorenbaum graduated in Medicine with Honorary Mention from the National Autonomous University of Mexico (UNAM), Mexico City. He holds specialties both in Pediatrics (University of Western Ontario/University of Ottawa) and in Psychiatry (University of Toronto), and a postgraduate Diploma in Child and Adolescent Psychiatry (University of Toronto). He completed his psychoanalytic training at the Toronto branch of the Canadian Psychoanalytic Institute. He is the former director of a day program for adolescents with psychotic disorders at the Hospital for Sick Children, Toronto, Ontario. In conjunction with his private practice, he is involved in supervising psychiatrists in training at the University of

Toronto. In addition, he has participated in multiple transdisciplinary projects in the field of the arts. By invitation, he has taught with Gordon Peteran in the Department of Industrial Design at the Ontario College of Art and Design (OCAD).

Diane Ehrensaft, PhD, is associate professor of Pediatrics at University of California San Francisco, and Director of Mental Health, Child and Adolescent Gender Center. She specializes in research, clinical work, and consultation related to gender expansive children. She is author of *The Gender Creative Child, Gender Born, Gender Made* and *The Gender Affirmative Model* (co-edited with Colt Keo-Meier, in press).

Dina Georgis is an Associate Professor at the Women & Gender Studies Institute at the University of Toronto. Her work is situated in the fields of postcolonial studies, queer theory, and psychoanalysis. She teaches and writes on Arab sexualities, aesthetic production, memory and affect, and war and culture.

Patricia Gherovici, PhD, is a psychoanalyst and analytic supervisor. She is co-founder and director of the Philadelphia Lacan Group and Associate Faculty, Psychoanalytic Studies Minor, University of Pennsylvania (PSYS), Honorary Member at IPTAR the Institute for Psychoanalytic Training and Research in New York City, and Member at Apres-Coup Psychoanalytic Association New York. Her books include *The Puerto Rican Syndrome* (Other Press, 2003), winner of the Gradiva Award and the Boyer Prize, and *Please Select Your Gender: From the Invention of Hysteria to the Democratizing of Transgenderism* (Routledge, 2010). She has published two edited collections (both with Manya Steinkoler), *Lacan on Madness: Madness, Yes You Can't* (Routledge, 2015) and *Lacan, Psychoanalysis and Comedy* (Cambridge University Press, 2016). Her latest book *Transgender Psychoanalysis: A Lacanian Perspective on Sexual Difference* was published by Routledge in June 2017.

Oren Gozlan, PsyD, ABPP, is a clinical psychologist and a psychoanalyst in private practice in Toronto, Canada, and the Gender and Diversity Committee (IPA) Representative for North America, International Psychoanalytical Studies Organization (IPSO). He is a faculty member at the Toronto Institute of Contemporary Psychoanalysis. His book *Transsexuality and the Art of Transitioning: A Lacanian Approach* won the American Academy & Board of Psychoanalysis's annual book prize for books published in 2015.

Aziz Guzel is a doctoral candidate in the Faculty of Education at York University. He has worked as a psychological counselor in student counselling. His work examines the question of care in the uses of the medical discourse in adolescent education.

Laine Hughes is a PhD candidate in Gender, Feminist and Women's Studies at York University. His doctoral research takes up a psychoanalytical approach to transgender identifications, and focuses on the intersection of mental health and surgico-hormonal intervention. He has received the support of the Social Sciences and Humanities Research Council of Canada, and the Ontario Graduate Scholarship.

Atalia Israeli-Nevo is a graduate student in the Department of Sociology and Anthropology at Ben-Gurion University of the Negev. Her main fields of interest are BDSM, transsexuality, queer temporality, and necropolitics. She is currently writing her thesis on cisgender identity, and has previously published in *Somatechnics*. She is a performance artist, among the coordinators of the Queer Reading Group at the university, a member of Project Gila—a trans grassroots organization for trans people in Israel/Palestine. She works at Zochrot, an NGO dedicated to commemorate the Nakba and develop ways to implement the Palestinian right of return.

Kinnon Ross MacKinnon is pursuing a PhD in public health at the University of Toronto, where he is also a member of the Re:Searching for LGBTQ Health group. Kinnon's program of research considers health equity issues for sexual and gender minority populations, while his specific doctoral research project investigates transgender persons' interactions with the mental healthcare system. He holds a Bachelor of Arts from Saint Mary's University (gender studies and history); a Bachelor of Social Work from York University (honors); and a Master of Social Work from Ryerson University. Kinnon integrates health equity advocacy with his passion for sport and physical activity. Influenced by unique triumphs as a gold-medal transgender powerlifter, he volunteers his time as a coach with Special Olympics and acts as the Canadian director of an international LGBTQ powerlifting federation. He was named a 'Sports Hero' by the 2015 INSPIRE awards.

Trish Salah is a poet and assistant professor of Gender Studies at Queen's University. Her books are *Wanting in Arabic*, and *Lyric Sexology: Vol. 1*, and she is co-editor of special issues of the *Canadian Review of American Studies* and *TSQ: Transgender Studies Quarterly*. At the University of Winnipeg she organized the conference Writing Trans Genres: Emergent Literatures and Criticism, and the symposium Decolonizing and Decriminalizing Trans Genres.

Erik Schneider, MD, is a psychiatrist and psychotherapist and works on a freelance basis in the fields of medicine, law, educational sciences, and ethics. The main focus of his work includes critique of definitions and categories, gender binary and variability, dynamics and power relationships between medicine, in particular psychiatry, and law and educational science. He is co-founder of the association Intersex & Transgender Luxembourg.

Silvia Tenenbaum is a registered clinical psychologist in the province of Ontario, providing therapy, training and supervision to a team of incoming mental health workers under her own practice (drsilviatenenbaum.com), as well as teaching at several post-secondary institutions in Canada. Silvia has been working with youth since her own youth in Montevideo, and under military dictatorship.

Elroi J. Windsor is an Assistant Professor of Sociology at Salem College in Winston-Salem, North Carolina, and the Chair of the Department of Sociology and Criminal Studies. Windsor's research focuses on gender and embodiment within healthcare institutions. Currently, Windsor is working on book based on an ethnographic study of healthcare professionals who work with body parts and dead bodies.

INTRODUCTION

Oren Gozlan

Is the field of Trans Studies at a crossroads? Many of the authors in this collection argue that it is. Recent developments in the emerging field of Trans Studies suggest that, just as queer theory did twenty years ago, trans scholarship has the potential to produce significant intellectual and political impact on the ways in which we conceive of gender embodiment, sexuality, and identity. As an interdisciplinary field, Trans Studies crosses conventional knowledge boundaries as it engages the conceptual, historical, sociocultural, and political dimensions of transgender living. In addition, a burgeoning collection of gender-queer fiction available for various audiences, including children and young adults (e.g. *Luna* by Ann Peters [2004], *Drew* by T. Cooper and Allison Glock-Cooper [2014], *I am J* by Cris Beam [2011]), as well as memoirs and testimonies (e.g. Janet Mock [2017], Caitlyn Jenner [2017]) that narrate in the first person stories of gender-becoming, have contributed to this landscape of vigorous intellectual production. Among contemporary lively discussions in the field is Susan Stryker and Stephen Whittle's *Transgender Reader* (2013), which is key in mapping the geography of voices and experiences of transitioning with the attempt at making a case for variety and plurality of experiences in gender. With this collection, we want to intervene in the emerging conversation and advance the debate beyond the issues of rights, access, and equity, as well as to explore the ways in which transsexual narratives and discourses may overcome the deadlocks of identity politics. Yet, how does one approach a signifier that is unruly?

The term that gives name to this collection – transsexuality – is a contentious signifier, and as the collection makes clear, debates over terminology have been foundational in the field. Readers will see that throughout the collection the terms trans, transsexuality, transgender, gender-non-conforming, and so on are used either interchangeably or chosen explicitly to make a point about the implications, both theoretical and political, of certain choice of terms. These terms, however, are unstable, and different author conceive of them differently. Some emphasize the problem of legibility and representation and use the term "transgender" to examine the shifting social and political discourses around non-conforming gender identities. Others use the term "transsexuality" to emphasize the fluid, incomplete, and in-process qualities of gender identity by emphasizing its inseparability from sexuality and its constitutive opaqueness. Still others radically reject the term transsexuality, which they see as inevitably marred by the pathologizing discourse of psychiatry.

The field of Trans Studies draws upon a discursive history that has framed how we experience, understand, and represent transsexuality. The term "transsexuality" has a long history, beginning with Magnus Hirschfeld, a German physician and sexologist, who introduced the term "Transsexualismus" in 1923 to refer to individuals wishing to become members of the sex to which they do not belong. David Oliver Coldwell was the first author to use the term in reference to individuals desiring physical sex change, and the first as well to introduce the term to English usage. The term was then disseminated by Harry Benjamin and entered the Diagnostic and Statistical Manual of Mental Disorders (DSM) in 1980 as a psychological disorder. More recently, the term "transsexual" has been subsumed under the umbrella designation "transgender" as a concept describing a sense of discordance between one's gender expression and assigned gender at birth, and it includes individuals who do not wish to undergo physical transition. The term transsexual has been rejected by those who see gender identity to be the loci of transitioning and view identity as separate from sexuality. Likewise, the term "transgender" has been rejected by some individuals who have undergone physical transitioning and view their transition as a process of aligning their bodies with consistently experienced gender identity.

The controversies around terminology reveal the shifting ways of understanding the relations between sexuality and identity, gender and politics. Like every other social movement, transsexual activism is a highly politicized movement, and it is rightly preoccupied with the nature of naming itself. There are two main problems associated with the term "transsexuality": first that the term is burdened with the history of medical pathologization of gender non-conformance, and second that some see the term as problematically compromised by dichotomous gender thinking, and therefore resistant to the deconstructive effort to overcome the binary.

Many activists have claimed that the term "transsexual" cannot be rescued from its earliest history. The opposition to the term is grounded in the argument that what transitions is not sex – a biological marker – but gender identity, assumed to be linked to psychological traits and social roles. Christin Jorgensen, for instance, publicly rejected the term transsexual in 1979 and identified herself in newsprint as transgender: "gender doesn't have to do with bed partners, it has to do with identity". One could argue, however, that this understanding of sexuality as merely concerned with object choice – dichotomously understood, by the way – pre-emptively annuls the very important question of the relation between identity and sexuality.

Gender, on the other hand, seems, for some, to offer an escape hatch from the impasse of biology, although it is a loophole that generates a new dilemma insofar as it could potentially limit identity to its social manifestations and become tied to rigid notions of femininity and masculinity that circumvent the complexities of gender identification. Some (Valentine, 2007) believe that although the term "transgender", as used by activists, has an inclusive quality, many non-gender conforming people do not necessarily identify with the term.

At the heart of the tension between the terms transsexual and transgender, I would suggest, lies a question that is continually raised but to which we can seldom give a consistent answer: when we talk about transitioning, are we talking about sexuality or are we talking about gender? Every term carries a history, intervenes in, and points to particular constellations of meaning. The question is whether we are able to use terms in ways that contest old and rigid imaginaries, potentiate new forms of thinking, and challenge gender normativity.

I have chosen to keep to the term transsexuality for the title of this collection for several reasons. I conceive of the notion of *sexuality* not in biological terms (e.g. sex), but rather in agreement with psychoanalytic thinking about the drives and their representation through phantasy. There is a collapse, I suggest, between sexuality and sex in the opposition to the term transsexuality. Along psychoanalytic lines, however, sexuality does not equate with physical sex, and in fact, largely exceeds the problem of sexual difference or object choice. It is rather conceived as a drive for life and death – a fort-da movement that signifies a constant psychic tension that refuses stability. As such, the term transsexuality carries within it the effervescing and unpredictable force of sexuality which is a source of both angst and creativity and which can never be subdued nor subsumed under any identity form or subject position, no matter how radical or subversive. It signifies an in-process, in-between, and ephemeral subjective position that engages gender in the ways in which we understand and transform ourselves. Under the term transsexuality, therefore, this collection investigates both the creative openness of new gender formations as well as their defensive manifestations; it examines critically the use of the polysemic and ambivalent term "transsexuality" as a signifier that, on the one hand, promises cohesion and legibility, and, on the other, connotes the capacity to play and to live creatively in the interstices between what is found and what is created in gendering processes (Winnicott, 1971). So approached, this collection mines the heuristic potential of transsexuality to engage the larger question of the relation between sexuality and identity.

The problem of sexual difference is, for obvious reasons, of paramount importance in the field of Trans Studies in general and in this collection in particular. A number of psychoanalysts, myself included, have challenged binary gender oppositions (Gozlan, 2008, 2011, 2015; Glocer Fiorini, 2017; Gherovici, 2017 among others) that lean on the symbolic oppositions between phallic/castrated, masculine/feminine, and absence/presence. Much of this work has as its backdrop clinical formulations which have laid the ground for new theoretical formulations. I offered, for instance, the case of Aron, a post-surgery F to M patient, to argue that transsexuality offers a way of challenging the conceptualization of gender as tied to biological origin as "the body moves from being a historical entity determined by an originary point to a body that incurs its history through a re-creation, a body, that is, that comes to terms with the instability of its own archive" (Gozlan, 2015, p. 5). I have used the case of Aron to argue for a psychoanalytic conceptualization of difference not tied to a phallic opposition between having and not having (a penis) but understood rather as an irreducible tension that requires a symbolic link with inherent otherness through a personal narrative that becomes engendered, retroactively. As Glocer Fiorini (2017) argues, "Equating castration with a category of absence is a construction responding to a very precise logic and narrative and does not constitute an a priori truth" (p. 142). Conceptualizing sexual difference in terms of femininity and masculinity as a strict dichotomy creates "universal axioms . . . thereby disavowing the singularity of desire and identification, and ignoring the enormous complexity of processes of construction of sexed subjectivity" (p. 140). There is something about sexual difference that leans disturbingly on the objective contrast between sexed bodies, but such difference is not determined by the genitals, as Freud has insisted: sexual difference is a psychic conundrum whose imaginary and symbolic meanings and implications cannot be exhausted by the factuality of genital difference.

There is a fetishization of gender, I suggest, that is played out both in essentialist transsexual narratives, and in dominant medical and psychological theorizations. Both discourses attempt to secure the meaning of transsexuality through the politics of identity that essentializes difference and transforms the many manifestations of gender non-conformance into self-contained identities. Studies of transsexuality often reflect a latent wish for stability and certainty manifested in the pinning down of categories of normative sexual development or in the medicalization of transsexuality; while in multiple medical and psychological approaches, transsexuality continues to be viewed as pathology, a failure to mourn sexual difference, or as a violation of nature. In these discourses, the ideality of gender is animated by a fantasy of certitude. The proliferation of modes of representation and naming both opens and forecloses our experience of gender and sexuality, where categories may provide options for representation or, conversely, create notions of selfhood as claustrum (Meltzer, 1992) which strive for absolute recognition through the exclusion of what is other to it. What is forgotten in this search for certainty is that our understanding of gendered sexuality is fraught with anxieties and laden with unconscious meanings related to presence and absence (e.g. of genital organs), love and hate, intelligibility and confusion that repeat older and forgotten vicissitudes in the history our own gender identifications.

As the field of Trans Studies is itself transitioning, the emancipatory potential of new understandings of transsexuality has yet to be actualized. Indeed, whereas the notion of transitioning has traditionally been seen as an either–or question, what is now being put into question is the notion of gender itself. As gay and lesbian theories have successfully denounced heteronormativity and stabilized the notion that object choice is independent of gender, transsexual discourses are deconstructing cisgenderism as the hegemonic and, therefore, invisible ideology of sexual difference, putting into question the male/female dichotomy. And yet, essentialist tropes of origin continue to stubbornly permeate both cisgender and trans accounts: in the first, through recourse to biological and naturalistic understandings of sexual/gender identity; in the second, through the belief in a "true gender core" hidden under layers of facade, or through narratives of being trapped in the wrong body. Whereas the former signals a refusal of the renewed categories brought forth by the gender revolution, the latter betrays a holding on to uncritically assumed notions of authenticity and identity. These narratives may work in political contexts to advance or secure equity demands, effectively functioning as forms of "strategic essentialism" (Spivak, in Morton, 2003, p. 75). I would argue that claims to authenticity may limit our understanding of the potential of trans thinking and scholarship to combat the assumed marginality of non-conforming trans identities and subjectivities.

The contributions in this collection suggest that transsexuality is a field traversed by political, ethical, and affective tensions, and, therefore, that the ways in which discourses around transsexuality mirror remain trapped, or become complicit with cisgender and heteronormative hegemonic discourses and practices, as well as with biomedical ideologies, require critical self-reflection. Rather than claim neutral objectivity, the contributors engage explicitly with the problematic meanings and implications embedded in the very terms we use to make sense of the experience and concept of transsexuality, compelling us to consider how "the new" emerges as we work through the force of historically sedimented repressions, disavowals, forgettings, and repetitions. In this sense, this book is simultaneously a collection of a record – of a broken record – and an attempt at breaking the record.

Over the last hundred years and as medico-technological advances have made it possible for individuals to radically reshape their gendered body, transsexual choices have raised critical and urgent moral and epistemological questions: Does one have the right to change one's gendered body? What are the psychic potentials, challenges, and limits of such transformation? How are body and gender related? What is gender anyway? While these questions are constitutive of the scene of transsexuality, they interpellate us all, compelling us to consider anew the potential and limitations of self-transformation *vis-à-vis* the symbolic arrangements and imaginary registers that govern our intersubjective entanglements – always already traversed by gender.

The collection considers sociocultural, therapeutic, experiential, and literary approaches to the concept of transsexuality, as well as clinical, social, and legal case-analyses of the status of transsexuality in the field of mental health. It places in tension transsexuality as a concept, social identity, subject position, and subjectivity, and engages the cleavages and contradictions that emerge between these differing points of view. It reflects on the conflicting ways in which political and cultural change affects self- and other representations of the transsexual person in situated and shifting contexts, revealing its instability as both concept and experience.

Each chapter in this collection delineates a conceptual geography of questions, challenges, and paradoxes pertaining to the concept, experience, and social positioning of transsexuality. The contributions have been grouped around four grand themes addressing current transformations in medical and psychosocial models, the social experience of becoming transgender, the history of trans activism, and transsexual interpellations through popular culture.

The collection is not meant to impose a univocal point of view – the reader is invited to associate with, rather than feel instructed by, the various approaches to questions of diagnosis, psychotherapy, social identity, and activism, among others. Yet, the differing facets of the conversation will also confront the reader with the desire for integration and its inevitable frustration, which inheres in each discourse's inability to provide a complete understanding, a solution, or a cohesive set of coordinates through which to navigate the field. This undecidability effect is not only inevitable but desirable, as any premature foreclosure of the crucial and urgent questions raised in this collection can only stall thinking by returning us to the comforts of the illusion of understanding. The pedagogical value of this collection lies in its challenging univocal accounts of the concept of transsexuality and of the experience of gender transitioning, and in contributing to the de-literalization of gender. The following section describes the three overarching themes that give shape to this collection.

Aesthetic tensions

Anxious reactions to transsexuality, I suggest, enact an anxiety inherent to gender. We experience difficult knowledge and uncertainty as attacks that cause us to defensively stabilize our experience, killing our curiosity in the process, and resorting to concretization, diagnosis, and dismissal of what is Other. We have an inherent difficulty with ambiguity. We insist on knowing whether we are X or Y, and we cannot imagine not knowing the other. "There is an insistence on relying upon fixed and legible markers of identity that forecloses potential insight into our unconscious reality and the indelible remainder that escapes" (Gozlan, 2016). The ideality of identity as a stable category and the pathologizing of transsexuality reveal how all transformations – conceptual, psychical, or physical – require coming to terms with the confusion and ambivalence that follows once we decide to let go of safe and familiar coordinates. Idealization of observable "facts", empirical knowledge, or the authority of the DSM, which characterizes many approaches to transsexuality, translates into attempts to fend off questions around identification, avoid of painful conflicts between love and hate, and preserve culturally constructed understandings of sexual difference as given or natural.

Meltzer and Williams's notion of aesthetic conflict (1988) helps us to dislodge transsexuality from its saturated meaning, to imagine it as psychical experience, allowing us access to questions of truth, beauty, and knowledge, and the tensions between them, as traversed by sexuality (Gozlan, 2015). Meltzer approaches these questions in relation to the infant's encounter with the enigma of the maternal body, which is the grounds for curiosity as well as anxiety, and which calls forth a wish to possess the mother's body. Meltzer's conceptualization of the apprehension of beauty as an encounter with an unknown and the hesitation borne of the contradictory nature of affect captures the paradox of grasping and simultaneously being unsettled by the enigma of the other's body. As I have argued elsewhere, this paradox is also experienced in relation to the transsexual body, thus producing an ambivalent affective scenario (Gozlan, 2015, p. 5). Yet, the enigmatic qualities of sexuality, and the inadequacy of our imagination to make sense of it, threatens our sense of identity, self-cohesiveness, and legibility.

What will become evident to the reader are the ways in which the debates themselves are affected by the enigma of sexuality. The nature of sexuality both disrupts the social, and at the same time insists upon unity (as articulated through Freud's notion of Eros as both a raising of tension and a wish to cathect). The polymorphous unpredictability of sexuality structures identity, but at the same time, the domesticating effect of identity alienates us from the enigmatic qualities of sexuality. This insoluble paradox makes sexuality a great inconvenience that propels us to anxiously believe that we coincide with our own self-definitions. But sexuality is a drag.

Diagnostic phantasies in the (failed) quest for authenticity

The essays in this collection all attempt to disassemble prejudicial orientations to the everydayness of transsexual living by engaging the broader dilemmas of identity in transsexual narratives and in the clinic. While in some chapters the concept of authenticity is explicitly linked to the question of reality or truth, in others it signifies originality or the first move towards the universal need to feel cohesive. So why is authenticity such an incitement? Authenticity is both a legitimate claim and an impossibility because the body and our experience of embodiment is constantly changing. Yet, we cling to ideas of authenticity as that which is given, permanent, and cohesive, as that which guarantees the legitimacy of our identity claims: I always was and *will always had been* gender-coherent. This understanding of authenticity emerges more forcefully as our capacity to change and represent our bodies in manifold ways becomes enhanced.

Authenticity, therefore, is a sliding signifier – both a coveted fantasy and a charge against the transsexual subject viewed as a facsimile. But the issue of authenticity is also deeply entangled with the problem of recognition and legibility; in short, with how we are apprehended by the other. This is where the question of authenticity finds its proper intersubjective dimension, given that transsexual subjectification not only concerns the relationship with one's body but also with the Other – a relationship filled with psychical entanglements, with transferences and counter-transferences that actualize themselves through the complex and multifaceted process of transitioning. As debates over gendered washrooms and the agency of the gender non-conforming child reveal, the instability and constructed nature of our gender identifications compel us all to recognize the fragility of gender conceptions grounded on genital morphology or chromosomal make up.

Underlying the concept of "mental health" is an obvious concern over mental illness and we are reminded here of John Rickman's definition, as noted by Winnicott, that mental illness "consists in not being to find anyone who can stand you" (in Britzman, 2015, p. 102). Indeed, the dilemmas concerning gender, sexual difference, identity, and intelligibility are inherently linked with the Other and with the anxiety over whether an other will be able to accept and receive our peculiarities. The capacity to "stand oneself" is inextricably tied with finding others who can stand us – and stand up for us. Grappling with the challenges and dilemmas of transsexual subjectification involves the capacity to stand the unknowable nature of sexuality and the complexity of identification. We can never fully know the reasons for our reasons, including the reasons that support our identifications and desires.

Cultural montage

Social visibility of transsexuality has increased in the mid-twentieth century, where a number of cases involving reassignment surgeries has caught the public's attention, gradually raising awareness about the question of gender transitioning. But transsexuality is surely not a new phenomenon: its social history began to be documented in the 1930s and 1940s with individuals such as Lili Elba and Christine Jorgensen who challenged prevailing notions of sex, sexuality, gender categorization, and representation. Post-World War II era's interest in science and sex (Meyerowitz, 2002, p. 2) was further heightened in the 1950s and 1960s with a gradual movement away from understanding sex as a question of visibility (genitals) and into the elusiveness of chromosomes through the "microscopic gaze" (p. 2) – an understanding still bound to biology and to the fantasy of what counts as "natural".

This new conceptualization had both broadening and narrowing effects on the meanings of gender and sexuality, since it continued to understand sex as biologically determined while, at the same time, it began to think anew secondary characteristics, gestures, and behaviours as not attributable to biology. These changes occurred simultaneously with significant advances in medical technology for reassignment surgeries. Increased visibility and representation of transsexuality and gender non-conformity has allowed the emergence of new narratives that cut through and challenge monolithic notions of sexuality and mental health. Terms such as transvestite, transsexual, and transgender, which were used to describe disparate identities, began to multiply in the late twentieth century to include bi-genders, two-spirited, cross-genders, and genders benders, among others. The meanings of these terms have not only changed throughout history, they have different meanings and social histories in non-Western cultures, as exemplified by the term "Hijra" in India and Pakistan, "Travesti" in Brazil, and "Kathoy" in Thailand.

As salient issues of access, recognition, and equity in regards to transsexual, transgender, and non-conforming gender identities become less controversial, at least in the global North, the space to rethink sexuality and sexual difference outside and beyond issues of identity has broadened, compelling us to approach sexual difference as enigmatic and in excess of sociocultural determinations that can never fully reconcile us with the mysteries and paradoxes of being sexed beings. This collection intervenes in the process of thinking transsexuality beyond the deadlock of identity politics while questioning narrow understandings of transsexuality divorced from larger sociocultural contexts, thus contributing to articulate the intricate connections between gender politics, social representation, mental health institutional practices, and embodied experience.

Chapter descriptions

David Dorenbaum's essay "Revisiting the Friends of the Place Blanche: the transsexual imaginary through the photographs of Christer Strömholm" opens the section *Aesthetic tension*. Dorenbaum's contribution engages the problems of singularity and stability of the subject's gender through an analysis of Strömholm's photographs of members of the Place Blanche transsexual community in 1950s Paris. Exploring the tension between the visible and the legible – between what can be seen and what can be understood – the author argues that Strömholm's photographs confront the spectator with the lack that sets in motion gender differentiation through the question: from where am I seeing? Through his analysis, Dorenbaum draws our attention to the performative aspects of these photographs in inscribing gender anew.

Dana Amir's essay "The two sleeps of Orlando: transsexuality as caesura or cut" addresses the question of gender transitioning through the lens of temporality. Drawing upon her reading of Virginia Woolf's *Orlando*, Amir conceptualizes gender as the basis for the splitting that grounds dichotomous thinking and delineates the conditions that propel an experience of transitioning as a rich and layered process between break and continuity, thus mobilizing the saturated terms of the gender binary.

Dina Georgis's essay "Gender transitions and aesthetic possibilities" engages the question of the non-deterministic yet universal relationship between trauma and sexuality. Georgis examines how the narratives we create about our past stabilize our self-knowledge, while making us vulnerable to the loss from which our sense of self emerges. Offering a reading of Chase Joynt's experimental documentary *Akin* – where the artist explores a history of sexual trauma – Georgis examines both the vulnerabilities inherent to (trans)gender embodiment and its potentials for a creative re-invention of self.

Atalia Israeli-Nevo's "Taking (my) time: temporality in transition, queer delays and being (in the) present" examines the question of time in the experience of gender transitioning. Thinking through her own autobiographical narrative as a transwoman in transition, she challenges the dominant before-and-after narrative trope and argues for a conception of temporality that may accommodate the present and allow for a consideration of existence in the "now" of the process of transitioning. Israeli-Nevo draws from key transcultural films and novels to further examine the meanings of "taking time", importantly drawing attention to class and racial implications for non-hegemonic trans subjects.

Opening the section *Diagnostic phantasies in the (failed) quest for authenticity* is Patricia Gherovici's discussion of the vicissitudes of psychoanalysis's historical encounter with transsexuality. Her essay "Psychoanalysis needs a sex change" reflects critically on the role of transsexuality in broadening the clinic's perspective on gender and sexuality. It also proposes an important shift in thinking about trans experiences that moves our attention away from the literal question of sexual difference and into an examination of trans embodiment as an affirmation of "livability". As such, Gherovici's contribution considers the notion of the death drive as central to an ethics of desire.

Sheila L. Cavanagh takes up recent Lacanian literature in her essay "Principles for psychoanalytic work with trans clients" in order to deconstruct clinical approaches that frame transsexuality as a psychotic symptom. Building on Gherovici's insight that transsexuality illuminates the failure in the Symbolic to decipher the conundrum of sexual difference, Cavanagh invites us to see transsexuality as an epistemological and aesthetic opening of the phallic logic that governs the symbolic articulation of gender.

Diane Ehrensaft's essay "Realities and myths: the gender affirmative model of care for children and youth" compares three mental health intervention approaches to gender non-conforming children and adolescents: the "learning to live in your own skin" approach, the "watchful waiting" perspective, and the "gender affirmative" model that she endorses and practices. Besides outlining comparatively the benefits and limitations of these approaches, she discusses pervasive myths in the field and cautions against their potentially damaging implications for gender non-conforming children and adolescents.

Erik Schneider's essay "Transition and childhood: querying the medical approaches" addresses the question of hormonal intervention in children and adolescents and problematizes the passive role of the child in the decision-making processes by examining a series of anxieties that are not easily situated or assigned. Whose anxiety, Schneider asks, is being addressed in the psychological or psychiatric evaluation: the child's or their parents'? The essay offers a critique of medical discourses that do not address the child's concerns which, in Schneider's view, are far removed from questions of diagnosis.

In her essay "Golden ticket therapy: stigma management among trans men", Elroi J. Windsor examines the various ways in which transgender people navigate the medical system and negotiate the expectations of health professionals as they request access to hormonal therapy and/or surgery. Windsor discusses the barriers that are placed as a condition to access, and identifies key strategies that help transgender individuals increase their probabilities of success. Windsor highlights the ethics of transitioning and the instability of knowledge, as transgender people strategically accommodate their narrative to the expectations of healthcare gatekeepers.

Silvia Tenenbaum-Magid's essay "Borders of belonging: challenges in access to anti-oppressive mental healthcare for Indigenous Latino gender-fluid youth" addresses issues of access to anti-oppressive mental healthcare services for Indigenous Latino gender-fluid youth in Toronto. Drawing from their own "border-narratives", Tenenbaum-Magid proposes an analysis of the systemic and intersectional barriers faced by this population and proposes guidelines for a culturally relevant and social justice-oriented approach to mental health intervention.

Mehrdad Eftekhar's essay "Transgenderism in Iran" takes up the question of how heterosexism, patriarchy, and binary notions of gender affect the presentation of transsexuality, as well as how medical and legal discourses shape the experience, perception, and expression of transsexuality in Iran. Specifically, Eftekhar offers an analysis of how the understanding of transsexuality as a return to a true gender identity has become a stabilizing response to cultural anxieties over ambiguous sexual identity and non-normative gender roles in Iran.

Trish Salah's essay opens the section *Cultural montage*, the last in this collection. Her contribution titled "To return to Schreber: trans literature as psychoanalysis" proposes a reading of Schreber's memoir that contests canonical Freudian interpretations and subsequent psychoanalytic readings. Whereas historically, psychoanalytic interpretations of the case have presented a plea for normative sexuality, Salah's return to Schreber's own account decentres both psychoanalytic and social constructivist understandings of transgender subjectivity. Approaching Schreber's memoir as trans literature, rather than as case study, Salah interrogates the history of cisnormative reception that has overdetermined its meanings and imagines novel interpretative paths for a productive re-encounter with Schreber.

Laine Hughes's essay "Wronging the right body narrative: on the universality of gender uncertainty" uses an interdisciplinary standpoint that combines trans theory, disability studies, and psychoanalysis to examine the problematic uses and shortcomings of the "wrong body" narrative. The author argues that as a hallmark for obtaining access to surgico-hormonal interventions, the narrative imposes a trans-normativity that reinforces dominant notions of normalcy and forecloses the capacity to imagine the body as a potential space. Hughes proposes the notion of "better than before" as a contestation to the phantasy of bodily cohesion that may release the subject from the imperatives of gender certitude.

In "Biopower and the medicalization of gender variance: a Foucauldian analysis of trans subjectivity", Kinnon Ross MacKinnon uses Foucault's theory of bio-power to investigate the ways in which gender-variant bodies have been regulated, disciplined, and categorized through medicalized discourses. One consequence of this biopolitical intervention, Mackinnon argues, is the imposition of the "gender/anatomical sex misalignment" narrative as a condition for trans intelligibility. MacKinnon goes on to explore potential forms of resistance to biopolitical regimentation through non-linear transition trajectories and other alternative subjectifications and embodied gender practices.

Aziz Guzel closes this collection with a critical analysis of the medical diagnosis of "gender dysphoria" in his essay "The professional recourse to the adolescent body: the bathroom wars and the limit of thinking in education". Guzel presents the case study of a high school student who sued his school over the right to use the bathroom and examines the educational, clinical, and legal responses to the student's request for access. Arguing that the complexities of adolescent sexuality challenge dominant frameworks in these institutional spaces, Guzel proposes a view of mental health unencumbered by the idealization of the DSM and more attuned to the interrelations between sexuality, development, and learning in adolescence.

To conclude, *Current Critical Debates in the Field of Transsexual Studies: In Transition* showcases diverse perspectives and shifts in current understandings of transsexuality. The collection challenges univocal accounts of the concept of transsexuality and of the experience of gender transitioning, and contributes to the de-literalization of gender through engaging a wide array of medical, clinical, legal, literary, and cultural discourses. These contributions broaden traditional understandings of femininity and masculinity, challenge normative discourses of gender, and highlight the instability of terms such as "sex-change", "gender transitioning", and "non-conformity", thereby revealing tensions between differing discourses and the desires and anxieties articulated through them. It is my hope that the essays in this collection allow us to meet at the threshold between our desire for stability of knowledge and the ever-present enigmas posed by our condition as sexed beings.

References

Beam, C. (2011). *I am J.* New York: Little, Brown & Company.
Britzman, P.D. (2015). *A psychoanalyst in the classroom.* New York: SUNY Press.
Cooper, T., Glock-Cooper, A. (2014). *Changers, book one: Drew.* New York: Akashic Books.
Gherovici, P. (2017). *Transgender psychoanalysis: A Lacanian perspective on sexual difference.* New York: Routledge.
Glocer Fiorini, L. (2017). *Sexual difference in debate: Bodies, desires, and fictions.* London: Karnac Books.
Gozlan, O. (2008). The accident of gender. *Psychoanalytic Review*, 95, 541–570.
Gozlan, O. (2011). Pictogram: Identity and the myth of sexual difference. Other/Wise, the online journal of the International Forum of Psychoanalytic Education. Retrieved from https://ifpe.wordpress.com/2011/04/15/pictogram/
Gozlan, O. (2015). *Transsexuality and the art of transitioning: A Lacanian approach.* New York: Routledge.
Gozlan, O. (2016). The transsexual's turn: Uncanniness at Wellesley College. *Studies in Gender and Sexuality*, 17(4), 297–305.
Jenner, C. (2017). *The secret of my life.* New York: Hachette Book Group.
Jorgensen, C. (1979). *Winnipeg Free Press*, October 18. Retrieved from: http://research.cristanwilliams.com/2011/08/21/christine-jorgensen-transgender-woman/
Meltzer, D. (1992). *Claustrum: An investigation of claustrophobic phenomena.* London: Karnac Books.
Meltzer, D. & Williams, M.H. (1988). *The apprehension of beauty: The role of aesthetic conflict in development, art and violence.* London: Karac Press.
Meyerowitz, J. (2002). *How sex changed: A history of transsexuality in the United States.* Cambridge, MA: Harvard University Press.
Mock, J. (2017). *Redefining realness: My path to womanhood, identity, love & so much more.* New York: Atria Books.
Morton, S. (2003). *Gayatri Chakravorty Spivak.* New York: Routledge.
Peters, J.A., (2004). *Luna.* New York: Little, Brown & Company.
Stryker, S., Whittle, S. (2013). *The transgender studies reader.* New York: Routledge.
Valentine, D. (2007). *Imagining transgender.* Durham, NC: Duke University Press.
Winnicott, D. W. (1971). *Playing and reality.* London: Tavistock Publications.

PART I
Aesthetic tensions

1
REVISITING THE FRIENDS OF THE PLACE BLANCHE

The transgender imaginary through the photographs of Christer Strömholm

David Dorenbaum

> Incomprehensible body, penetrable and opaque body, open and closed body, in one sense. I know very well what it is to be looked over by someone else from head to toe. I know what it is to be spied from behind, watched over the shoulder, caught off guard when I least expect it. I know what it is to be naked. And yet this same body, which is so visible, is also withdrawn, captured by a kind of invisibility from which I can never really detach it. This skull, the back of my skull, I can feel it, right there, with my fingers. But see it? Never. This back, which I can feel leaning against the pressure of the mattress, against the couch when I am lying down, and which I might catch but only by the ruse of the mirror. And what is this shoulder, whose movements and positions I know with precision, but that I will never be able to see without dreadfully contorting myself? The body—phantom that only appears in the mirage of the mirror, and then only in fragmentary fashion—do I really need genies and fairies, and death and the soul, in order to be, at the same time, both visible and invisible?
>
> *Foucault, 2006, pp. 229–234*

What is at stake as the image traverses the body? How can we understand the capability of visual language to render the body legible, but also to make gender take place through the body, as a discourse inscribed in it, through lived experience? From a Lacanian perspective, the subject is an effect of language and does not hold the discursive power of the performative (Lacan, 1973). In other words, the subject is not in charge: rather than addressing gender, the subject is addressed, indeed revealed by the performative power of gender.

Inspired by Swedish photographer Christer Strömholm's work from the 1950s in Paris, I will approach the meaning of the term *transgender performativity* from a

Lacanian angle, specifically its register of the imaginary. How is it possible that, in the face of the un-representable experience of transgender subjectivity, which defies any stable representation, Strömholm's photographs have attained such levels of extreme visibility? We find in them a rare equilibrium that permits us to read their performativity in spite of their incomprehensibility.

This essay looks historically at the creative process behind the narration and transition of the members of a particular transgender community. It considers their transgender subjectivity as a form of kinship, a mode of connection. The methodology employed by the photographer in this instance engaged not just his gaze but his literal corporeality, too. Everything is presented on the surface. Without hierarchy, Strömholm makes bodily essence perceptible and affecting, expressing the entirety of its human qualities. I maintain that whatever ethic we attribute to Strömholm's practice, his photographs celebrate the human body as it appears to us in those images: both material and transparent.[1]

Having moved to Paris in the 1950s, Strömholm found himself at the heart of the district inhabited by a transgender community. Strömholm's first contact with this community, according to Örjan Kristenson, Strömholm's assistant and a photographer himself, followed an evening photographic session with a model. When Strömholm delivered the finished material the next day to the address in Paris that had been given to him, a man he had not previously met opened the door and said: "Perhaps you won't recognize me. Yesterday I was Dolly." According to Kristenson, this encounter awakened Strömholm's curiosity (Orjan, 1999, p. 63).[2] "It was because I didn't understand it myself," Strömholm recounted, half a century later.

> I hadn't given it a thought until I met them. We met by chance and I realized very soon, that as soon as you ask yourself why their lives are the way they are, it becomes difficult not to take pictures. After fifty years of photographing I still don't know exactly what I do when I pick up my camera. I know when I sit down and think about it. But it isn't one picture in particular I'm looking for, but many. I often get pictures that are not necessarily visible on the surface. The picture isn't obvious. This way of seeing and taking photos appears gradually.
>
> *Knape, 2001, p. 5*

In photographing the transgender people he encountered at Place Blanche, Strömholm immersed himself not only in their lived experiences, in their interactions with others and with the world—some had prostituted themselves, for instance, to finance their surgeries in Casablanca—but also in their inner lives and internal conflicts. He was by no means the passive witness of their own narrative. Instead he propelled himself and his protagonists into spaces that initially seemed protected, tapping into the realm of their imaginary and, needless to say, into his own as well. His camera served as a device that provided him the possibility of addressing the performative power of gender. As Kendall Gerdes (2014) writes, this power works not merely to "make bodies legible" from having gendered characteristics but to make "gender itself take place" through bodies (p. 149). Gender is "performative," she points out, "because it inscribes itself as a discourse each time it inscribes itself on a body, as a lived experience."

Strömholm quickly dispels the widespread notion, as decried by Diane Arbus and others, that an image is stolen by a photographer, that a photograph taken of a subject is actually *taken from* that subject (Arbus, 2003, p. 147). On the contrary, in Strömholm's work we can see the complexity of the drama unfolding and moving toward the unfamiliar on both sides of the lens. The gaze takes on a mimetic quality. Photography here, as Sara Davidmann (2014) puts it, operates as "an interactive social process with a dynamic potential for envisioning the transsexual intimate partnerships beyond the authority of textual representation" (pp. 636–653). We can think of Julia Kristeva's term *interactive subjectivity* that captures the essence as the expression of what is not accounted for by the "active–passive dichotomy" (Kristeva, 2005, p. 44). Incidentally, by transcending the elementary active–passive opposition between photographer and photographed, and by operating as the reflector of every other participant, Strömholm arrives at his own self-portrait.

The following are excerpts from the text that Christian Caujolle, then director of the Vu agency in Paris that represented Strömholm, wrote as part of the publication produced by the Hasselblad Center, on the occasion of Strömholm's being presented with the prestigious Hasselblad Award in 1997:

> Because I am French and interested in photography, his work, "Place Blanche," was one of my reference books. I had been fascinated by his lack of voyeurism on a tricky theme that is normally dealt with in a spectacular way in order to please the grubby watcher who is hungry for "shock" pictures; by his respect and complicity shown towards transvestites and transsexuals in Paris by night; by an absence of anecdotes, or, to be more precise, by a rejection of anecdotal stories; by the profound humanity of his expression; by his dark yet not despaired vision that showed tenderness and smiles; by his mix of conspicuousness and mystery that underlay pictures which wanted to fool us or at least raise questions under their "report" style; I considered this a tremendous documentary work. I was completely ignorant.
>
> *Caujolle, 1998, p. 6*

> The people of the world who are not a majority do not live or populate it. They are here, they have no specific occupation, they are not in agreement with space. With the significant exception of the "birds of the night" on Place Blanche that foster between themselves and their own body readable relationships which often undergo identity questionings. Male and female face features that we meet are often impossible to define.
>
> *Kristeva, 2005, p. 44*

This remarkable body of work that Strömholm produced over ten years for *Place Blanche* constitutes, if not the first, at least one of the earliest attempts to portray the singularity of the individual's experience of transgender subjectivity (Strömholm, 1983). The consistency, the body, and the flesh of these photographs release an eroticism, which in turn infuses the images with an astonishing flexibility and freedom of movement. They incite us, in Nikki Sullivan's (2006) terms, to rethink the ways in which bodies are entwined in (un)becoming, rather than presuming that they are simply mired in being unless they undergo explicit, visible, and identifiable transformational procedures (p. 561). We feel the wind blowing, and it blows from all directions. In these portraits the photographer has located the site of the transgender experience in a personal space of indeterminacy and decisions linked to existence. This site is not just a surface but also a space of potentiality, infused with a psychological relationship to time, in which the future emerges from a dialectical reconfiguring of the past.

Strömholm's photographs of transgender subjects could be viewed as *anachronistic montages*, a term coined by the art historian and philosopher Georges Didi-Huberman (1997) to describe images structured by many layers that resist forming part of the "great chronologic discourse" (p. 114). He suggests that their dialectic presentation is meant neither to resolve contradictions nor to transcend the opposition between the visible and the legible. On the contrary, according to Didi-Huberman there is a play of figuration which constantly activates the contradiction, exposes it, dramatizes it. We are left suspecting that something remains yet to be seen, something that imposes itself on the exercise of our gaze, which belongs to the private dimension and therefore remains opaque. We are left in doubt, which contravenes the certainty that "what you see is what you see," the certainty of "being in front of the thing itself" (Didi-Huberman, 1997, pp. 78–79).

The estrangement and intensity of these images derive from their temporal paradoxes, from their anachronisms. They are charged with a formidable dialectic capability, a tremendous evocative power with a "poetic effect," to paraphrase Lacan. Strömholm's images disrupt the temporal stability of photographs. The progression of the sequence, as is our reading of the presentation of transgender, does not seem to unfold in chronological, linear time. Instead, we are presented with the experience of a "temporal augmentation," to take up an expression by art historian Adrian Stokes (1978, p. 22). It is evident that these images result from a confluence of multiple time relations that would never have appeared to us under ordinary circumstances. As the product of an inherently creative act, however, the photograph is capable of capturing the essential creativity embedded in the individual's experience of transgender subjectivity (Gozlan, 2015, p. 1). In seizing the instability and the complexity that characterizes the time interval of the expected arrival of the transformative event, "transitioning," Strömholm manages to hold in suspense the disclosure of an enigma (Carter, 2014, p. 149). The photographs of *Place Blanche* are splashed with enigmatic traces.

How can we understand the enigmatic quality of these images? In a June 7, 1961 lecture from the seminar *The Clinic of Transference*, Lacan refers to a primordial image derived from his theory of the function of the mirror:

as something . . . suddenly proposed to him in which he does not simply receive the field of something in which he recognizes himself, but of something which already presents itself as an *Urbild-ideal*, as something which will always be, something which subsists of itself, as something before which he essentially experiences his own fissures as a premature being, as a being who experiences himself as not yet even—at the moment that the image comes to his perception—sufficiently coordinated to respond to this image in its totality.

For Lacan, the *Urbild-ideal* is a very particular kind of image formation that operates outside of time. The notion can be linked with what would later become for Piera Castoriadis-Aulagnier the concept of the "pictogram," which she describes as a "pre-mirror stage formation" constituted by the earliest representations of heterogeneous stimuli that reach the mind. According to Castoriadis-Aulagnier (2014), the "pictographic representation" consists of metabolizing this heterogeneous information into homogeneous material capable of embodying experience (pp. 47, 51). The pictogram acts as a bridge to one's own representation of the body in its totality, which is fundamental to achieving a sense of integration of the body as a unit. However, in its un-integrated state, the pictogram can also be the cause of disintegration, giving way to fragmentation anxieties. Although Strömholm's photographs pose an intriguing synthetic quality, it is not surprising that, given their pictographic overload, in approaching these images one is also faced with many inevitable cracks, the cracks that speak of the body's exposure to the real.

A few years after his seminar on *The Clinic of Transference*, near the conclusion of his January 9, 1963 lecture from the seminar *On Transference*, Lacan proposed to add to his theory of the mirror stage:

something comparable to the Moebius strip, something which does not have a specular image, the *object a*, [which causes the mirror image] to become the strange and invasive image of the double, becomes that which happens little by little at the end of the life of Maupassant when he begins by no longer seeing himself in the mirror, or when he perceives in a room something which turns its back on him and regarding which he immediately knows that he is not without some relationship to this ghost, when the ghost turns back, he sees that it is himself.

Lacan's shift from the mirror image to the image of the double puts into question the presupposed idea of the stability of the mirror image itself, stability understood here as the capacity of the image to encompass in itself all the visible elements constituting the object, without any one of them missing. In other words, an image derives its stability from being capable of reflecting the object without anything interfering with the totality of its imprint.

The Lacanian double constitutive of the transgender imaginary is ubiquitous in Strömholm's images. In them we experience how the introduction of the *object a*—in not being interchangeable, compatible, or visible with the mirror image—disturbs the stability of the mirror image and unveils the lack of stability in the image of the body. As a consequence, in Strömholm's photographs the mirror image is bound to remain linked to the uncanny, described by Freud as the unfamiliar in the familiar (Melenotte, 2005, p. 136). As Lacan puts it, if psychoanalysis did not exist one would still know it, from the fact that there exist moments of the object's appearance which throw us into a completely different dimension. Since it is given by experience, this alternative dimension merits detachment from the primal, which is the dimension of the strange, of something which can in no way allow itself to be grasped (Lacan, 1962).

At the same time, but operating in yet another dimension, alternative even to Lacan's alternative—a third dimension, then—in Strömholm's photographs we can see that the incorporation of the *object a* into the mirror image endows this transfiguration with the full scope of its erotic capability. The *object a*, in tying the knot of the un-interpretable, favors the intermittent cascading of a sexual force, as highlighted by Lacan:

> The intermittent springing forth of its force, is what everything that I could call a series of images, that are easy to put before your eyes, of an eroto-propaedeutics, indeed even properly speaking of an erotics, gives a quite easy access to. A crowd of images of this type, Chinese, Japanese and others and, I imagine[,] ones that are not difficult to find either in our culture, will bear witness to it for you.
>
> *Lacan, 1963b*

George Bataille's (1986) notion of eroticism, as "the disequilibrium in which the being consciously calls his own existence in question," is applicable here. "In one sense, the being loses himself deliberately," Bataille claims, "but then the subject is identified with the object losing his identity. If necessary I can say in eroticism: I am losing my-self" (p. 31).

How does one think of the dialectic of these images so full of contradiction? Through Strömholm's lens, the gaze occupies a privileged vantage point. What is most striking about the photographic sequence of the transgender members of the Place Blanche community is that by intensifying and magnifying their gaze, the photographer activates their imagination. Strömholm's lens also provides him with the possibility of articulating whatever is located between the visible and the invisible, another way of naming of the real.

The Lacanian concept of *semblant* comes to mind in connection with these images. As Lacan clarifies, the *semblant* highlights the opposition between the object and its representation. It operates as the veil that covers the lack, veils the fire from the object, its irreducible excess, while at the same time generating the luminosity that exposes it. Lacan suggests that this "imaginary formation" also operates as a signifier (Lacan, 1971). As the *semblant* conceals the fire from the object, it awakens the image of the fire in the viewer. He locates his image at the limit of the imaginary, yet not quite fully belonging to the realm of the real; in the opposition between seeing and being seen; at the point where the gaze is actualized and one is confronted with a nuclear element, a phantasm (Nasio, 1992, pp. 52–53).

Indeed, the "suggested position of the phantasm," according to François Lyotard (1993),

> which makes of it something like a manufactured object, a product the "consumption" of which would be the voluptuous emotion itself, is, in this regard at least, fully affirmative: the pieces of the postured body which produce pulsional force and which are vainly consumed as intensities of joissance, are then conceived as substitutes for nothing, they are those very things engendered by the impulsion by means of its intensification and circulation, are pieces "invented" and added as a patchwork to the libidinal band. The phantasm here is not an unreality or a dereality, it is "something" which grips the crazy turbulence of the libido, something it invents as an incandescent object, and which it instantaneously adds to the band traced by its trajectory.
>
> *pp. 72–73*

Strömholm's mind is full of images. His photographs are the result of transforming thoughts into images. These images are filled with questions. Who is the creator in the photographic act? How does the shaping of one's narrative contribute to the shaping of the body? From his own observations we can see many parallels between his manner of working and that of a psychoanalyst. Through his lens, "transsexuality is approached as a particular embodiment of sexual difference that captures the universal enigma at the heart of subjectivity" (Gozlan, 2015, p. 12). Clearly this masterful interpreter is in possession of a great analytic virtue: the exercise of patience. "In the early 60's I used to live in rue Constance," Strömholm recalls.

> Every night I would come downstairs to the Brasserie de la Place Blanche with my old Leica, a few reels of tri-x and my hesitating French. Everybody knew what I was doing. I never took photos in hiding. I only worked with the existing light, and frequently it was neon. Since I developed my own photographs upstairs in my room at the hotel, I could quickly review the negatives. If the exposure had not been the correct one, or if I had committed any other mistake it wasn't grave. I had the availability of many other nights. For me it was a question of securing the negative.
>
> *Kristenson, 1999, p. 63*

Each one of Strömholm's photographs addresses the question: what is the primary matter in photography? As in psychoanalysis, his way of working in photography is linked to the construction of the Subject. However, in both instances the process could also be understood "not only as the work of creating but also the work of un-creating" (J. McDougall, personal communication, 1996). For Strömholm to achieve this paradigm, it was necessary to dismantle the envelope of reality that surrounded and concealed the real. In his photographs we are able to perceive the intrusions of the real. "I make images and they are not necessarily photographic pictures," he has asserted. "What's important to me is what the picture says. The impression of the picture is what matters. That is even more important than the truth—a photographic truth" (Knape, 2001, p. 6).

Through his ability to capture the *sameness* but also the diversity in the identities of the transgender subjects, Strömholm's photographs expose an absence. In his images the *sameness* is advanced forward to the point of crossing the threshold beyond which the original subject is no longer recognizable. The photograph no longer resembles the *original* subject. Instead, as Jean-Luc Nancy (2007) explains with respect to portraiture, it resembles "the idea of resemblance of the original" (pp. 45–48). In other words, the photograph operates as the "original" of the "resemblance of itself" of a subject in general, but also of a singular subject in particular. Nancy reminds us that it is only in our own portrait that we can encounter our sameness, and that in each portrait we will identify a different resemblance. "[W]hat stands *behind* a face," Nancy (1993) wonders,

> —but also behind a hand, a belly, a buttock, a breast, a knee—the *he* or *she* who hides behind a face stands entirely outside of this face, and this is why first of all, there is no face. There is first, skin detaching from the world, from other skins, but detaching itself only while remaining attached, attached and exposed, attached by its detachment from the body. Absolute skin.
>
> *pp. 205–206*

In setting out to photograph the intimate lives of transgender people and their transitional and ambiguous forms of relatedness, Strömholm is able to facilitate the establishment of both a fictional space and a structural space—an intermediate area of experience—which operates as the "transitional space" described by D.W. Winnicott (1971) as integral to the presentation of the Subject (pp. 104–110). The area of the transitional space, according to Winnicott, constitutes a psychic space as such between inside and outside, a "potential space" in which he sees "the origins of creativity." This intermediate area of living experience that is neither fantasy nor actual reality is, at the same time, both—"an essential paradox" (Winnicott, 1989, p. 204). Winnicott considers it essential to the development of the human being that this paradox be accepted and respected, rather than questioned or resolved. From his perspective, the status of "transitionality" is inherently paradoxical.

The range of affect shown in these photographs makes them captivating, playful. There is clearly a strong *coup du théâtre* coming from the experience comparable to that of the opening and closing of the curtain of a psychic theatre. In setting up so masterfully this theatricality, Strömholm establishes an inside and an outside, which in fact are not separate. They are not even grounded in opposition. The theatrical effect is only the mirror of the subjective mise-en-scène of the photographed. Multiple references populate the field: everything is a sign, the sign of singularity, and everything is what it is because each thing resembles another thing. "The body remains the dark reserve of sense, and the dark sign of this reserve," writes Nancy (1993). "But in this way, the body is absolutely trapped by the sign of this reserve" (p. 193).

In addition, Strömholm unmasks the void that invades the scene. There are parts of the photograph that escape our vision, that operate as a negative reference. Or as Lacan (1962) says,

> it allows there to escape something of this primitive cathexis to our being which is given[,] it is this non-imagined residue of the body which comes by some detour—and here we are able to designate this detour—to manifest itself here at this place provided for the lack, to manifest itself in this fashion and in a fashion [which,] since it is not specular[,] becomes henceforth unlocatable: this lack of certain reference points is effectively a dimension of anxiety.

Looking at these photographs from the perspective described above, it is clear that they correspond precisely to a period when an original sense of completeness was lost, to the playing out of an essential lack, which simultaneously implies gender differentiation. However, gender differentiation here should not be understood in a binary mode, since gender—unlike sexual difference—is not constructed as a binary. Instead, gender emerges from these images as an ancillary feature where female and male, woman and man, homosexual and heterosexual, active and passive, nudity and disguise, time and timeless, all present themselves as invariably intertwined, just like Eros and Thanatos (Verhaeghe, 2004, p. 63).

Lyotard (1993) reaffirms that it is important to change references: "the two principles of Freud's pulsional theory," he writes,

> are not two instances each endowed with a distinct functional principle allowing their identification from their respective effects or symptoms in the "psyche" or on the body. According to him, it is not the case that Eros is the producer of wholes, systems, compositor or master builder, and that the death drives *on the other hand* are the destroyers of systems, the deconstructors, the unbinders. There is a pulsional machinery put in place, which functions on its own account, and this machinery does not work according to death or according to Eros, but according to both, erotic as a regulated machine, lethal as a deregulatory machine, but also mortal as regulated, and alive

>   because of its deregulation, because it attests to the fact that the libido circulates and invests over the organic body, in its unpredictable displaceability.
>
>   *pp. 52–53*

What position are we to take before these images? Perhaps, as Oren Gozlan (2015) points out, "it is a question that can also be asked as we encounter the fragility of our gender imaginary through the concept of transsexuality" (pp. 78, 93). He reminds us that "identity emerges through the mirror stage as a retroactive construct," that "no one escapes the imaginary of gender," and that each individual confronts the question: what is the state of "this" imaginary? The unity of the bodies of the people photographed in Place Blanche presents itself in an infinitely precarious state, in a perpetual "glorious metamorphosis" and simultaneously, paraphrasing Jean-Bertrand Pontalis (1981), in "a fatal '*amorphosis*'" involving continuity and a radical transformation at the same time (p. 88). By suspending the prevailing codes, the accursed energies of the suppressed codes are unbound. There is a concentration of the force of a charged energy. Strömholm's photographs manifest the coalescing of the two sides of the oppositions, and they lead to suppressing contradictions.

Through our binary gaze, the visual representation of the non-binary transgender body has the potential to challenge our own bodily experience, our body image, and the belief in the organizing principles of the binary sex and gender systems (Davidmann, 2006). In calling into question the stability of gender as a category, Strömholm's images put the spectator in a difficult position. As Joyce McDougall (1995) writes, "we depend on the tension that emanates from this dichotomy, with its depressive potential it impels an eternal quest for resolution and, indeed, provides a vital, ever-present substantiation of all forms of adult love and sexuality" (p. ix). Consequently, as Susan Stryker (2014) points out, "transgender phenomena flicker across the threshold of viability, simultaneously courting danger and attracting death even as they promise life in new forms, along new pathways" (p. 40). How can the two principles of Eros and Thanatos be considered, if they cannot be differentiated through their two functions?

Judith Butler (1999), on the other hand, raises the question,

>   Is the breakdown of gender binaries . . . so monstrous, so frightening, that it must be held to be definitionally impossible and heuristically precluded from any effort to think gender? . . . how do non-normative sexual practices call into question the stability of gender as a category of analysis? How do certain sexual practices compel the question: what is a woman, what is a man?
>
>   *pp. viii, xi*

In viewing the transsexual body through the normative categories of female and male, the two sexes and two genders system underpins our perception to such an extent that we actually see through the binary categories. Butler claims that:

even 'seeing' the body may not answer the question: for *what are the categories through which one sees?* The moment in which one's staid and usual cultural perceptions fail, when one cannot with surety read the body that one sees, is precisely the moment when one is no longer sure whether the body encountered is that of a man or a woman. The vacillation between the categories itself constitutes the experience of the body in question. When such categories come into question, the *reality* of gender is also put into crisis.

p. xxii

Strömholm's photographs from *Place Blanche* could be viewed as a mise-en-scène of Lacan's idea concerning the mirror as constitutive of the body:

This body is not to be taken either, for its part, in the pure and simple categories of the transcendental aesthetics. This body is not[,] in a word, constitutable in the way that Descartes establishes in the field of extension. It is a matter of our seeing that the body in question is not given to us in a pure and simple fashion in our mirror, that even in this experience of the mirror, there can occur a moment where this image, this specular image that we think we have in our grasp, is modified: what we have face to face with us, our stature, our face, our pair of eyes, allows there to emerge the dimension of our own look[,] and the value of the image then begins to change[,] especially if there is a moment in which this look which appears in the mirror begins to look no longer at ourselves, *initium* aura.

Lacan, 1963a

Christer Strömholm has generated photographs that transfer the idea of the image into a static form. As a result of the process, however, far from being frozen they are elastic, polymorphous, corporeal, embedded with time. Highlighted here is their relevance not only to the field of photography but also to all disciplines interested in a deeper understanding of transgender subjectivity. In a world in transition, photography itself, of course, has been the subject of ongoing transformations. Contemporary photographic practices continue to focus on alternative forms for representing gender variances, exploring the question of how photography acts through the body, how photography can advance beyond itself, even surpass itself. Experimenting with new technologies and new forms of affiliation has, interestingly enough, required returning to the visual archive, reimagining the past. This essay has focused on one of the earliest attempts at portraying the multiple compositions of transgender subjectivity: photography navigating in uncharted territories.

[The photographs by Christer Strömholm were made available with the permission of Joakim Strömholm from the Christer Strömholm Estate.]

FIGURE 1.1 Cynthia, Hôtel Idéal, 1966. Christer Strömholm Estate.

FIGURE 1.2 Jacky and Adèle, Chanel mannequin, 1960. Christer Strömholm Estate.

FIGURE 1.3 Sonia, 1962. Christer Strömholm Estate.

FIGURE 1.4 Gina and Nana, 1963. Christer Strömholm Estate.

FIGURE 1.5 Soraya and Sonia, Hôtel Pierrots, 1966. Christer Strömholm Estate.

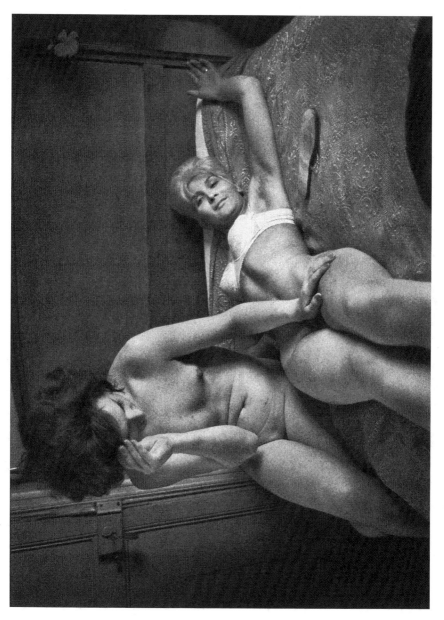

FIGURE 1.6 Susannah and Silvia, Hôtel Pierrots, 1962. Christer Strömholm Estate.

FIGURE 1.7 Kissmie, 1962. Christer Strömholm Estate.

FIGURE 1.8 Nana, 1960. Christer Strömholm Estate.

Notes

1 Unless called for otherwise, throughout this essay I will employ the multifaceted term transgender as an umbrella term for describing a range of gender-variant identities such as the terms transvestite, transsexual, crossdresser (Williams, 2014, pp. 232–234).
2 Kristenson assisted Strömholm until the latter's death in 2002.

References

Arbus, D. (2003). *Diane Arbus: Revelations*. New York: Random House.
Bataille, G. (1986). *Erotism: Death and sensuality*. M. Dalwood (Trans.). San Francisco, CA: City Lights Books.
Butler, J. (1999). *Gender trouble: Feminism and the subversion of identity*. New York: Routledge.
Carter, J. (2014). Transition. *Transgender Studies Quarterly* 1(1–2), 149.
Castoriadis-Aulagnier, P. (2014). *La violencia de la interpretación. Del pictograma al enunciado*. V. Fischman (Trans.). Buenos Aires and Madrid: Amorrortu Editores.
Caujolle, C. (1998). Christer Strömholm or photography at work. In *Imprints by Christer Strömholm: The Hasselblad award 1997*. L. Hall & G. Knape (Eds.). Sweden: Hasselblad Center.
Davidmann, S. (2006). Border trouble: Photography, strategies, and transsexual identities. *SCAN: Journal of Media, Arts, Culture* 3(3). Retrieved from http://scan.net.au/scan/journal/display.php?journal_id=85.
Davidmann, S. (2014). Imag(in)ing trans partnerships: Collaborative photography and intimacy. *Journal of Homosexuality* 61(5): Trans Sexualities, 636–653.
Didi-Huberman, G. (1997). *Lo que vemos, lo que nos mira*. Translated by Horacio Pons. Buenos Aires: Manantial.
Foucault, M. (2006). Utopian body. L. Allais, C. A. Jones, & A. Davidson (Trans.). In *Sensorium: Embodied experience, technology, and contemporary art*. Curated by B. Arning, J. Farver, Y. Hasegawa, & M. Jacobson. Cambridge: MIT Press, 229–234. This publication accompanied the exhibition: List Visual Arts Center. Retrieved from http://monoskop.org/images/a/ad/Foucault_Michel_Utopian_Body_1966_2006.pdf
Gerdes, K. (2014). Performativity. *Transgender Studies Quarterly* 1 (1–2), 148–150.
Gozlan, O. (2015). *Transsexuality and the art of transitioning: A Lacanian approach*. New York: Routledge.
Knape, G. (2001). Interview with Christer Strömholm by Gunilla Knape. In *Christer Strömholm exhibition catalogue*. L. Peracaula (Ed.). Barcelona: Fundació la Caixa.
Kristenson, Ö. (1999). Un homenaje a la mujer. In *Christer Strömholm. Nueve segundos de mi vida*. M. Hörnell & R. Vázquez Díaz (Trans.). Mexico: Centro de la Imagen.
Kristeva, J. (2005). Some observations on female sexuality. S. Leighton (Trans.). In *Dialogues on Sexuality, Gender, and Psychoanalysis*. I. Matthis (Ed.). London: Karnak Books.
Lacan, J. (June 7, 1961). Seminar 24. In *The Seminar of Jacques Lacan. Book 8: The Clinic of Transference, 1966–1967*. C. Gallagher (Trans.). Retrieved from www.lacaninireland.com
Lacan, J. (December 12, 1962). Seminar 5. In *The Seminar of Jacques Lacan. Book 10: Anxiety*. Retrieved from www.lacaninireland.com
Lacan, J. (January 9, 1963a). Seminar 7. In *The Seminar of Jacques Lacan. Book 10: Anxiety, 1962–1963*. C. Gallagher (Trans.). Retrieved from www.lacaninireland.com
Lacan, J. (March 26, 1963b). Seminar 16. In *The Seminar of Jacques Lacan. Book 10: Anxiety, 1962, 1963*. C. Gallagher (Trans.). Retrieved from www.lacaninireland.com
Lacan, J. (January 13, 1971). Seminar 1. In *The Seminar of Jacques Lacan. Book 18: On a discourse that might not be a semblance, 1971*. C. Gallagher (Trans.). Retrieved from www.lacaninireland.com

Lacan, J. (January 16, 1973). Seminar 5. In *The Seminar of Jacques Lacan. Book 20: On Feminine Sexuality: The Limits of Love and Knowledge, 1972–1973*. C. Gallagher (Trans.). Retrieved from www.lacaninireland.com

Lyotard, J.-F. (1993). *Libidinal economy*. I. Hamilton Grant (Trans.). Bloomington and Indianapolis, IN: Indiana University Press.

McDougall, J. (1995). *The many faces of eros: A psychoanalytic exploration on human sexuality*. New York: W.W. Norton.

Melenotte, G.-H. (2005). *Sustancias del imaginario*. S. Pasternac (Trans.). Mexico: Editorial Psicoanalítica de la Letra.

Nancy, J.-L. (1993). Corpus. *The Birth to presence*. C. Sartiliot (Trans.). Stanford, CA: Stanford University Press.

Nancy, J.-L. (2007). *La mirada del retrato*. Buenos Aires and Madrid: Amorrortu Editores.

Nasio, J.-D. (1992). *La mirada en psicoanálisis*. Barcelona: Gedisa.

Pontalis, J.-B. (1981). The elusive in-between. In *Frontiers in psychoanalysis. Between the dream and psychic pain*. C. Cullen & P. Cullen (Trans.). New York: International Universities Press.

Stokes, A. (1978). *The critical writings of Adrian Stokes*. Vol. 2. London: Thames & Hudson.

Strömholm, C. (1983). *Vännerna från Place Blanche (friends from Place Blanche)*. Sweden: ETC Förlag.

Stryker, S. (2014). Biopolitics. *Transgender Studies Quarterly* 1 (1–2), 38–42.

Sullivan, N. (2006). Transmogrification (un)becoming other(s). In *The Transgender Studies Reader*. S. Stryker & S. Whittle (Eds.). New York: Routledge.

Verhaeghe, P. (2004). Fallacies of binary reasoning: Drive beyond gender. In *Dialogues on sexuality, gender, and psychoanalysis*. I. Matthis (Ed.). London: Karnac Books.

Williams, C. (2014). Transgender. In *Transgender Studies Quarterly* 1 (1–2), 232–234.

Winnicott, D.W. (1968/1989). Playing and culture. In *Psycho-analytic explorations*. C. Winnicott, R. Shepherd, & M. Davis (Eds.). Cambridge, MA: Harvard University Press.

Winnicott, D W. (1971). The place where we live. In *Playing and reality*. New York: Basic Books.

2
THE TWO SLEEPS OF ORLANDO
Transsexuality as caesura or cut

Dana Amir

Gender dichotomy is probably the most primary dichotomy internalized in human thinking. It acts as a prototype for all the later dichotomies, in a sense inaugurating dichotomous thinking in general—first within the imaginary of the parent who holds the soon to be born infant in his or her mind—and afterwards within the mind of the infant itself. This chapter focuses on the conditions that enable the establishing of a dialectic and unsaturated gender space—one that enables both a concrete and fantasized creative mobility between the two gender poles—versus the conditions that generate a polar, saturated, gender dichotomous stagnation and stasis.

One of the most famous literary illustrations of the idea of an unsaturated gender space is Virginia Woolf's *Orlando* ([1928] 1949). This is perhaps her most eccentric book: a clever and ironic wink, as Haim Pesach (2007) writes in the introduction to the Hebrew translation, a moment of mischief in this brilliant and tragic author's oeuvre. The book deals with the relationships between men/women and gender identity through the story of a young man who, after an extended deep sleep, turns into a woman and continues to lead a social life of romance and love for over three hundred years.

Twice in the course of the book, Orlando falls into what may be a sleep or an inexplicable coma. The first instance occurs when he is abandoned by his girlfriend and falls into an extended dissociative sleep in order to overcome his heartbreak. In the second sleep, somewhat reminiscent of God's creation of Eve out of Adam's body ("And the LORD God caused a deep sleep to fall upon Adam, and he slept: and he took one of his ribs, and closed up the flesh instead thereof"; Genesis, 2:21), Orlando undergoes a transformation in which he changes from a man into a woman. I would like to begin by identifying the different characteristics of these two "sleeps" of Orlando, subsequently connecting them to two types of gender crossing: gender crossing (or gender mobility) that enables the transformation of "gender excess," as opposed to gender crossing that is in itself an acting-out of this excess rather than an act of transformation.

Orlando's first sleep (Woolf, [1929] 1949, pp. 63–64) presents, in fact, an episode of dissociative detachment. During his seven-day sleep, Orlando is ridded of his painful memories, and when he wakes up he can continue his life supposedly from the point where it was interrupted. Yet this is a mechanical, somewhat hollow continuity that does not enable him to maintain a vivid continuum as to himself or to his life. In effect he loses the "function of the inner witness" (Amir, 2014), or the function of the "biographer" as Woolf calls it throughout the book: the inner function that enables the subject to be in touch with experience and at the same time deviate from it and reflect on it. Orlando, who, from the moment he wakes up, lacks the ability to bear witness to the story of his life as his own story, can only take either one of two positions: allowing himself to experience the unbearable but then take the chance of suffering another collapse, or bearing witness to his story as if it were not his, namely by holding on to the facts without an emotional connection to the experience—and thus to stay alive at the cost of losing his liveliness. Either way his mental existence remains incomplete, and this is his condition until he undergoes the second transformation that allows him a renewed access to the memories that were lost during the first sleep.

Orlando's second sleep (Woolf, [1928] 1949, pp. 121–128), unlike the preceding one, culminates in a real transformation. But this transformation from man to woman does not come at the cost of dissociation. Not only doesn't it block access to existing memories, it repaves a pathway to the memories blocked by the first sleep's dissociation. The difference between Orlando's first and second sleep is that while the first sleep erected a barrier between him and his previous life, the present sleep enables him to simultaneously maintain who he was as well as who he is; that is, to integrate the man and the woman within one speaking person: "The change of sex, though it altered their future, did nothing whatever to alter their identity" (ibid., p. 127). Thus he becomes not only "she" but also "they"—that is, the third person plural, which includes both man and woman, past and present, interior and exterior in a consecutive and continuous way. In this context, the allusion to Genesis's episode of the creation of Eve out of Adam's body is interesting. Genesis's episode supposedly created two separate entities whose dichotomy, once constituted, does not allow reduction. Virginia Woof, on the other hand, reverts the dichotomous scene to its pre-dichotomous state by hinting that since the two identities were created out of one body they will always contain one another somehow, albeit with varying degrees of balance.

Both of Orlando's sleeps are a reaction to his encounter with excess. In the case of the first sleep, it is an excess of pain that is related to his beloved's treacherous act of abandonment. In the case of the second sleep, an excess of admiration is showered upon him which reaches its hysteric peak on the evening prior to his falling asleep: "Women shrieked. A certain lady, who was said to be dying for love of Orlando, seized a candelabra and dashed it to the ground" (ibid., p. 120). However, while the first sleep was a way to create dissociation of the excess—the role of the second sleep was to transform it.

Bion's notion of the "Caesura" ([1977] 1989) simultaneously contains a break and a continuity. A break beyond which there is no continuity is a cut rather than a caesura. Bion himself situates the caesura between the pre-catastrophic state and the post-catastrophic state of change, treating it not as a static point in space or time but rather as a rich dynamic space in itself: "It is in course of transit, in the course of changing from one position to another that these people seem to be most vulnerable—as, for example, during adolescence or latency" (ibid., p. 53). However, this vulnerability is precisely why the state of caesura constitutes the richest potential for change. Bion compares the dividing of the world into polar states that exclude one another with the state in which two different views or perspectives function together in a dialectical, caesura-like and productive manner (Aharoni and Bergstein, footnote 48 in the annotated translation to Hebrew, 2012). Development is always related to the preserving of different views in a non-saturated state, thus avoiding the fixation of the components of consciousness in a stasis that does not allow them to absorb new meanings.

Transsexuality: caesura or cut?

One of the most important questions that arises in this context is whether we formulate transsexuality[1] in terms of caesura or in terms of a cut, or even more precisely: under which conditions should transsexuality be formulated in terms of caesura, and under which in terms of a cut?

As said, gender dichotomy is probably the most primary dichotomy internalized in human thinking. As with any dichotomy, it may collapse into a saturated state, becoming fixated in a way that enables it only a minuscule degree, if any at all, of transformability—or, alternatively, it may remain unsaturated and in this sense contain movement, richness and layered meanings. When does gender dichotomy become a rich dialectic—as opposed to being constituted as a saturated excess, that is, as a dichotomy whose two poles are not only distinct but also exclude each other?

An excess of saturated gender dichotomy forms in conditions that a priori encourage saturated divisions. The propensity for saturated divisions may be innate or acquired, always related to an anxiety of ambiguity and the need to defend oneself through rigid thinking against the unexpected and the impermanent. In most cases this propensity for saturated divisions is a general inclination of thinking and language that is not solely related to gender dichotomy but it becomes especially charged in children who do not find themselves at the "expected" end of the gender dichotomy. In such cases, the combination of the primary gender ambiguity and the acquired propensity for saturated dichotomies might evolve into a need to situate oneself on one gender pole, losing the freedom to experience (even in fantasy) dialectical movement between the poles. Where gender categories do not serve thinking but rather block it, children whose primary "gender experience" is ambiguous might feel trapped in a saturated dichotomy in which they cannot find their place.

In his article "The Other Room and Poetic Space" (1998), Ronald Britton develops the notion of the "other room" as the space of imagination and fiction. He suggests that the "other room" emerges as the subject imagines the parents' intercourse rather than observes their actual sexual relations. It concerns the unwitnessed primal scene rather than the actual one: the one we have imagined as happening in our absence and which exists only in our imagination, thereby becoming the space for fiction. Unlike Winnicott, who defined the transitional phenomenon as the psychological space arising from the relations between infant and mother, and hence situated between "me" and "not me"—Britton argues that the creative space emanates from the internal triangular space. Similar to Melanie Klein (1924) and Otto Rank (1915) who argued that the origins of the theatrical stage are in the imaginary location of the parental sexual act, Britton claims that there is a "primal romantic couple", a "phantasised ideal, super-sexual parental couple", consisting of mythical figures, a kind of primal Adam and Eve, who are "the stars of the screen and the objects of endless media voyeurism." Expelled from Heaven, we are compelled, as non-participating observers, to imagine *their* Paradise. That Paradise becomes our "other room," forever unfulfilled, accompanied with the pain of longing (Britton, 1998, pp. 122–123). Borrowing the terms "this room" and "the other room" from the field of poetic creativity and applying them to the field of gender, I would like to suggest that when gender becomes a "saturated object" what is damaged is exactly this ability to create movement between "this room" of actual gender, and the "other room" of the phantasmatic gender. The possibility of establishing a rich and layered gender space crucially depends on the creative movement between "this room" and the "other room," without each negating the other. When such a situation is possible, even a child whose initial gender experience is an ambiguous and layered one will feel that s/he can creatively move between the gender poles without this mobility (in its concrete and non-concrete aspects) posing a threat. One can say that such movement between the different gendered spaces is an integrated movement that includes all rooms, as well as the areas of overlap and interface between them, within one house, that is, within one self. As opposed to the stagnation and stasis that characterize the polar, saturated, gender state—within what I refer to as a "gender space," there is living movement between the polarities.

In my book *On the Lyricism of the Mind* (2016) I previously suggested a "lyrical dimension" of mental space, which is in charge of the integration of two experiential/perceptual modes: the continuous mode, which perceives the world as predictable, explainable and logical, and the emergent mode, which perceives the world as unpredictable, unexplainable, and constantly changing. The integration of these two modes of experience, which Bion (1970) originally identified as constituting the container/contained interaction, yields the capacity to presuppose constancy and continuity, on the one hand, and to tolerate severe deviations from that constancy and continuity without losing one's sense of "identity" and "biography," on the other hand. Formulating his notion of the *container contained* interaction, Bion (1970) pointed at three possible types of this interaction, of which the one with the most powerful capacity for change is the symbiotic interaction, while the one with the most destructive power is the *parasitic* (in between Bion posited a somehow neutral interaction he entitled "commensal"). If we formulate the interaction between the emergent and the continuous principles of the self in Bion's terms we may suppose that wherever the interaction between the emergent and the continuous is parasitic in nature or takes the form of a "malignant containment" (Britton, 1998, p. 28) one of two things might happen: the continuous self may smother the emergent self, leaving the latter no space for movement or development; or alternatively, the emergent self might stretch the continuous self beyond its breaking point, crashing through its boundaries. Bion (1970) argued that the sense of catastrophe that attends such an interaction between the emergent and the continuous is related to the fact that the psychic space is unable to supply an experience of constancy beyond change, a constancy that is actually the primary condition for change. When the continuous principle prevails, the psychic space becomes lacking in depth and resonance, while when the emergent principle takes over the psychic space turns into a terrifying nightmare. If, by contrast, the interaction is compatible integration may occur, inaugurating the lyrical dimension of the psychic space. The emergent is the force that preserves things in their unsaturated condition, whereas the continuous is the saturated state. The more fertile the interaction between the two, the more likely one is to experience oneself as owning a historical and biographical continuum, on the one hand, and as being a singular individual whose creativity is allowed to interrupt this continuum, on the other hand. "Gender excess" can also be formulated in terms of the relationship between the continuous and the emergent: for example, an excess of a "continuous" gender experience as opposed to an "emergent" gender experience could damage the possibility of establishing a "gender space" which holds the continuous and the emergent in a fertile dialectic relation. On the other hand, an excess of "emergent" gender experience, in which every shift threatens to change the deep nucleus of identity, may undermine the possibility of a cooperative relationship between the two poles of gender dialectic (the actual and the phantasmatic). Gender is constantly in the process of emerging. Yet every emergence needs a continuous container for its forcefulness and volatility. When there is a "continuous" gender that can contain the various gender emergences in a way that doesn't force the self to undergo a catastrophic identity change "a gender space" is created.

However, where the continuous (which manifests itself, for example, in the a priori propensity towards saturated dichotomies) is too fragile and rigid, and its encounter with the volatile and powerful emergent threatens breakdown, parasitical relations may form between the actual and the phantasmatic gender, resulting in anxiety that further builds up fragility and rigidness. Whether these parasitical relations end in confinement within the original gender or whether they lead to a concrete sex-change procedure—they share the same "parasitic" quality that refuses transformation. In this sense, even if they lead to gender crossing, this is a "saturated crossing," one with the characteristics of a "cut" rather than a caesura; one in which the new gender demands ongoing maintenance on account of other areas of experience and thought, and, above all, one that does not enable free mobility to the "other (previous) gender" that has now become, in retrospect, an ostracized and forbidden territory. Since saturated objects are characterized not only by rigidity and lack of transformability, but also by fragility, the more saturated the object—the more threatened it becomes by any movement or change. This is why amongst transsexuals this fragility is at times manifested in extreme subjugation to the new gender's stereotypical characteristics in a way that is only a different version of the same saturated gender dichotomy which was the source of their suffering in the first place.

One form this kind of "saturated" crossing may take is some transsexuals' refusal to look back at their childhood photo albums or even show them to others, much like their refusal to mention their previous name or to somehow otherwise contain their previous identity in their new one. This refusal creates a defensive split between themselves and the entire parts of their lives as well as the lives of those surrounding them, parts whose inclusion in the continuous sequence of life and identity is of paramount importance.

Quinodoz (1998), who describes the analysis of Simone, a transsexual woman, writes in this context: "Simone complained of having 'forgotten' her pre-surgery past and, in particular, the feelings that belonged to that period of her life" (p. 95). Further on she writes:

> What she was in fact doing was unconsciously rejecting her past—and it seemed to me that this aspect . . . did indeed fall within the purview of analysis. Without analysis, I could not see how Simone could ever become reconciled with a part of herself she thought she hated. In my view, she could not readily achieve a sense of inner cohesion and personal unity without coming to terms with the first half of her life.
>
> *Ibid., p. 99*

It is precisely in such cases that it is important to think of psychotherapy or psychoanalysis as a process that encourages the possibility to contain the myriad shades of gender in the new gender, rather than forgo them. The distinction between pathology and growth in relation to gender crossing has to do with the question whether it is an act that undermines the saturated areas of thinking and experience or is itself a form of an enactment of this gender excess. When gender (old or new) becomes an addictive subjugating object in itself, crossing becomes a saturated state that obstructs development rather than enabling it. This could of course be a temporary state, a natural result of anxiety, expressing the obsessive hold of what is still experienced as transient, threatened and unattainable; but it is important to expect that with time a person will be able to relate to the new gender with the same degree of flexibility and freedom that we would expect of him or her when relating, in an intact situation of a priori congruence, to their original gender.

The treatment of transsexuality must therefore focus on establishing a continuum between the identities and an integration between the different states of psyche and soma, rather than generating a growing split between them. To return to Orlando, one can think of the treatment of transsexuality in terms of the second transformative sleep, which enabled integration, while being careful not to encourage forms of cutting as manifested in the first sleep's dissociative rift.

Quinodoz (1998, p. 99) distinguishes between transsexuality deriving from a very early experience of being "imprisoned" within the wrong actual gender, as opposed to transsexuality deriving from unprocessed hatred towards the actual gender, not because it contradicts the natural experience but because it arouses psychotic anxieties. Yet can we really discriminate between these two situations? Undoubtedly we often witness a mixture of both, with the anxiety towards the actual gender being related to it being experienced as nullifying the phantasmatic gender (which is experienced as the natural one). Perhaps the distinction here should not refer to the conscious and unconscious reasons for gender crossing, but rather to the level of their symbolic organization. Certain instances of transsexuality are indeed related, as the case below bears out, to a concrete or imagined significant object that becomes a saturated object, and the identification with which becomes malignant. When this occurs, crossing might be a psychotic-fetishistic expression of the wish to become that very other, a wish that dangerously and deceptively hides, through the possible physical transformation, a psychic transformation that could not have taken place.

From a cleft lip to a cleft tongue

Dan, a twenty-nine-year-old male, seeks psychotherapy in the midst of sex-change procedure (MTF). After approximately two years of hormonal treatment, he turns to me for consultation since he feels that the psychiatrist who has been treating him thus far is "pushing" him to complete the full transition, whereas Dan himself does not feel ready for it. He is terribly anxious and does not know how to explain why now, of all times, a moment before his planned surgery, he suddenly hesitates. Recently he has also reverted to using his original name, presenting himself alternatively as a male (Dan) and as a female (Dania).

Dan is a twin brother to Anne. They were born to relatively old parents (both in their forties) after years of fertility treatments and painful miscarriages. From the moment they were born, Dan recounts, there was a division of roles between them. Anne was a beautiful, fragile, and sickly girl who attracted a lot of attention and evoked great concern. Dan, on the other hand, was a chubby and robust baby, healthy and lively, but since he was born with a cleft lip his face was, at least in his own opinion, "damaged" in relation to Anne's face. He remembers how for years—even after the aesthetic defect was surgically corrected by two successive plastic operations—people would avert their eyes, as if searching for a more "comfortable" place to "rest" on. That "more comfortable" place was Anne's pretty face. Although Dan was in every way a clever and talented boy, he felt that he was living in her shadow or, more accurately, in her light. He always felt that he must protect her—yet he remembers feeling completely exposed when he was not by her side. He describes the gazes of others, to which he was exposed whenever Anne was not with him and her face could not serve as his refuge—as intolerable and persecutory. The relations between brother and sister were symbiotic in many ways, including early experiences of joint masturbation and sharing everything they were given or owned: toys, clothes, food. When Anne was diagnosed with celiac disease Dan stopped eating the foods she was forbidden to eat. When Dan suffered insults from fellow players in his football team Anne ripped pictures of herself in the team uniform from the walls of her room. This symbiosis was not without a price. They had very few friends who were not shared; their attachment to one another limited their areas of interest; and above all, Dan recounts, their togetherness left out their parents. They both felt that all they needed was each other. Except for their physical care neither of them remembers their parents having a significant role in their concrete or emotional lives. Dan recently felt this loss when meeting his father in the hospital where his mother was recovering from a heart attack, realizing how little they knew about each other. It seems as if, very early on, the parents gave up on any attempts to penetrate their children's symbiotic dyad. Dan describes their emotional connection to their children, as well as to one another, as distant and poor.

Dan remembers himself, already at an early age, jealous of Anne's beauty and wanting to be like her. Most of all, he was jealous of her face. While he experienced his own face as "mutilated," hers was the ideal image of the face that he could or should have had. He remembers standing next to her by the mirror, looking at her reflection instead of at his own. He also remembers the fantasy he had about his face having been mutilated during their birth (and not prior to it, as is the factual truth) and believing the cleft in his upper lip to be the result of his having sacrificed his face in order to let Anne be born whole and unharmed.

Dan recalls experiencing the words he was trying to utter as "spilling out of his mouth" in the most concrete sense: "every word was accompanied by spitting, I couldn't articulate a single word without it coming with something physical in the form of spit or, if I had been eating, chewed food that would spill out along with the words." He remembers many social occasions on which he would let Anne complete his sentences since it was more convenient for him not to "use his mouth," and since "she always knew what [he] intended to say anyway." Thus, words constituted "somatic" objects rather than symbolic ones. This bears a huge significance, as will be discussed later, when it comes to Dan's decision to undergo the physical transformation which in many ways substituted for his incapacity to work through his feelings.

Anne seemed to have served as Dan's perfect imaginary image. He remembers feeling at a very early age that since Anne was born a girl she had somehow appropriated what should have been his: the beauty, the delicateness, the caring she received—all these were attributed to her being a girl rather than to her being who she was. He recalls his envious passion for everything she had had: her clothes, her makeup accessories. In her wardrobe closet there were several dresses and shirts she bought and kept especially for him, pretending they were her own. He detested his body, which he experienced as cumbersome and damaged, and the early signs of puberty only added to his abhorrence. He fell in love with girls, but felt that he loved them as a girl and not as a boy. He wanted them to caress his hair, to touch his breasts. His sexual fantasies were never related to penetration but rather to friction, and in masturbation he always visualized his genital as a female genital rubbing against another female genital. The few sexual experiences he had were indeed experiences in which he "masturbated against" a woman's body without penetrating her. His sexual wish was to "come on her" and not to "come inside her," and he repeatedly emphasized this. This phrasing might hint at the aggression, envy, and hatred towards women (which for him were all extensions of Anne) concealed behind his desire to become a woman. This hatred may also explain the anxiety that arose during the process of preparing for sex-change surgery, which will be described further on.

The symbiotic twinship with Anne along with the critical physical difference between them created an inner environment of splitting: her perfect face as opposed to his damaged face, the love that she aroused as opposed to the aversion and embarrassment he aroused, at least in his own experience—all these were attributed to the gender dichotomy, turning it simultaneously into a rigid and an extremely fragile dichotomy. When he reached the age of eighteen he began to speak openly about his wish to undergo a sex change. His parents reacted with "shocked alienation or alienated shock," as he put it, but nevertheless supported the process. In the course of it, however, many misgivings began to emerge. Dan felt he could not find himself in his new body (which due to the hormone treatment was beginning to show feminine characteristics). He did not want to return to his old body, which he detested, but then did not feel "at home" either in the new body he had developed. Even as a woman he still felt awkward and damaged compared to Anne; he wanted to be as pretty as her, but discovered that in actuality he was not going to become a prettier woman than the man he had previously been. Gradually the therapy sessions revealed that his unconscious phantasy was not to be a woman—but to be Anne herself. She was the object of his admiration and passion, and the process he had begun was a process whose purpose was not to join her but to be her, perhaps even to replace her.

Another aspect, emerging from Dan's dreams, was related to mutilation. As I previously mentioned, Dan's fantasy was that his face had been "mutilated" in order to allow Anne to be born flawlessly. Now, instead of experiencing the gender-change procedures as remedial, he experienced them as "adding mutilation to mutilation." In one of his dreams he is lying on the operating table. One of his legs is apparently longer than the other, and the purpose of the operation, so he is told by the doctor, is to shorten the longer leg which will enable him to walk without limping. During the operation, however, it is his short leg that is mistakenly shortened, and he completely loses his ability to walk.

I understand this dream as touching upon Dan's immense anxiety around his body's change processes: the surgery that was supposed to fix what he had experienced as an a priori failure was revealed in the dream as likely to bring about an even bigger and irrevocable failure. The longed-for surgery reflecting his wish to undo the prenatal mutilation became the enactment of this mutilation. At this stage, it was clear that the wish to undergo a sex change was related to the excessiveness of Anne as a saturated object of identification. The splitting and projections that characterized Dan's relationship with her positioned Anne as an object of persecutory wholeness, the identification with which had a psychotic-fetishistic tone, accompanied with the phantasm of wholeness without lack (the lack, for him, was signified by his cleft lip). In effect the only way to get rid of this persecutory object was by fusing with it; that is, by becoming it. Yet the sex change was experienced as a cut rather than a caesura: a moment in which he would murder and be murdered, losing both Anne and himself. Dan's transsexual desires may be understood as a wish to unite with an object of *jouissance*, but, no less than that, as a way to annihilate this object by appropriating its identity. The gender dichotomy in this case was psychotically charged by the splitting between Anne's whole face as opposed to Dan's mutilated face, and between her "whole lip" and his "cleft lip," while the gender crossing was aimed at acting out that excess. It is thus possible to relate to Dan's psychotherapeutic treatment as a treatment intended to turn "the cleft lip" into a "cleft tongue"; that is, to transform the actual cleft into a symbolic one, which can be worked through rather than acted out.

The difference between transsexual states that are based on a psychotic organization, like in the case described above, as opposed to transformative transsexual states, involves the degree by which the new gender is constituted as a concrete actualization of the phantasm of wholeness. When gender crossing comes to confirm the illusion that it is impossible to fill the essential, inherent lack (Lacan, 1958), then, disguised as the realization of subjectivity, it actually undermines this very subjectivity. Oren Gozlan (2015) writes beautifully in this context that "surgery in itself becomes irrelevant to the question of pathology, because what distinguishes an Act from an acting out is not the activity but its ability to be enjoyed as lacking" (p. 54).

"To be enjoyed as lacking" means to preserve the state of lack that enables desire and movement; it means to preserve the unsaturated quality of the concrete "act" in a way that enables the new state to be constituted and reconstituted in various modes, always absorbing new meanings; it means preserving the unsaturated quality of the new body and gender so that they turn from an object of *jouissance* into a transformative object, namely into a source of psychic movement and change. Danger appears where gender crossing loses its symbolic quality and becomes a concrete act, one that psychotically regenerates the illusion of incestuous union with the original Real object. In such cases what is at stake is the act itself erasing the experience of lack, thus turning into an act that nullifies, through the concrete gratification it enables, the need to create meaning.

This can also be formulated in Bion's (1965) terms as different transformations: In "rigid motion transformations", a model of relationship is transferred as-is, from one relation to another, without any change. In the context of transsexuality, one can think of a "rigid motion gender crossing" which transfers the typical pattern of saturated gender dichotomy from the old gender to the new gender without enabling a greater freedom vis-à-vis the new gender than was enabled vis-à-vis the old one. One can also think of transsexuality as a state of "projective transformations," in which "acidic" contents are projected onto the actual gender, forming a relationship of mutual negation with it and paving the way for a gender crossing that negates the negation. Transsexuality can of course be a function of "transformations in hallucinosis"; that is, a process whose aim is the evacuation of intolerable contents which cannot be thought of or represented. Finally, transsexuality may be a function of "transformations in K"; that is, an attempt to know the other and otherness, perhaps even take possession of one's otherness.

My assumption is that every gender crossing includes all these transformations in varying degrees of dominance. To return to Dan's case, one can formulate his transsexuality as "rigid motion transformations" that transfer the saturated gender dichotomy from the male pole to the female pole, without constituting any change in his attitude towards gender itself. One can refer to his transsexuality also as "projective transformations," within which acidic persecutory elements were projected upon the actual gender, engaging in a relationship in which anything negative was considered a result of this actual male gender, thus "pushing" him to concretely negate his masculinity though its surgical undoing. In addition, one can recognize in Dan's transsexuality elements of "transformations in hallucinosis"; that is, the use of the sex-change procedures as a form of evacuation and emission of intolerable elements that cannot be thought of or represented. In this type of transformations we can include the psychotic delusion that the mutilation of his face was what enabled Anne to be born intact, as well as the hallucination that as a result of the surgery he would not only turn into the same sex as Anne, but would actually become Anne. Though one might be misled to perceive Dan's transsexuality as transformations in K, the key element in the wish to "fully know the otherness of Anne" was not really related to the wish to know her, but rather to his unconscious phantasy to take possession of her otherness. All these can explain why in Dan's case the gender crossing expressed a psychotic delusion rather than a real wish to undergo change. In other transsexual situations, however, transformations in K could indeed be dominant, and transsexuality can be understood as a real striving towards life and liveliness.

From trans-disciplinarity to inter-disciplinarity

Adrienne Harris (2011) suggests that to work on the phenomenon of transgender subjectivities is to work "trans-disciplinarily" as an enactment of the richness of dimensions and points of view that characterize this phenomenon which obviously "transgresses" the limits of our imagination and thought. One may perhaps say that the therapeutic work that offers the richest response to the transsexual phenomenon is not "trans-disciplinary" but rather "inter-disciplinary": one that focuses not on the actual linear passage from one side to another but rather emphasizes the integration of both sides and the everlasting movement between them. It is my belief that only therapeutic work based on such integration may enable the creation of a rich caesura in a place that has thus far been formulated overwhelmingly in terms of a cut.

Note

1 I use the term "transsexuality" rather than "transgenderism" when I refer to the actual transitioning from one sex to another. Transgenderism, unlike transsexuality, does not necessarily refer to an "actual" transitioning from one sex to another but rather to a broader space of expressions, behaviors, and a general sense of self.

References

Aharoni, H. and Bergstein, A. (2012). On the Caesura and Some More Caesuras, foreword to the Hebrew edition of "Caesura" by Wilfred Bion (trans. Aharoni and Bergstein). Tel Aviv: Bookworm.
Amir, D. (2014). *Cleft Tongue: The Language of Psychic Structures*. London: Karnac Books.
Amir, D. (2016). *On the Lyricism of the Mind: Psychoanalysis and Literature* (trans. Mirjam Hadar). London: Routledge.
Bion, W.R. (1962). *Learning from Experience*. London: Heinemann. [Reprinted London: Karnac Books, 1984.]
Bion, W.R. (1965). *Transformations*. London: Heinemann.
Bion, W.R. (1967). "Catastrophic Change. Unpublished paper.
Bion, W.R. (1970). Container and Contained Transformed. In *Attention and Interpretation*. London: Tavistock [Reprinted London: Karnac Books, 1984.]
Bion, W.R. (1977). *Two Papers: The Grid and Caesura*. Rio de Janeiro: Imago Editora. [Reprinted London: Karnac Books 1989.]
Britton, R. (1998). *Belief and Imagination*. New York: Routledge, 120–127.
Gozlan, O. (2015). *Transsexuality and the Art of Transitioning: A Lacanian Approach*. New York: Routledge.
Harris, A.E. (2011). Gender as a Strange Attractor: Discussion of the Transgender Symposium. *Psychoanalytic Dialogues*, 21: 230–238.
Klein, M. (1924). An Obsessional Neurosis in a Six Year Old Girl. In *The Writings of Melanie Klein*, Vol. 2, eds R. Money-Kyrle, B. Joseph, E. O'Shaughnessy, and H. Segal. London: The Hogarth Press, 1975.
Lacan, J. ([1958] 2007). *Écrits* (trans. Bruce Fink). London: W.W. Norton.
Pesach, H. (2007). Introduction to V. Woolf, *Orlando: A Biography*. Israel: Yediot Books (Hebrew).
Quinodoz, D. (1998). A FE/Male Transsexual Patient in Psychoanalysis. *International Journal of Psychoanalysis*, 79: 95–111.
Rank, O. (1915). Das Schauspiel im Hamlet. *Imago* 4.
Woolf, V. ([1928] 1949). *Orlando: A Biography*. London: The Hogarth Press.

3
GENDER TRANSITIONS AND AESTHETIC POSSIBILITIES

Dina Georgis

Following Oren Gozlan's (2015) view that "transsexuality can be thought of as a placeholder for the incommensurability between gender and sexual difference" (p. 7), this chapter extends the definition of transsexuality as not only a way to identify people who transition from one gender/sex category to another, but also to understand the psychic capacity from which the variabilities of gender are possible in the first place.[1] In psychoanalysis, sexual difference is understood as imposing ontological radical heterogeneity and this inaugurates the human subject into a lifetime of living with and defending against uncertainty. Indeed, because the trauma of sexual difference is the loss of the illusion of wholeness, gender is the elaborate fantasy that fills lack and provides narrative sense or cohesiveness to unbearable uncertainty, while transsexuality is the psychic mechanism for reiterating gender, which may or may not find expression in the desire to change sex. Importantly, gender transitions are not the choices individuals make to stabilize what they know but are instead confrontations with what feels uncertain which might bring forth new and imaginative ways of embodying gender. This is a perspective, following Gozlan (2015), that understands "transsexuality as belonging to signifying chains involved in and affected by the formation of the unconscious" (p. xi). Gender, in other words, is the psychic outcome of meaning-making under the pressures of instinctual life and the subject's encounters with otherness and difference.

The premise of this chapter challenges our popular and academic conceptions of transsexuality to think beyond the minoritizing logics of gender identities. My hope is that Chase Joynt's aesthetic text *Akin* (2012) will help elucidate why it is valuable to think about transsexuality capaciously and why the filmmaker is compelled to make a comparison between his sex change and his mother's conversion to Judaism. Specifically, this nine-minute video, which tells the story of Joynt's shared experience with his mother of sexual trauma, beautifully expresses the confusion and creative possibilities in the aftermath of events that psychically rupture the ego. As my reading of *Akin* will illustrate, an aesthetic text is more capable of exposing the affective "truths" of loss and trauma on the subject. That is because the process of aesthetic creation is in and of itself a process that helps repair or rewrite the self. Joynt's *Akin* cobbles together his "truth," but the text is hardly straightforward and is indeed saturated with hints that invite a creative engagement.

What follows is my interpretation of *Akin*, which I describe as my "playful" response to the hints that this aesthetic work makes space for. With the aesthetic, insights can be made outside the very frameworks and knowledge in which the aesthetic object is produced. The intention of this chapter is to demonstrate how the aesthetic impulse is an attempt to represent an interior reality or a wanting that is not fully available to consciousness. In this way, the aesthetic is a method for encountering unconscious knowledge. But more importantly, the aesthetic is implicated in the creative transitions of the human. In other words, creative expression does not only belong to artistic creation but to how life is creatively lived, embodied, written, and rewritten. My hope is that my reader might be incited to join me in imagining what it would mean to think openly and creatively about what enigmatic knowledge is communicated in aesthetic expression and what modes of inquiry are possible from understanding transsexuality as the creative process of becoming from ontological difference.

Chase Joynt's video *Akin* begins melancholically inside a moving car. The camera is positioned between the driver's window and the windshield. Though vision is blurred by the weather and by the wipers that squeak back and forth to clean the falling rain, the homes of a "nice" middle-class suburb are seen to pass by. The scene, which foreshadows the challenges of seeing and knowing in the aftermath of trauma, ends with the viewer catching a glimpse of the filmmaker's mother through the rear-view mirror after she announces that she would never want to move back "here," here being the neighborhood where she and presumably her former husband started their lives together and had a family. "Here," she explains to her son, is "not who I am . . . I'm not sure who I am but it's not this . . . it wasn't who I was then either." "I'm not sure who I am but I know it's not this" might be the words the younger Chase might have shared with his mother when he was ready to come out to her as trans. Chase here is hinting at how something in their experiences have an uncanny analogous composition, even if he himself can't quite fully articulate its significance.

Akin demonstrates the aesthetic impulse to create and repair damage caused from the past. D.W. Winnicott's (1971) view on creativity is that it is motivated by the active search for a self. This search begins early—at the moment when the child realizes its dependence on the mother and loses the illusion of omnipotence and undifferentiated unity with her and must therefore learn how to separate from her and emerge from that separation as an autonomous being (of course the child is never fully autonomous and the adult similarly never loses their dependency on the other). The work of achieving this ontological development occurs in the real and imaginary space between mother and child. In this space, the child creates a world by playing with toys, which act as transitional objects for helping the child find its place in reality and learn how to be alone. The success of how well the child achieves "aloneness" is contingent paradoxically on how well a parent is able to create a space where the child does not feel abandoned and is strong enough to stand alone.

Akin, a film that documents the artist/son's visit to his childhood home with his mother, seems to delve into the world of primal longings. This is not a place of weakness. On the contrary, Chase, the son, has become strong enough to let his adult illusions of omnipotence perforate and is reaching for transitional objects in order to re-find, maybe even (re-)create his self. The mother both real and symbolic is once again called upon to adapt to this need, to act as the good enough mother who will facilitate the transition. The challenge of the "good enough" mother as understood by Winnicott (1971) is to hold the space—to be there and not be there in small doses so that the child can feel securely alone. No child ever grows up feeling perfectly secure because the mother's task in producing the perfect outcome from a perfect recipe of there and not there is impossible and as such she can only ever be good enough. But with a good-enough mother, the child is able to take the objects handed to him/her and begin the process of discovering a self through play.

For Winnicott, play is not only foundational to selfhood but also the basis of art and culture. Play in other words is and can be a highly sophisticated and complex activity, and from a psychoanalytic perspective is also the means through which we negotiate conflict and work through the confusions and conflicts that surround sexual difference, desire, and loss. In *Akin* the relationship of loss and art is more transparent. The film, which is narrated by Joynt in the form of a letter, is written to his mother after spending a day with her in the suburbs visiting the homes they used to live in. In it he is clear about the purpose of the visit, which is also arguably the purpose of the film, when he tells her, "there were open doors in need of closing and I knew you and I had the only keys." His pronouncement begs the question: must one walk through a door and venture into space, even spend some time playing there, before returning to it and closing it? In the film, mother and son never actually open the car door and step out, let alone knock on the doors of the houses they used to live in. Parked in front of the house, they look out through the screened windows of the car, at a safe distance. A door, in other words, does not necessarily feel like a welcoming invitation. I am reminded of Kafka's parable "Before the Law" where a man who seeks admission through the door insists on getting permission from the doorkeeper. The doorkeeper never grants it to him, but also never denies him admission to a door that had actually been left open for him all along. For the artist and his mother, the door and doorkeepers might be the ghosts of the past whose appearances might feel like frightening obstacles in the way of the door but are paradoxically responsible for keeping it open in the first place. The door might also be an unconscious symbolization of the anxieties that surround a difficult past and simultaneously the transitional object needed for creative reparation and healing.

As mother and son drive by the dream house that the artist's father and mother built together, Joynt remarks, nothing looked as it did when they had lived there: the house had become completely transformed. Mother tells her son to stop filming, as though the event of visiting the house had been rendered meaningless by the changes. Chase does not push her to be curious and stay (you can never force curiosity on anyone). Noticing her defensive reaction, in his letter to her he says: "we both knew your reasons [for wanting to leave] had nothing to do with those changes." If the mother is symbolically the object that creates the condition for play and reparation, Joynt's mother both "succeeded" and "failed" to help her son open (and close) the door: she joined him on the journey back but did not walk him through every door. Chase was left alone but not abandoned to face the house and the painful memories that lay disguised within its altered walls. If what compelled him to come back was to mourn and transition into a new place, then it was a journey only he alone could make even though the son may have yearned for his mother help take him there.

The theme of transitions runs through *Akin*. Much like the house they had once lived in, both mother and son had also changed and reconstructed themselves: she had converted to Judaism and he had had a sex change. Within the first few moments of the film, the artist makes a comparison between these two transitions. He wonders: "I'll never forget the day you told me you were converting from Christianity to Orthodox Judaism. I thought to myself, I wonder if this is the appropriate time to tell her I'm transitioning from female to male. I always knew it would make a great story." As he narrates these words, still pictures from the past flash across the screen of mother and child looking content and connected. He goes on to say, "The truth is I think I've remained so focused on telling the story of our differences, because I've always been so afraid of telling the story of why we're the same." Joynt is insinuating that perhaps his insistence on their difference has served to shelter or defend against a truth rendered to silence and obfuscation, but still painfully connects them to one another. That shared truth, we ascertain, is the experience of sexual violence, likely to have happened inside that dream home. Much like the house that no longer resembles what it was, so too do mother and child look very different from what they were and also from each other. The filmmaker is suggesting that their turn towards difference, or to radically different reconstructions of their selves, might be the very thing that makes them the same.

To make a comparison between a religious conversion and a sex transition is indeed tricky, especially when they are being linked by a shared experience of sexual trauma that would render their identities as causal, symptomatic, and therefore pathological. This linkage indeed threatens the popular discourses that explain transsexuality as neither a choice nor a pathology.[2] For many trans people, to be trans is not a choice but rather about being born in the wrong body. Essentialist narratives about trans identity mitigate against pathologization of gender dysphoria. Such insistences cannot be separated, in Trish Salah's (2014) words "from the ways in which transsexuals [have] been subalterned by both feminist transphobia and medical discourses" (p. 201). Considered a mental disorder by the psychiatric community, on the one hand, and attacked for bolstering the gender binary or copping out from the difficulties of living in an ambiguous body, on the other, trans people tell their story between a rock and a hard place. "Born this way" is the best possible story under hostile conditions and attacks that render trans people monstrous, delusional, or weak. Indeed, the emotional logic of "born this way" defends trans people's right to exist in a dignified way. It positions their sex change as an empowered and conscious choice made in keeping with who they "essentially" are.

All this to say that there is a great deal of pressure to write the story of transsexuality correctly. If you are seeking surgery, that story has to cohere with officially sanctioned rationales. Your gender identity has to be fixed and stably conform to your stated gender choice. But the imperative to produce identity coherently and in a linear story of transition has had the effect of reducing the origin story of transsexuality as either biological (born this way) or, from an academic point of view, as socially constructed.[3] Both stories, Oren Gozlan argues in *Transsexuality and the Art of Transitioning*, refuse uncertainty. They also refuse incoherence and variance on how to be trans. These strategies encourage compliance to their respective temporalities. Collective strategies for transition are not only practical in helping people through the stages of transition, but also offer safety in community and discourses that help trans people stand up to transphobia and transphobic institutions. These are psychological solutions, unique in content but are not exceptional to trans people.[4] And like all strategies of survival, they can be ontologically limiting and potentially punitive to those for whom the script feels wrong or if there are competing pressures and temporalities (from family, ethnic community, etc.), conscious or unconscious.

Defined psychically, however, transsexual temporality has no predetermined intent and a defined future but is an unsettled process with queer desires, with the failures and breakdowns of symbolic articulation of gender, and with embodiment. One might say that transitions are made from an affective logic not a discursive one. They are motivated by affects and intensities and the enigmas of sexual difference that demand to be expressed, heard, and materialized. In psychoanalysis, sexual difference is not reducible to sexual identities of male and female (Gherovicci, 2010, p. 61). Sexual difference is the raw field of desire, perversion, and trauma that shape subjectification but remain inaccessible to the subject. One might think of sexual difference as the psychic challenge that puts pressure on the subject to settle the trauma of difference into coherent identities. In other words, gender settles the Real of desire, using Lacan's term, or the dilemmas of our polymorphous perverse origins, as Freud put it. It is the psychic strategy made from the loss of having to renounce the carnal and the perverse for the right to be loved. While Winnicott's object relations' theory undermines the sexual/erotic dimensions of subjectification that I spoke of earlier, for the context of this chapter especially it is important to understand the "problem" of sexual difference with the "problem" of love and relationality. Sexual difference as undifferentiated otherness becomes implicated and entangled with the actual Other, who comes to stand in for difference in phantasy. In this way, sexual difference, Gozlan (2015) writes, "is not simply a problem for the transsexual subject" (p. 2); it is rather a problem for the psyche, which must transform radical or queer heterogeneity into a cohesive self that can live with and be loved by others.

Gender and other constructions of culture is the price we pay to be socially recognized. Implicated in loss, it is fundamentally and constitutively ambivalent. Not everyone, however, is equally or similarly ambivalent. And not everyone notices or explores their ambivalences equally—nor do they negotiate them similarly. In this way, transsexuality is not exceptional, but in Gozlan's (2015) words a "metaphor for the aporia of gender" (2015, p. xiii). Indeed, for Gozlan (2015), gender rests on "unmetabolized affect" (p. 84), or what I refer to as queer affect (Georgis, 2013), against which the subject must persistently defend to sustain a version of gender and social identity they have settled into. These unmetabolized or queer affects are the remains of loss from a carnal/familial relationality that had to be discarded or sublimated to become an acculturated properly gendered human. When they return, though disorienting and difficult, they make space or create an opening for re-finding the self in reparation. One way to understand reparation is to think of it as the aesthetic impulse for transformation, which for Winnicott was only possible through creative play.

Motivated by the hope that a return "home" would open and close some painful doors, Joynt's *Akin* is arguably a film about what it means to have creative or aesthetic reparation. But since his story of trauma is told alongside the story of his sex change, it is also a bold account of transsexuality. Whether intended or not, Joynt's story of his transition articulated alongside his story of shared family violence does not comply with most discourses of trans identity, academic or popular. His story instead asks us to confront transsexuality's kinship to trauma. Nothing in the video suggests that his sex change is a causal outcome of violence, but the opposite is also true. The question of causality is a red herring, as is the demand for origins. While there might be an "origin" to gendered being, or more precisely multiple psychic origins/events and phantasies that shape gendered being, none will ever be fully accessed or understood.[5] All attempts for narrative coherence are eventually undermined as uncertainty arises in queer affects. But when narratives are given permission to breathe, in this case by way of aesthetic play and expression that give voice to wounds, the story has a chance to change and the identity the space to transition. This is the reparative moment—a break from the compulsion to repeat—what Freud termed "working through" (1914) which in his mind was an interminable process of transformation and reparation. Freud was not interested in his patients uncovering the truth about their identities, in the parlance of contemporary discourse; rather, he helped his patients disassemble their defenses, relieving them from debilitating symptoms. Indeed, the work of uncovering the symptom reveals a story about the patient's personal history of trauma and suffering, otherwise lost to memory. In gaining insights into symptom-formation, the story of the self actually changes—it is rewritten so to speak. Indeed, with such insight, the individual can even claim the symptom in a sinthome, Lacan's concept that explains the capacity for individuals to creatively identify with their symptoms and relate to it in, writes Gozlan (2015), "a creative product of the self." (p. 49). Here the truth about the self is located in psychic history—not in choice, or social construction, or pathological dysfunction. And it is a malleable shape shifting truth because psyches are capable of transitions. In his artist bio Joynt asks: "I wonder what it might mean to tell personal stories without claiming personal truths? And furthermore, I wonder what it might mean if the story of me didn't have to inherently disprove and/or de-authenticate the story of you?" (Artist Bio, para. 4). As I see it, Joynt is imploring his interlocutors to read his stories curiously, as playful openings, not as conclusions to gendered being with reductive truth claims. His art, and specifically *Akin*, is giving voice to the ineffable wounds of gendered being and from this viewpoint does indeed authenticate everyone's story.

Joynt's story of sex change is affectively linked to his story of family violence and the transitions that took place in its wake. If the confrontation with sexual difference is a confrontation with the loss of the illusion of wholeness (unity with the Other), with lack and with uncertainty, and if we come into gendered being to preserve love and our dependency on the Other from the threat of separation and aggression (Butler, 2004; Kristeva, 1982; Winnicott, 1971), then violence is not a unique experience of some individuals but intrinsic to the possibility of gender and to the capacity for love and connectedness. In both psychic realms, dissolution to various degrees is inevitable. Gender resolves sexual difference and organizes love and dependency to a socially acceptable other, but there are no guarantees for stability in either realm. When love is undone, as it often does, we return to the queer space of confusion, aloneness, and uncertainty—sometimes destabilizing gender identification—and creating the conditions for creative reconstructions and transitions, gendered or otherwise. Alternately, experiences of gendered uncertainty often unravel love and sometimes alter what objects an individual would want to love. Suggested here is that creative transitions and reconstruction is how we survive or repair what comes undone. In this way, the transitions of mother and son are analogous, psychoanalytically speaking. *Akin* invites the possibility that trans identity is neither a social construction nor biological but an "aesthetic" response and a psychic transformation, perhaps "akin" to other forms of psychic transformations. Indeed, mother and child have to rebuild their lives from the difficult and confusing remains of violence

With the filmmaker and his mother, we are witness to two reconstructed humans. It is clear that they have survived well. The shattered pieces of their egos have been glued together and they are, so to speak, on the other side of abjection, unbearable affect, and incoherence. And yet Joynt is unsettled. Perhaps what is disconcerting is how settled they have both become. He says he can't believe it's been a decade since they've been back to the suburbs. In all likelihood, it took that long to find enough strength to make the return and to risk being undone by it. Looking at her son through the rear-view mirror as she speaks in the third person (as if to distance herself from her experience?), mother says, "it's another life, yes it impacts you, but don't go back to it because it keeps you stuck back there instead of facing forward." Though Chase, the son, is silent at this moment, Joynt, the filmmaker, presents an ambivalence to the value of moving forward while avoiding the past. Not prepared to corroborate her story for why there was no point in filming a house that had changed so much, Chase in his narration seems to want her to know that he could see that she was affected by the journey back—that even after a decade, it was not so easy to open the door, step out of the car, and stand in the presence of a house whose walls might emit a muffled cry. Joynt might have been attempting to express a difficult truth for which he may have needed his mother to act as transitional object; namely, that conversions/transitions can disguise the residual fragility brought on by trauma if the creative reinvention of the self becomes too hardened or, or as Patricia Gherovicci (2010) points out, is treated psychically "as a way out" (p. 11) from the challenge of living with difference. In other words, a transition, for psychoanalytic trans theorists Gozlan and Gherovicci, is not an end in itself but merely a beginning, or one transition among many transitions.

In a published interview with Joynt, Hannah Dyer asks: "Was it your hope that the car ride would give language to affect not yet named but nonetheless present?" (Dyer and Joynt, 2017, p. 215) The film is shot almost entirely inside the car: mother at the wheel and son in the backseat filming her. Very little of their conversation is recorded. But we know from the narrator that they don't talk about the time, in his words "when you [mother] went away to recover from past violence and that while you were gone that same violence found me." It would seem that this set-up reproduces the psychic environment of mother and son. The son looks to mother for answers but is instead met with silence. The wish that the car ride to the house would bring transformation or answers to a painful history falls short of its intentions. But does *Akin*, as an aesthetic attempt "to loosen control of the narrative" (ibid., p. 215), have reparative effect? In the interview, Joynt remarks: "*Akin* has afforded me an opportunity to breathe air into an otherwise claustrophobic engagement with a stagnant history; but has also revealed the limits of storytelling as method" (ibid., p. 218). Joynt's comment exposes an interesting slippage. What has afforded him an opening and an engagement with the past is not in spite of the limits of storytelling, as I see it, but a direct outcome of it. In *Akin*, arguably a story about his family, Joynt embarks on a journey where he is confronted with how knowledge is resisted. Put differently, it is only in the telling of the story that resistance is brought to bear and something in the claustrophobic narrative is loosened.

In *Akin*, defensive narratives are foregrounded and simultaneously undone. One way this occurs is in Joynt's insistence on identifying sameness between mother and son despite the different paths taken by them. In his narration, he says, "I find great comfort in these moments, of recognizing all that is changed by finding something that rather remarkably has stayed the same." He is talking about their shared pretty eyes here, but it is followed by this remark: "The strength of our family is rooted in the survival of women, one of them being you and one of them being me. It's a history now kept secret under the veils of religious modesty and the illusions of a gendered dream." In this segment of the film, the camera is shifting from street to sky. It is not a transcendental move because things seen are connected to the ground:

the tips of bare trees, streetlights, power lines. There is an insistence on not forgetting, on not disconnecting what was from what has become: to see the past in the present. Underneath the wig and behind the gendered impression is a shared history of violence, of vulnerability and of strength. People see the present version of a mother and son. But underneath those versions is the truth of messy hair and visible scars.

Chase, you might say, is asking his mother to be, quoting Carson, a historian, "one who asks about things," to pause and be curious about the queer feeling she had while parked in front of the dream house. In a caption at the end of the video he quotes Anne Carson who writes, "the asking is not idle. It is when you are asking about something that you realize you yourself have survived it, and so you must carry it, or fashion it into a thing that carries itself." Transsexuality is Chase's queer survival. For him to communicate this in *Akin* is not undermining his identity, but actually carrying it. Transsexuality might be regarded as a different kind of embodiment in the world, but as a psychic phenomenon, it is not special. It encapsulates the transitions that the psyche must make to negotiate the conflicts of sexual difference and polymorphous perversion. Transsexuality, as Gozlan (2015) writes, "captures a universal enigma at the heart of subjectivity" (p. 12) and as such helps us theorize the psychic transformation of difference required to produce a cohesive self – a self that is also always in transit (in the film, this is metaphorized with the moving car). Similarly, Joynt understands transness as a method of theoretical inquiry—as a way to make insight into gender as opposed to settle it. Perhaps this explains his non-compliance to identity and why he can attribute the strength of his survival and the strength it took to become a man to come from what it means to be a woman. Indeed, for Winnicott, compliance shuts down playful, inventive, and creative living. *Akin* is a plea for mourning and creative survival in non-compliance. His sex change does not settle into a psychic state that covers over the loss and the fragilities from which he needed to survive, but is instead a resource for challenging psychic complacency. In this vein, he asks his mother the hardest question of all: "How do we talk about a shared history of violence when the only man we talk about is me?"

This chapter has aimed to understand sex transitions from the queer excesses of narrative and language. It offers a theoretical approach that universalizes gender and its transitions in ways that do not create a binary between trans and non-trans people. For me, the queer space of the non-verbal is the place of loss, or lack, and its legacies. Gender fills the space of lack. It is the symbolic conclusion of the demand to settle the "problem" of sexual difference and the enigmas of sexual being. Joynt's film might be understood as the method through which something new is birthed in himself. Arguably, he engages in a playful transitional process, not unlike a sex change where parts of oneself are opened up and imaginatively stitched together (Gozlan, 2015, p. 54–55) to re-create what was there. Indeed, for Gozlan (2015, citing Gherovicci, p. 54), surgery itself is a narration that accompanies the physical act. Transition, in other words, is an aesthetic process. In describing the act of painting, Marion Milner (1973) explains that the creative process "is a plunge that one could sometimes do deliberately but which also sometimes just happen[s], as when one falls in love" (p. 31). The outcomes and meanings then made from painting, filming, falling in love, transitioning can never be anticipated because what is being expressed is born from the queer within—from a non-logical non-discursive space in the body that expresses imaginatively and calls us to be open to understand its illusions and to be transformed. My suggestion here is that the transitions are akin to how I define aesthetic creation: the impulse to give form and value to the self's enigmas. When we are moved by the aesthetic, as I was by Joynt's film, then we are submitting to the urge and desire to unpack its riddles.

Notes

1 Readers will notice that I exclusively use the word "transsexual" rather than "transgender" in this chapter, despite the fact that transgender is the umbrella term for non-normative gender identity. Though the nomenclature for gender identities has proliferated over the years (gender queer, non-binary, etc.) and exceed these two terms, my chapter is interested in what ties them together rather than what sets them apart. For the purposes of this chapter, the distinction between, for instance, transgender and transsexual is not relevant to my argument. But because transsexuality is normally understood to involve transition—psychosocial and/or physical—it helps me define the psychic mechanisms that destabilize gender and render it vulnerable to transitions.

2 To understand more deeply why the trans community has had to defend against the discourse of pathology, Patricia Gherovicci's *Please Select Your Gender* offers a cogent analysis of how trans people have been pathologized by Freud's theory of hysteria, which interestingly helped him conceptualize his theory of the unconscious. But Gherovicci (2010) works with the very conceptual tools of psychoanalysis to help her think against transsexuality as a pathological identity. In psychoanalysis, she writes, "the body is not a natural entity governed purely by biological laws and cannot be reduced to projections or representations ... Psychoanalysis has the advantage of being able to operate in this problematic intersection between the signifier and the flesh, between body and language" (2010, p. 61). Hysteria, she argues, is culture specific—it is the collective sense make of disease (2010, p. 56). Though hysteria in actuality defies definition, it has provided the definition of transsexuality in psychoanalytic history, challenged not only by Gherovicci but by other contemporary psychoanalytic thinkers (Cavanagh, 2015; Salah, 2014).

3 As I've argued in former work (Georgis, 2013), postmodern and social construction theories of identity have largely been responses to the violences of modernity and colonial imperialism. While they effectively give us tools to resist essentialist reductive depictions of subjectivity, they fail to demonstrate how people affectively and ambivalently negotiate social identities. Indeed, a psychoanalytic perspective on identity makes space for the possibility that social constructions are psychically motivated and that the psyche is interminably affectively reconstructing itself. So while it might feel safe to arm oneself with social construction critique to defend against hate, it can put a constraint on the processes of becoming. In other words, a social construction as defense can stifle. The main objective of social construction theory is critique. The invitation here is not re-creation or reconstruction of self but to resist the forces that oppress you—resist pathologization, resist victimization, resist the perpetrators of violence. Non-compliance to the way things are gives way to new possibilities and transitions, even social change, but as an end in itself, we become subjected to the stable narratives and discourses of protest that may not offer reparation for suffering or make space for re-imagining and reconstructing life. In so doing, protest itself becomes the life-line. In the absence of being given permission to create or become, resistance becomes the *raison d'être* of marginalized groups. When you are not given the space to create, you may think all you can do is resist.

4   Early in queer theory history, Eve Sedgwick (1990) had suggested that we should be very careful with minoritizing positions on homosexuality. She draws on Freud who in his theory of sexuality argued that our sexuality is in essence polymorphously perverse, suggesting that sexuality has no focus but merely aims to maximize pleasure from any part of the body and with any other body. Heterosexuality, from this view, is the achievement of culture, not essence. For Sedgwick, a minoritizing principle on sexuality renders identities stable and essentialist. But more importantly, a universalizing principle means that sex and gender is protean and that no one is safely who or what they think they are.
5   For Melanie Klein (1937), phantasies are not outside reality for the child, but the unconscious expression of libidinal and aggressive impulses as the child encounters the outside world, namely the child's primary (m)Other. As such, even though our origins are rooted in human experience, they will forever be enigmatic to us.

References

Butler, J. (2004). *Undoing gender*. New York: Routledge.
Cavanagh, S. (2015). "Transsexuality and Lacanian psychoanalysis." In Dina Georgis, Sara Matthews, & James Penney (eds), *The Freudian legacy* (Canadian Network of Psychoanalysis), 1, 104–124.
Dyer, H. and Joynt, C. (2017). Aestheticizing trauma and the remains of childhood secrets: A Conversation with Chase Joynt's Akin. *Psychoanalysis, Culture and Society*, 22 (2), 212–219.
Chase Joynt Bio. Retrieved March 12, 2017 from http://chasejoynt.com/about/bio/
Freud, S. (1914). Remembering, repeating, and working through. *The standard edition of the complete psychological works of Sigmund Freud: Vol. XII (1911–1913)*. Edited and translated by James Strachey, in collaboration with Anna Freud, assisted by Alix Strachey and Alan Tyson. 24 vols. London: Hogarth, 145–156.
Georgis, D. (2013). *The better story: Queer affects from the Middle East*. Albany, NY: SUNY Press.
Gherovici, P. (2010). *Please select your gender: From the invention of hysteria to the democratizing of transgenderism*. New York: Routledge.
Gozlan, O. (2015). *Transsexuality and the art of transitioning: A Lacanian approach*. New York: Routledge.
Joynt, Chase. (2012). *Akin*. Canada.
Klein, M. ([1937] 1998). The importance of symbol-formation in the development of the ego. In M. Klein, *Love, guilt and reparation, and other works, 1921–1945*. London: Hogarth Press, 219–232.
Kristeva, J. (1982). *Approaching abjection, powers of horror*. New York: Columbia University Press.
Milner, M. (1973). *On not being able to paint*. New York: International Universities Press.
Salah, T. (2014). Notes on the subaltern. *TSQ: Transgender Studies Quarterly*. "Inaugural Issue: Keywords for Trans* Studies," 1 (1–2), 199–203.
Sedgwick, E. (1990). *The Epistemology of the closet*. Berkeley, CA: University of California Press.
Winnicott. D. W. ([1971] 2005) *Playing and reality*. London: Routledge.

4

TAKING (MY) TIME

Temporality in transition, queer delays, and being (in the) present[1]

Atalia Israeli-Nevo

I wasn't born a transwoman.

This statement could be considered provocative, reactionary, subversive and/or trivial. It raises some questions about the temporality of trans narratives and bodies. If gender isn't necessarily a trait, is the passage through linear heteronormative time is what determines it? If so, what makes us trans people? Do we change over time? Do we turn from one gender to another? From cis to trans? If so, what causes this shift?

As a woman who wasn't born trans, my trans identity took time to settle. It is still settling throughout time, unfolding, while manifesting itself in the present. This notion of "doing identity" in the present and embracing past identities, rather than erasing them, is important when talking about trans subjectivity and embodiment.

This chapter examines the practice of being/making/creating/developing trans identity through the notion of "taking one's time." I will begin with my autobiographical narrative as a transwoman, taking her time while transitioning. I will then discuss more general notions of what it means to take one's time, the bodily and affective reactions this practice leads to, and the classist and racial implications of such a notion. In general, I wish to demonstrate the ways in which "taking time" is embedded within the present, and to trace the meanings of this process.

This chapter is a theoretic and creative conjunction of personal narratives, public narratives, and trans cultural pieces such as films, series, and novels. In addition, throughout my analysis I will use theories of trans and queer temporalities. I will begin with an analysis of what I call "classic" trans temporalities, which I will explain through a narrative reading of Caitlyn Jenner's public coming out. Following that I will elaborate on my own experience as a transwoman taking her time transitioning to suggest a different kind of temporality that disrupts the progressive force of the classic ones. After that I will use Imogen Binnie's novel *Nevada* and John Greyson's series *Murder in Passing* to demonstrate the introspective sides of taking time. The films *Jupiter Ascending* and *Tangerine* will aid me in my discussion of the classist and racial implications of such a practice. Finally, I will conclude with some of the problematic aspects of taking time, and the potential it has to the notion of being (in the) present.

"Classic" trans temporalities

Temporality and narrative are interwoven with one another. In fact, narratives are the tool with which subjects incorporate time and chronology into the anecdotal pieces of their daily life. This is especially clear in trans narratives, embedded within a change of gender identity and holding a need to sort time in order to incorporate it within the gender change.

I would like to illustrate two ways in which time is incorporated in trans narratives that have become almost hegemonic within past and contemporary trans politics. I would like to show how these temporalities are manifested by looking at the commercialized story of North America's most recently famous trans person, TV personality and former decathlete Caitlyn Jenner.

Jenner talked about being a transwoman for the first time in April 2015, in a two-hour-long interview with Diane Sawyer on ABC's *20/20* television show. With almost 17 million viewers, the interview had one of the highest ratings in the show's history (Kissell, 2015). Right before she finished introducing the long anticipated interview, the broadcaster gave a note about the pronouns used to refer to Jenner: "In this moment [. . .] Jenner says we should use the familiar pronoun for him, as we try to tell his story" (ABC News, 2015).

Jenner insisted on using her male pronouns until her debut on *Vanity Fair* in June 2015, in which she announced her new name Caitlyn and asked people to refer to her as "she" (Bissinger, 2015). Her insistence on using male pronouns even after she came out publicly as a transwoman can be read as an attempt to subvert gender norms and highlight the fluid nature of gender identities. Indeed, that it takes one's time to change from one gender to the other, and thus that gender can be perceived as a fluid category. However, it seems that Jenner's use of male pronouns came from the need to wait until she could be "fully" seen as a woman, or rather revealed as one: her appearance on the magazine's cover complete with white dress and loose long hair represented a stark contrast to her appearance at the *20/20* interview, in which she kept her then-familiar public appearance (a buttoned blue shirt and a ponytail).

The point of this description is not to critique Jenner's individual choices regarding her body and her identity, but rather to trace the trans narratives and temporalities with which her public story and appearances resonate. It seems that this particular shift between her publicly known "male figure" to her "female figure" as Caitlyn contains in itself an "extreme makeover" storyline: an over-the-top, incredible, and almost impossible transformation from one sex/gender to the other. In one of the chapters in *Second Skins*, Jay Prosser analyzes transsexual autobiographies and calls these reoccurring shifts a "conversion," a critical moment in which one transforms and changes from one life form to the other (Prosser, 1998, pp. 100–101).

This narrative assumes a deep gap between the former gender identity and the new one. It identifies one moment of somatic change that allows the subject to move to the other side of the gap (without looking back), and change everything. Jenny Sundén claims this kind of narrative is infused in a futural temporality, in which the "spark of difference" between the genders ignites a split between (in Jenner's case) the male past and the female future (Sundén, 2015, pp. 204–205).

At the same time, a different temporality is produced in Jenner's interview. Showing Jenner a picture from one of her athletic competitions for males in the past, Diane Sawyer asks for her aid: "Help . . . Everybody's struggling with what this is" (pointing at one of the pictures). In response, Jenner points at the picture expressively and says, "That is me, that is her" (ABC News, 2015).

This is a different narrative, in which the new/aspired gender was "always there." This is a narrative created in the junction between trans subjects who wish to change their bodies and the medical institutions which hold means to change one's gender/sex. The physicians are looking for a very specific narrative, in which the somatic changes are merely a means to reveal and relieve the "real" gender trapped inside the wrong body (Spade, 2006). This is a temporality in "past tense," in which the aspired gender "has been there all along as an affective force of the past in the present" (Sundén, 2015, p. 200).

Although they are temporally different, these two narratives have one thing in common—the turning from one gender into another is complete. They are linear, whether this linearity comes from a direct transformation or from a reimagining of the past in the present. In both cases, they are moving towards the future without looking back: The first narrative puts its emphasis on the future that comes after the "conversion," and although the second narrative is in "past tense," its point of reference is also the future, because it revisits past life experiences from a "futural gender" point of view. They are representing a jump between the past and the future, without addressing the present.

What are other possible narratives? What do they produce in terms of the linear and progressive notion of classic trans temporalities?

Disrupting the progress

It took me almost a year from the point I began openly living as a transwoman to the time I chose to put female hormones in my body. This decision was not an easy one to make. Deliberately and artificially changing one's body is not an act one can make on a whim. What was harder than the decision itself was actually giving myself the time and not rushing myself to decide.

Everywhere around me I felt enormous pressure either to forfeit this "trans escapade," or to "go on with it." The cis people around me were puzzled, anxious, and sometimes angry with the fact that I demanded to be addressed with female pronouns and considered a woman without (at least seemingly) making any efforts to pass as a woman, except for wearing dresses and skirts. On the other hand, a lot of trans people were puzzled as well, and decided that the fact that I did not immediately choose to take hormones and pursue top and bottom surgery made me genderqueer, and were sometimes baffled by the fact that I dared to call myself a transwoman.

Taking hormones made me feel good with my body. It didn't change my body in ways I imagined it would, but that was mainly because I wasn't sure even how to imagine my body. I liked the idea of forming it in the present, and not trying to fit it into something I wasn't even sure I had imagined in the past. As a transwoman who wasn't born one, I have the privilege of constantly imagining and reimagining my identity and my body, having different images of myself which can affect the ways I act and change my body in the "present tense."

Taking my time to decide if I wanted to take hormones or not made me realize that I wanted to intentionally "take my time" with my transition, examining from every possible angle every decision I make. Though this is possibly a partial outcome of a need for constant control, I am not convinced that this is the whole story. Nasser Abourahme discusses both the dangers and opportunities of a halted present to postcolonial subjects. In his discussion of a temporal present after failed Palestinian revolutions, he argues that this present holds a "blurring of temporal markers" in which the past and future are more closed and yet more present (Abourahme, 2016, p. 153). This halting of the past and future, and at the same time the holding of them, allows an indeterminacy to the subaltern subjectivity. Similarly, I would like to argue that as trans subjects in this transphobic world, we are encouraged and forced into a position of not being present. We are dissociated from our bodies, our loved ones, and our general environment. This dissociation throws us into a far future in which we are safe after we have passed and found a bodily and social home. However, this future is imagined and unreachable, resulting in us being out of time.

Thus, taking one's time has a potential to put the trans subject's emphasis on the present, to pull him/her/them back into the time cycle. This is a mindful embodied present, in which one has a chance to halt and delay his/her futural aspirations regarding his/her identity and explore them. This mindful element of the present will be discussed below, both in my autobiography and in the other trans cultural texts.

The decision to "take time" has direct implications on my appearance and my passing status. The fact that I am taking my time to decide whether I want to remove my body hair, in what way and on what parts, results in being able to pass as a woman with hair on my legs and occasionally on my chest. This causes me to stay, for a while at least, in a liminal state "in between genders," in which I am unable to be fully read or categorized by the cis gaze. It is in this state where cis subjects often mistake trans subjects as cis, but are then left feeling deceived. This is one of the most dangerous affective moments in trans lives. As Kristen Schilt and Laurel Westbrook (2009) have shown, the feeling of being "tricked" leads cis subjects (mostly cis men) into being physically aggressive, and sometimes fatally violent, towards trans subjects (ibid., p. 452).

This phase disrupts the progressive linearity of classic trans temporalities. During one of these liminal times, I met an old acquaintance on my way out of the campus, with whom I took some courses during my BA. He hasn't seen me for maybe two years, and although he knew I was transitioning, he didn't recognize me when I greeted him. "You've changed," he told me, referring to me with the male pronoun, and then immediately corrected himself.

What did he see, in that moment? What affects were generated when he turned his gaze to me when I greeted him? It would seem reasonable that he wouldn't recognize me because I am already transitioning and passing more as a woman. Then again, the fact that I'm taking my time with it (and, sometimes, go a few days without hormones for various reasons) probably causes him to see me differently than what he had probably imagined. The pronoun confusion shows that this moment represents a distortion of a trans linear temporality, sending it back and forth like a ping pong ball, or more like a quantum particle, being potentially in a range of different places. The fact that I can pass at the same time as a man, a woman, and something in-between, creates an excessive affective moment, in which the person in front of me is temporally delayed and pulled into the mindful present, forced to recognize his/her confusion.

Another affective process that comes into being is an (un)intentional politicization of trans identity. A personal example may come in handy here:

> I have been asked to talk at an LGBTQA+ youth group about trans identity. During a short break, after I've been talking for almost an hour about my experience of my body and my life as a transwoman, one of the group facilitators approaches and sits by me.
>
> Hesitantly but eagerly, she inquires: "I've been meaning to ask you. I see that you don't shave your legs. Is that for feminist reasons?"
>
> I am puzzled by the question, not sure how to answer, or even take it. A bit taken aback, I say: "Well … I think that when I first started transitioning it was for feminist, or political, reasons, but now I'm not sure. I think it's got to do more with the fact that it's hard to face my body issues, even more in an electrolysis treatment, being vulnerable in front of other people who might be not that trans-friendly."
>
> Without even thinking about what I just said, she blurts out: "So it's for feminist reasons."

It seems that once the practice of transitioning is perceived differently from one trying only to reach the other gender as quickly as one can, it is perceived as having a say on reality, as political. Although I have chosen to take my time with removing my body hair for various reasons, it seems that the facilitator could not but interpret it as a feminist—and therefore a political—act.

Politicizing trans identity, especially a transfeminine one, is an uncommon thing. Transfeminist scholars have shown that hegemonic and radical feminist analyses perceive trans identities as heteronormative and essentialist because they embody gender normative ideological norms (Jeffreys, 2014; Serano, 2012; Noble, 2012). Some of these critics have gone even further to claim that trans identities depoliticize gay/lesbian/queer identities, in the sense that they are transforming sexual political subversion into idealized hegemonic notions of gender and sexuality (Moraga, 2011). This is even more true to MTF identities, criticized harshly because they embrace femininity. In that sense, trans identities are perceived as a-political. Although the facilitator is prying and objectifying, she unintentionally (or intentionally) politicized and gave subversive meaning to my identity.

It seems, then, that taking time with one's transition is queering linear trans temporalities. It distorts the forward motion force of these classic temporalities, moving them back and forth, and therefore enables a politicization of trans identities. This distorted movement between perceived norms of trans bodies and their counterparts in reality allows to pause and linger on the subversive politics of trans subjectivity, and the fluidity of gender itself. As Elizabeth Freeman puts it, this temporality constitutes "sensations [. . .] of uncanniness, untimeliness, belatedness, delay, and failure" (Freeman, 2007, p. 163). These queer delays and "failures" subvert hegemonic paradigms. They are a productive and subversive force that, as Jack Halberstam states, are associated with "nonconformity, anticapitalist practices, nonreproductive life styles, negativity, and critique" (Halberstam, 2011, p. 89).

Queering trans temporality requires a careful introspection. While queer and trans identities, narratives, and times are often linked together and find mutual ground in certain arenas, queer theories of temporality (as in other areas of queer theory) use trans subjects to explain queer temporalities on the one hand, but also use trans narratives and bodies to criticize trans practices and temporalities for their normative standards (Amin, 2014, p. 220). In order to evade these kind of problematic reading, I would like to situate my reading of "taking time" from a trans perspective as a form of reading a way of experiencing time, thus situating my reading in the trans subjects themselves and our cultural imagination.

Hung up out of fugue states

In order to broaden the perspective of what it means when one is taking time in his/her transition, I wish to articulate the theoretical framework within which I discuss the notion of "taking time." Writing from a postcolonial context in Australia, Michelle Bastian (2013) discusses what she calls a "double temporal logic": her main argument is that dominant Western cultural law perceives (linear) time both as discontinuous, in which there is a split between the past and the present and future, and at the same time continuous, in which the present and future are continually connected to the past (ibid., pp. 104–105). Both these temporal logics work to include and exclude politically members of various communities; the fact that both of these temporalities are linear and forward-moving results in excluding members of the community still haunted by the past.

In contrast, she tries to avoid this oppressive colonialist temporal logic and offers a radical way of thinking of time. Drawing from Aboriginal and Western continental philosophic notions of time, she carefully suggests a notion of "sharing time," in which multiple temporalities are expressed, where time is experienced through different cultural and societal perspectives to a point where it becomes "disjointed and dislocated" (ibid., p. 117). Similarly, I would like to argue that taking time delays the linear progressive rush of what Freeman calls "chrononormativity," the creating of a temporal space in which the present becomes the main reference point and the future becomes unforeseeable (2010). Taking time is a way of thinking and experiencing life and body through delay and untimeliness. It may cause moments of deep introspection about trans identity, both in the trans subject and in the people surrounding him/her/them.

Imogen Binnie's novel *Nevada* is a good example of that. *Nevada* tells the story of Maria Griffiths, a 29-year-old transwoman living in New York City. Upon discovering that her girlfriend has lied to her, they break up and Maria embarks on a journey to the west coast, stopping at the fictional city of Star City, Nevada where she meets a young person who's not sure of his gender identity and tries to guide him through his troubles (Binnie, 2013).

The novel consists of two parts, the first one ranging over more than half of the book and can be regarded as a form of introduction. In it, Maria mainly travels around New York City, takes long escapades from her bookstore shifts, rides her bike during the night, and ponders issues such as being trans, transmisogyny, capitalism, and so on. On one of those night trips, she realizes that she's late for her hormone shot:

> she's late for a shot of estrogen. Like, a week late.
> Eureka, motherfucker. Maria is supposed to take a shot of estrogen every two weeks; [...] And man, if you do not keep your estrogen levels consistent, you become a useless and fucked up mess. It's just like, it hadn't even occurred to her that she was going on romantic late-night adventures and drinking herself stupid because she needed a shot. [...] It also explains why she'd been so goddam hung up on being trans. Her body is telling her, hey fucker, I am a trans body, you need to do the things that you do to take care of a trans body.
>
> *Ibid., p. 51*

By not injecting hormones, Maria is taking her time with her transition, literally bringing it to a halt or delaying it. This delay has physical reactions: her body feels uncomfortable, and this feeling of discomfort allows her to be "hung up" on being trans, to be introspective about her gender and her life. She starts writing her blog again, decides to break up with her girlfriend, and comes to the conclusion that she is stuck at a certain stage in her life. She even claims one morning to have had "four epiphanies" (ibid., p. 67).

Maria's hard and often exhaustive introspection is reflected also in the novel's structure. Approximately half of it is dedicated to her long days in New York City and mostly to her long monologues over activist and political issues. In this sense, the plot itself takes some time to be introspective, allowing the reader to ponder and take time to think of trans identity and issues concerning it.

An even more direct approach is taken by the Canadian whodunit web-series *Murder in Passing*, directed by John Greyson. The series follows the investigation of the murder of Mars Brito, a trans bike courier in the fictional town of Passing, British Columbia. The series consists of forty-two 30-second episodes, and it was broadcasted during January and February of 2013 on Pattison Outdoor Advertising's video screens in the Toronto subway system (Mills, 2013). It was later uploaded to YouTube as a web-series, in which a 30-second opera aria was added to each episode, usually depicting various lead characters riding bikes and lip-synching the aria (Greyson, 2013).

Visualized in a film noir aesthetic and some dark humor, the series depicts several issues familiar to trans lives. Deadly violence is represented by Mars' murder. Living in stealth is depicted through the character of Detective Epicene who was given the task of investigating the murder and is secretly a transwoman. Cis–trans relationships are depicted between Mars and his fiancé and Epicene and her love. Among other issues depicted are relationships between trans children and their parents and municipal neglect (Greyson, 2013).

A verse that keeps repeating during the aria sequences of the series is lip-synced by the deceased Mars while he is riding a bike: "The sun says that a fugue has caught him, that a fugue has kissed her" (ibid.). A fugue here has a double meaning: The first and obvious one is a form of compositional technique for two or more voices that imitate one another (most of the arias in the series are composed as fugues). The second meaning refers to a fugue state, a rare psychiatric condition in which the subject enters a state of (reversible) amnesia that can cause him/her to forget memories and other identifying characteristics of their personality.

By putting this verse in the mouth of a murdered transman, the series can be seen as pointing a blaming finger towards the cis viewers, for falling into a fugue state, a temporal and convenient amnesia, in which they can forget the extreme daily violence against trans people. At the same time, the series' plot, broadcast, and small franchise around it invites the viewers to get out of their fugue state, to take time to get involved with trans issues and lives. By broadcasting the series on the screens of Toronto's subway stations, it was watched by hundreds of thousands of people traveling every day. In addition, the series encouraged viewers to guess the identity of the murderer by putting clues in the Toronto edition of the *Metro* newspaper, via Twitter, and through a contest on the series' official website (Greyson, 2013). Much like Binnie's *Nevada*, *Murder in Passing* invites its viewers to take their time to be introspective and think about trans lives. As another repeated aria in the series states, these pieces invite their consumers to stop forgetting about trans lives, to "flee your fugue state" (Greyson, 2013).

Seizing time

"Taking time" might not necessarily lead to introspectiveness and calling out trans neglect. It can also lead to classist and racial meanings and practices. I will demonstrate this through two films with trans elements in them: *Jupiter Ascending* (2015) and *Tangerine* (2015).

The Wachowski trans sisters' sci-fi space opera *Jupiter Ascending* is set in a universe in which ultra-rich royal families own hundreds of planets (including the contemporary Planet Earth), through which they produce a life serum that regenerates their body cells to their optimal genetic condition, thus allowing them to live for tens of thousands of years. This life serum is produced by the planets' populations. In this ultra-capitalist dystopian world, the royal families are "seeding and growing" populations in different planets, up to the point where the planet is genetically and evolutionarily developed. Then the planet is ripe for "harvest," in which the entire planet's population is wiped out in order to produce the life serum, the most valuable resource in this universe. Human life (and death) turn into a literal commodity that can be converted into capital to be traded and consumed (Wachowski & Wachowksi).

Kalique, a member of the Abrasax royal family, explains some of this to the film's protagonist, Earth-born Jupiter Jones:

> In your world, people are used to fighting for resources like oil, or minerals, or land. But when you have access to the vastness of space you realize there's only one resource worth fighting over, even killing for: more time. Time is the single most precious commodity in the universe.
>
> *Ibid.*

In the most literal, technocratic, and capitalist sense, the members of the Abrasax family are "taking time," treating it as the universe's ultimate resource, and seizing it. When they are taking their time, they delay the most obvious and apparent future of human life: death. They use the temporal space they open up by extending their own lives to linger in the present, slowing and halting the linear speeding time, without a seeming change in the future. This is an interesting futuristic disposition in which capitalists are seizing time in order to produce more of it for themselves so they can live a longer time.

This raises question about the relationship between a trans position of taking one's time, and socioeconomic location. Can I allow myself to take my time with my transition because I am in less danger of violence, as a white woman? This relates to José Esteban Muñoz's critique that the idea of a queer future, anti-future, and even time itself is embedded within a white middle-class imperative in which white queers have a future in which they can live safely and (relatively) unharmed, and it is forgotten that queers of color do not have this kind of imaginable temporal horizon (Muñoz, 2006, p. 825).

Am I allowed to take my time transitioning because of the fact that no matter what, I have a future, and I do not need to be in a rush to pass? While this may be true at least in part, other factors should be taken into consideration as well. Some trans subjects unwillingly take their time with transition because of a lack of resources, social neglect, and marginalization. An example for that can be seen in Sean S. Baker's *Tangerine*, a 2015 film that tells the story of two trans sex workers in Hollywood, Los Angeles on Christmas Eve. Sin-Dee Rella is released after serving a 28-day prison sentence, and meets with Alexandra, who accidently informs Sin-Dee that her boyfriend and pimp Chester has been cheating on her with a cis woman while she was away (Baker, 2015).

Sin-Dee and Alexandra are both women of color and are constantly marked and read as transwomen by the people around them (other transwomen, clients, police officers, and the general public). Although they are not content with how they look (Alexandra exclaims that "the world can be a cruel place," to which Sin-Dee sarcastically answers "Yeah, it is cruel. God gave me a penis."), they are unwillingly taking their time to transition (at least partially) due to lack of resources; towards the end of the film a group of cis men throw a cup of piss on Sin-Dee, causing her hair/wig to get dirty. Anxiously, she cries: "It's my fucking hair! I don't have no fucking money for new hair!" (ibid.). Their socioeconomic neglect is even more apparent when, during the touching last scene of the film, Alexandra gives Sin-Dee her own hair/wig while they wait at the laundromat for her clothes and hair to get cleaned. In this sense, they are both unwillingly in the mindful present, staying in a marginalized condition partially because they are in the middle of their transition.

Cinematically, the film was shot with three iPhone 5s smartphones, giving it a real-life aesthetic. It follows the two protagonists through the streets of Hollywood during one day, as they go back and forth from street to street (Sin-Dee looking for the cis woman with whom Chester cheated on her and then looking for him, and Alexandra looking for Sin-Dee). In that sense, the film itself is "taking its time," and is anchored in the present time of trans sex workers of color.

This trans present is quite similar to Tom Boellstroff's discussion of queer coincidental time: drawing from anthropological notions of time, he argues that queer temporality is rooted in "coincidence, intersection [and] admixture" (Boellstroff, 2007, p. 239). It is a cyclical present which disrupts straight (and in our case, cis) notions of the present and future, thus encompassing both social failure (which may lead to neglect such as the one experienced by the characters in *Tangerine*) and subversion (such as the earlier example of politicizing trans identity).

If we look back at *Jupiter Ascending*, this film can also be traced to the present. Although the film does not have any trans characters in it, or even mentions their existence in this fictionalized universe, I read it as a trans critique of hegemonic cis discourses. Earth-born Jupiter Jones, the film's protagonist, discovers to her surprise that she is the reincarnation of the head of the Abrasax family, Seraphi. In a process called "recurrence," Jupiter has the exact gene pattern as the late Seraphi, thus allowing her to inherit the privileges of the leader of the Abrasax industries and the title of the queen of the universe (Wachowski & Wachowski). The fact that Jupiter receives entire planets and possessions based on her gene patterns shows the vital part of biology in this world; the people are their genes.

But Jupiter denounces this stance; once she discovers how the life serum is made she refuses to take part in the industry, saving the lives of billions of people on the planets she owns. She renounces the claim that she and Seraphi are the same person, clearly stating to one of the Abrasax sons, "I am not you mother" (Wachowski & Wachowski). She is seizing a twofold transfeminine position: firstly, she refuses to agree that she equals her genes/biology, embracing an anti-essentialist stance. Resisting the genetic ideological hegemony, she refuses to take a part in a cis framework of thought that connects identity and biology. Secondly, Jupiter dismantles her privileges by refusing to claim them. In that sense, she denounces a futuristic stance (leaving behind the option of living for thousands of years) and prefers to stay in the halted present, taking her time to live and not seizing it on account of others' lives. She is taking her time differently from the oppressive ways in which the Abrasax family seize time. Instead, like in Boellstroff's cyclical queer time, she chooses to halt Earth's impending demise, pulling its course into the present, thus saving its inhabitants.

Conclusion: present dangers, present hopes

As I have shown here, taking one's time in transition, as in other arenas, takes on several meanings. Most importantly, it disrupts and distorts classic trans progressive temporalities and brings things to a queerly delayed halt, entwining us in the present. However, the present has its own dangers. According to Rasheedah Phillips, western, white, and capitalist societies are rooted in a notion of a linear mode of time, in which "the present moment is fleeting, but ever present" (Phillips, 2015, p. 12). The future is inaccessible because it always has to go through the present, which is always there (ibid.). This way of thinking and practicing time leaves us without any access to the future and with little information of the past, resulting subjects to be trapped in the present. This is especially problematic for marginalized populations such as black and postcolonial subjects, because the present is overloaded with oppression, loss, and trauma, and dictates the future accordingly, filling it not only with the uneven distribution of resources, institutional and social violence, but also with self-doubt and self-hate in the subjects themselves towards both their cultures and their individual identities.

The same could be said for trans subjects. In my transition, I am not always sure that I am deliberately taking my time, or rather that I accede to the traumatic experiences of being trans, thus evading and halting my transition and the things I want for my body. For example, I have postponed a few times my electrolysis treatment because I was taken aback by the very cis and normative standards by which I felt I was judged during treatments. This is where taking time blocks the trans subject from moving forward, keeping him/her/they confined in the halted present.

This is why upon finally embarking on her journey away from New York City, *Nevada*'s protagonist Maria eventually injects her hormones, exclaiming: "Not giving yourself your shot is like slamming your fingers in a car door over and over, or forcing yourself to drown a kitten every morning or something. Totally unproductive" (Binnie, 2013, p. 131). This is what allows her to finally move from her former life and former relationships into possible new ones, leaving the halted present in favor of an unknown future.

The dangers of the present I have noted above are infused in the existence of trans lives. Dislocated and marginalized in the cis linear temporality, we are dissociated from our bodies, identities, and close ones. We put our trust in the distant future, but are never able to reach it. Thus, I want to suggest taking time as a proposition, as a way of being (in the) present. It is a way of conceptualizing and experiencing our bodies in time, while at the same time distorting the oppressive hegemonic temporal logic and bringing forward new mindful experiences of delays, untimeliness, and multiple temporalities. Taking time may allow us to be present in the now, at least partially, to be introspective and to feel and be with and in ourselves.

Note

1   [This chapter was originally published under the same title in *Somatechnics* 7.1, special issue on "Trans Temporality" (2017), pp. 34–49. Reprinted by kind permission of Edinburgh University Press.]

References

ABC News. (2015, April 25). Bruce Jenner, in his own words—Interview with Diane Sawyer—20/20—*ABC news* [Video file]. Retrieved from https://www.youtube.com/watch?v=JaqLG3myKUk.

Abourahme, N. (2016). The productive ambivalences of post-revolutionary time: Discourse, aesthetics, and the political subject of Palestinian present. In A. Agathangelou & K. Killian (Eds.), *Time, temporality and violence in international relations: (De)Fatalizing the present, forging radical alternatives* (pp. 129–155). London: Routledge.

Amin, K. (2014). Temporality. *TSQ: Transgender Studies Quarterly*, 1(1–2), 219–222.

Bastian, M. (2013). Political apologies and the question of a 'Shared Time' in the Australian context. *Theory, Culture & Society*, 30(5), 94–121.

Binnie, I. (2013). *Nevada*. New York: Topside Press.

Bissinger, B. (2015, June 25). Introducing Caitlyn Jenner. *Vanity Fair*. Retrieved from http://www.vanityfair.com/hollywood/2015/06/caitlyn-jenner-bruce-cover-annie-leibovitz.

Boellstroff, T. (2007). When marriage falls: Queer coincidences in straight time. *GLQ: A Journal of Lesbian and Gay Studies*, 13(2–3), 227–248.

Freeman, E. (2007). Queer temporalities: Introduction. *GLQ: A Journal of Lesbian and Gay Studies*, 13(2–3), 159–176.

Freeman, E. (2010). *Time binds: Queer temporalities, queer histories*. Durham: Duke University Press.

Halberstam, J. (2011). *The queer art of failure*. Durham and London: Duke University Press.

Jeffreys, S. (2014). *Gender hurts: A feminist analysis of the politics of transgenderism*. London and New York: Routledge.

Kissell, R. (2015, April 25). Bruce Jenner interview ratings: 17 million watch ABC special. *Variety*. Retrieved from http://variety.com/2015/tv/news/bruce-jenner-interview-ratings-17-million-watch-abc-special-1201479968.

Mills, C. (2013, January 7). Murder in Passing is a whodunit unfolding on TTC subway screens. *The Star*. Retrieved from https://www.thestar.com/entertainment/television/2013/01/07/murder_in_passing_is_a_whodunit_unfolding_on_ttc_subway_screens.

Moraga, C. (2011). *A Xicana codex of changing consciousness: Writings, 2000–2010*, Durham and London: Duke University Press.

Muñoz, J. E. (2006). Thinking beyond antirelationality and antiutopianism in queer critique. *PMLA*, 121(3), 825–826.

Noble, B. (2012). Trans. Panic. Some thoughts toward a theory of feminist fundamentalism. In F. Enke (Ed.), *Transfeminist perspectives: In and beyond transgender and gender studies* (pp. 45–59). Philadelphia: Temple University Press.

Phillips, R. (2015). Constructing a theory and practice of black quantum futurism: Part one. In R. Phillips (Ed.), *Black quantum futurism: Theory & practice* (Vol. 1) (pp. 11–30). Philadelphia: AfroFuturist Affair.

Prosser, J. (1998). *Second skins: The body narratives of transsexuality*. New York: Columbia University Press.

Schilt, K., & Laurel, W. (2009). Doing gender, doing heteronormativity: "Gender normals," transgender people, and the social maintenance of heterosexuality. *Gender & Society*, 23(4), 440–464.

Serano, J. (2012). Reclaiming femininity. In F. Enke (Ed.), *Transfeminist perspectives: In and beyond transgender and gender studies* (pp. 170–183). Philadelphia: Temple University Press.

Spade, D. (2006). Mutilating gender. In S. Stryker & S. Whittle (Eds.), *The transgender studies reader* (pp. 315–332). New York: Routledge.

Sundén, J. (2015). Temporalities of transition: Trans-temporal femininity in a human musical automaton. *Somatechnics*, 5(2), 197–216.

Filmography

Hill, G., Wachowski, L., & Wachowski, L. (Producers), Wachowski, L., & Wachowski, L. (Directors). (2015). *Jupiter ascending* [Motion picture]. United States & Australia: Warner Bros.

Greyson, J. (Director). (2013). *Murder in Passing* [Web series]. Canada: Unknown Production Company.

Baker, S., Cox, K., Cox, M., Dean, D., & Tsou, S. (Producers), Baker, S. (Director). (2015). *Tangerine* [Motion Picture]. United States: Magnolia Pictures.

PART II
Diagnostic phantasies in the (failed) quest for authenticity

5
PSYCHOANALYSIS NEEDS A SEX CHANGE[1]

Patricia Gherovici

Psychoanalysis is overdue for a transition. For a very long time psychoanalysts have viewed transgender expressions as an indicator of underlying pathology—be it a precursor of narcissistic disorders (Oppenheimer, 1991; Chiland, 2003), transvestism or homosexuality (Limentani, 1979), borderline disorders (Green, 1986), or psychosis (Socarides 1970).[2] Understandably, feeling relegated to the realm of pathology and abjection, trans people rejected psychoanalysis. Psychoanalysis, however, has played a crucial part in the history of transsexualism. It is time both to historicize and theorize this loaded connection.

This chapter assesses the controversial yet central role of sex-change theory for psychoanalysis. Based on my experience as a clinician, I argue for the depathologization of transgenderism. My clinical work with gender non-conforming analysands has shown me that often those compelled to change gender do it because they are confronting matters of life and death. Challenging the pathologization of transgenderism historically enforced by psychoanalysis, I propose a new ethics of desire capable of fundamentally rethinking sexuality and of taking seriously the issue of death. I also argue for a productive confrontation between psychoanalysis and transgender discourses claiming that transgender people are actually changing the clinical praxis, advancing new ideas for the clinic that can be expanded to social and intellectual contexts.

Times are changing and notions of what it means to be a man or a woman continue to fluctuate and be re-shaped. Words like "cis," "transgender," "agender," or "genderqueer" have entered the everyday vernacular. In what has been named a post-gender era, we continue to hear reverberations of Freud's famous axiom combining "anatomy" and "destiny," but what he actually meant is up for discussion. Listening to the unconscious teaches us that the so-called "gender trouble" of those who identify as trans is in fact a universal phenomenon—for human beings embodiment is a complex process resulting from a series of both overdetermined and contingent identifications; if there is a destiny it is that language distorts the flesh and challenges any idea of biological pre-programming. It is my belief that the transgender experience has the potential to reorient psychoanalytic practice and make psychoanalysis fresh again.

Transgender activists and scholars have been wary of psychoanalysis and with good reasons: psychoanalysis has had a regrettable history of coercive heteronormatization and pathologization of non-normative sexualities and genders. However, such a homophobic and transphobic positioning was founded on a selective reinterpretation of the Freudian texts. It is of course true that many normative theories about sex and gender claim to derive from Freudian psychoanalysis and classify and adjudicate individuals according to sexual behavior. Freud's Oedipal Complex, it is said, starts with the recognition of anatomical sexual differences, before passing through "castration complexes" and "penis envy," culminating in the development of a mature, "normal" genital choice. This choice would entail fully assuming a heterosexual femininity or masculinity. In this reading, proper gender identification produces masculinity for males, femininity for women, and creates an adapted heterosexual desire that is purported to result in satisfying sexual lives. In fact, nothing could be farther from what Freud stated theoretically or from what he observed in his practice. All the previous claims are reductive distortions.

How could psychoanalysts after Freud talk about "normal" sexuality and reduce normalcy to heterosexual genital functions when Freud acknowledged that the supposedly normal mutual interest of men and women is "a problem that needs elucidating and is not a self-evident fact" (footnote added in 1915; Freud 1905, p. 146n)? As Dean & Lane (2001) highlight, one of the greatest paradoxes of the history of psychoanalysis is that its institutions have developed normalizing moralistic and discriminatory practices that are antithetical to psychoanalytic concepts. This is a pity because it has prevented psychoanalysis to make a valuable contribution to the field. Such contributions could have important implications for transgender theorists and activists, transgender people, and professionals in the trans field by enriching current debates about gender and sexuality.

To further contextualize our discussion, we can survey some canonical definitions of transsexuality, all as revealing as they are exemplary. This brief history of the evolution of the nomenclature will be helpful to see how the terminology has been linked to the domain of the pathological. It also shows the central and complex role psychoanalysis has played in the history of transsexualism.

The philosopher Michel Foucault made us aware that sexuality has a history, and that psychoanalysis has played an important role as a theory of the intersections of law and desire. His *History of Sexuality* (Foucault, 1990) states that a history of the deployment of sexuality since the classical age "can serve as an archeology of psychoanalysis" (p. 130.) For Dean & Lane (2001) this characterization, which makes it look "as if the book were really all about psychoanalysis" (p. 8), also highlights the fact that today we cannot think of sexuality without using psychoanalytic categories. In the case of transsexuality, then, the interrelatedness with psychoanalysis is not just referential, as we will see.

Cross-dressing

The term "transvestite" was coined by Magnus Hirschfeld in 1910 to describe those who occasionally wear clothes of the other sex. Hirschfeld, a passionate sex reformer and an activist, struggled for the legalization of homosexuality. He was also an occasional cross-dresser as well as a central political figure in Germany's incipient field of sexology. Hirschfeld developed a theory of sexual intermediaries, contending that the existence of two opposite sexes was an oversimplification and that one could observe many varieties of intermediates. A pioneer advocate for transgender people, he argued that transgenderism could not be reduced either to homosexuality, fetishism, or to any form of pathology. Hirschfeld's classic book *Die Transvestiten. Eine Untersuchung über den erotischen Verkleidungstrieb mit umfangreichemcasuistischen und historischen Material* (1910) was translated into English only in 1991, that is, eight decades after his initial publication in German. The translation's title was *Transvestites: The Erotic Drive to Cross-Dress*. Notably, its English title contains a word that belongs to basic psychoanalytic nomenclature: "drive," a term that reveals an engagement with psychoanalysis, even if the sense is clearly different.

In fact, Hirshfeld played a main role in the early days of psychoanalysis, and he published a number of psychoanalytic papers. Freud's own article "Hysterical fantasies and their relation to bisexuality' (1908) appeared in the first issue of Hirschfeld's new journal exclusively devoted to sexology as a science, *Zeitschfrit für Sexualwissencraft*. Subsequent issues published original work by Alfred Adler, Karl Abraham, and Wilhem Stekel (Bullough, 1994, p. 68.) Hirschfield was not just instrumental in the publication of psychoanalytic texts, he also co-founded with Karl Abraham the Berlin Psychoanalytic Society in August, 1908 (Gay, 1998). In 1911, at the third international Weimar congress of psychoanalysts, Freud greeted Hirschfeld as an honored guest and a "Berlin authority on homosexuality" (Bullough, 1994, p. 64). However, even with this recognition, Hirshfeld abruptly left the Berlin Psychoanalytic Society shortly after the Weimar meeting, despite Abraham's "attempts at persuasion" to stay (Falzeder, 2002, p. 139). It seems clear that Hirshfeld's departure had been precipitated by "an external cause" (p. 139), which has also been described by Abraham as "a question of resistances" (p. 140). In fact, it seems that Jung had objected to his homosexuality (p. 141.) Unlike Jung, Freud did not seem to mind Hirschfeld's political activism. Quite the contrary, Freud saw Hirshfeld's advocacy of homosexual rights as a positive development and from the beginning he had encouraged Abraham to work with him (Gay, 1998, p. 181). After Hirshfeld's departure, the Berlin Psychoanalytic Society decided, at Abraham's instigation, to work collectively on Freud's *Three Essays on the Theory of Sexuality*. The irony is that the *Three Essays* owe a lot to Hirschfeld's research (Freud, 1905, p. 1, credits in the opening page the "well known writings" of Hirschfeld along with other eight authors ranging from Krafft-Ebing to Havelock Ellis, all published in *Jahrbuch für sexuelle Zwischenstufen*, a journal under Hirschfeld's direction).

Hirschfeld's empirical data underline the non-pathological aspects of non-normative expressions of sexuality, revealing that transvestites included both men and women who were homosexual or bisexual and, contrary to popular belief, many were heterosexual. He observed that some transvestites were asexual (*automonosexual* was his term); the asexual group eventually led to the 1950s classification of transsexual. Hirshfeld broke new ground by proposing that transvestism was a separate sexual variation different from fetishism and homosexuality. However, as a clinician and researcher, Hirschfeld never wavered in his belief in a biological (endocrinological) basis for sexuality.

Paraphilia

Moving on from Hirschfield, perhaps the most influential post-Freudian psychoanalytic theory of transgenderism was that of Wilhelm Stekel (1930). He popularized the use of *paraphilia* for unusual sexual behaviors, the term was coined in 1903 by ethnographer, sexologist, anthropologist, and Freud's correspondent Friedrich S. Krauss (from the Greek *para*: beside, beyond, amiss, and *philia:* love). Evincing a Freudian influence, Stekel's book *Sexual Aberrations: The Phenomenon of Fetishism in Relation to Sex* (1930) makes explicit in its title the wish to systematize the structure of all sexual deviations as a single entity under the model of fetishism, the prototypical substitute for the maternal phallus. The book included a chapter on transvestism written by Emil Gutheil. For Gutheil ([1930] 1971), even though transvestism was not strictly fetishism, it was a compulsion to create a phallic female: the attraction for the genitals of the "other" sex was transferred onto the garments. Stekel and Gutheil are good examples of how former devoted disciples modified Freudian theories and popularized them by erasing any nuance, bringing them closer to the dominating medical model. As Bullough (1994) puts it, "Freud cannot be blamed for the excesses of his disciples" (p. 90).

During the first half of the twentieth century, in order to solve the problem of the mind, most post-Freudians inevitably relied upon the notion of the traumatic effect of childhood experiences. Castration anxiety accounted for a psychobiological etiology of transgenderism often confused with homosexuality (Bullough, 2000). Cross-dressing continued to be understood according to Gutheil's theories as an attempt to overcome the fear of castration, creating a phallic woman and identifying with her (Lukianowicz, 1959).

Psychopathia Transexualis

The word "transexualis" was first used in the popular journal *Sexology* in a 1949 article by David Cauldwell titled, in Latin, *Psychopathia Transexualis*. The spelling was with only one "s" because the term was a direct reference to the title of Krafft-Ebing's opera magna *Psychopathia Sexualis* (1886/1965), the monumental catalog of the "aberrations" of sexual behavior. Cauldwell talked of a psychological disturbance, of a "pathologic-morbid desire to be a full member of the opposite sex" (Cauldwell, 2006, p. 40). Already in 1923, Hirschfeld had used the German expression *seelischer Transsexualismus* (psychological transsexualism), attributing the roots of transgender inclinations to the psyche. Cauldwell in 1949 described "transsexuals" as "individuals who wish to be members of the sex to which they do not properly belong" (p. 275). Cauldwell also coined the term "sex transmutationist" (1947; 1951, pp. 12–16) and used both the spellings trans-sexual and transsexual interchangeably (1950). Cauldwell's (1949/2006) initially described transsexualism in terms of disease, considering as a hereditary condition of individuals who are "mentally unhealthy" (p. 275). By 1950, Cauldwell had clearly made some progress: "Are transsexuals crazy? One may as well ask whether heterosexuals are crazy. Some are and some are not. Some transsexuals are brilliant. Now and then one may be a borderline genius. Transsexuals are eccentric. Some of them are not of sound mind, but this is true of heterosexuals" (p. 4). Nevertheless, he strongly advised against "sex change surgery" claiming that surgery could not make a "real" member of the opposite sex (Cauldwell, 1955). Cauldwell is usually mistakenly credited as the first person to use the word transsexual but rarely quoted in the academic literature (except for Meyerowitz, 1998, p. 168–170, and Stryker & Whittle, 2006, pp. 40–52, who nevertheless caution the reader against his excessive pathologizing, p. 40; see also Ekins & King, 2001b).

Cauldwell's role as populist column writer of tabloid sex advice warrants a comment. As Stryker & Whittle (2006) observe, Cauldwell's quasi-scientific work is worthy of note because it reflects the earlier biologically inclined positions of Krafft-Ebing, Hirschfeld, and Havelock Ellis while it anticipates the controversial contributions of future transsexualism experts like Robert Stoller, Richard Green, John Money, and Leslie Lothstein (p. 40). Most of Cauldwell's popular booklets were published by E. Hadelman-Julius, an American publisher who reached a substantial readership with a sure formula—"sex, self improvement, and attacks on respectability and religion" (Ekins & King, 2001a). Cauldwell's position as a popularizer serves also as a cultural barometer. Being a medical practitioner, he developed a second career and explained transgenderism to the masses. This was indeed a prurient matter at the time, but also a subject which, according to Hadelman-Julius' winning recipe, was seen as a self-improvement. After World War II, Cauldwell switched to a more liberal attitude towards sexual matters, perhaps reflecting a new climate of more honest public discussion over sex (as exemplified by the Kinsey studies).

Transsexualism

The word transsexualism then became a popular term in the 1950s thanks to sex-change pioneer Harry Benjamin. Benjamin was a Berlin endocrinologist who relocated to New York in 1915. He had worked closely with Eugen Steinach, the gland specialist innovator who performed the first sex-change surgeries by gland transplants in the late 19th century and isolated the "sex hormones," and knew Hirschfeld, the sex reformer, from before the war. Benjamin relied on a biological concept to account for the etiology of transsexualism, despite the fact that he could not find any bodily confirmation for this claim. Notably, Benjamin advocated against psychotherapy. Benjamin borrowed Ulrich's formula of a female soul trapped in a male body, all the while looking for answers in the body, not in the soul: "the soma, that is to say the genetic and/or endocrine constitution . . . has to provide a 'fertile soil' in which the 'basic conflict' must grow in order to become the respective neurosis" (Hausman, 1995, p. 122).

Despite the use of the term "neurosis," Benjamin (1954) discouraged any psychoanalytic or psychotherapeutic intervention, seeing them as "a waste of time" (p. 228). Benjamin argued that psychoanalysis did not lessen the wish to change sex but rather forced patients to hide this desire and therefore live miserable lives. As his close collaborator Hamburger (1953) put it, "it is impossible to make a genuine transvestite [transsexual] wish to have his mentality altered by means of psychotherapy" (pp. 392–393).

Following the significant media impact of Christine Jorgensen's 1952 successful sex change, Benjamin chose to share publically his opposition to the psychoanalytic treatment of transsexuality at a symposium of the US Association for the Advancement of Psychotherapy. This was a symposium that Benjamin himself organized; it was attended by an audience of professionals in the "psy" field (Meyerowitz, 2002/2004, pp. 106–107). The landmark 1954 paper that came from this, published in the *American Journal of Psychotherapy*, became one of transgender studies' touchstones, as it spelled out the distinction that Benjamin was establishing between the transvestite (psycho-somatic) and transsexual (somato-psychic) phenomena. Physical bisexuality was the point of departure. Benjamin (1954) wrote: "Organically, sex is always a mixture of male and female components," but he suggested that mild cases (like transvestism) could be "principally psychogenic," while for true "transsexualists" "a still greater degree of constitutional femininity, perhaps due to a chromosomal sex disturbance, must be assumed" (pp. 228–229). Following British sexologist Havelock Ellis' contentions that travestism (that Ellis renamed eonism) was not an erotic impulse but an expression of the real self, Benjamin proposed a continuum of transgender behavior with crossdressing on one end, and transsexualism on the other. For transsexuals, Benjamin (1954) reiterated that therapy was of no use. He was also not naïve, admitting that for a male-to-female transsexual surgery "may not always solve [the transsexual's] problem. His feminization craving may never end" (pp. 228–229). He also warned against performing sex reassignment on patients with psychosis or who were in danger of suicide or self-mutilation. The conclusion to this paper reveals interesting contradictions: "Transsexualism is inaccessible by any curative methods at present at our disposal. Nevertheless the condition requires psychiatric help, reinforced by hormone treatment and, in some cases, by surgery. In this way a reasonably contented existence may be worked out for these patients" (Benjamin, 2006, p. 52). According to Benjamin, transsexualism was deemed "inaccessible by any curative methods," nevertheless it required specific treatments like psychiatry combined with hormone treatment and surgery. Benjamin considered that if psychoanalysis and psychotherapy could not cure transsexualism, they could not explain it either.

Meyerowitz (2002/2004) observes that Benjamin emphasized the biological aspect of transsexualism, which explained for him the failure of psychotherapy in treating the condition. The condition justified a surgical intervention. Benjamin maintained a negative bias against psychotherapy and psychoanalysis but he created a protocol for sex change in which psychiatrists were given the power to determine who would be potential candidates for surgery. Psychiatrists had the final word on the treatment decision but no say on the diagnosis. As Hausman (1995) observed, "this illustrates the ambivalent relation between the mental health specialist and the clinical endocrinologist in the treatment of transsexualism" (p. 124). The fact that Benjamin's choice of treatments affected and transformed the body (surgery, hormones) foreclosed a consideration of what may not be fully anatomical, as if the seeming efficacy of the interventions on the organism would preclude any consideration of other issues involved in the transition of sex.

Another close collaborator of Benjamin, the American psychoanalyst Robert Stoller, helped establish a pioneer sex-change clinic in the early 1960s. This was the Gender Identity Center at UCLA, which developed an influential notion derived from John Money's 1950s new vocabulary of gender by introducing the idea of an "environmental" psychological sex separated from the biological sex, and which took pains to offer a distinct transsexual psychic structure (Meyerowitz, 2002/2004, p. 114; Millot, 1990, pp. 49–59).

Money in fact further developed Kinsey's explanation of sexual behavior as the result of "learning and conditioning" (Kinsey et al., 1953, pp. 643–644) and proposed a behaviorist model for what he called "gender roles" (Money, 1955). Stoller further refined the notion of a separation of sex and gender with the idea of "core gender identity," which corresponded to the internalized idea of the individual's belonging to a particular sex. Stoller initially supported the idea of a biological force, a drive determining gender. "Gender identity" stressed more the subjective experience of gender and separated gender from sexuality. Based on the conviction of a distinct identity and the importance of the penis, Stoller systematized a distinction between the transsexual, the transvestite (cross-dresser), and the effeminate homosexual. He noted that in contrast with transsexuals, transvestites and male homosexuals identify as men; transsexuals abhor the penis, which for transvestites and homosexuals is an insignia of maleness and a source of pleasure (Stoller, 1975, pp. 142–181).

By 1968, Stoller, always a believer in bisexuality, had completely moved away from a biological model to a psychological one and emphasized the psychological forces that resulted in transsexualism. Stoller was mainly interested in male transsexualism, which he considered a "natural experiment" (Stoller, 1975, p. 281) to measure variables in the development of masculinity and femininity, but also a pathology of psychosexual development caused in early childhood by "excess merging with the mother" (p. 296). He recommended "sex-change surgery" for patients properly diagnosed as transsexual, requesting from his colleagues that "everything should be done to assist them in passing" (p. 279) and was quite humble about the goals of his treatment.

Stoller opposed any attempt at "converting" male transsexuals into masculine, heterosexual, or even less feminine people, because "the treatment of the adult transsexual is palliative; we must bear this and not, in our frustration, impatience, or commitment to theoretical positions, fail even to provide that much comfort to our patients" (p. 280). Despite his efforts at contributing to psychoanalytic theories of sexuality, and perhaps because he believed that transsexualism was a petri-dish for human sexuality, Stoller developed a simplistic explanation with psychological overtones that he summed up in the formula: "dominant mother, father pushed to the side, infant cuddly and lovable, mother–son too close" (p. 193). In cases of male-to-female transsexualism, the key was an essential femininity passed from mother to son: "What his mother feels is femininity; what he feels is femininity" (p. 204).

His model was that of mimetic imitation. If the son copied the mother; the mother's excessive closeness to the son was a negative influence. Stoller also talked about a bisexual mother, who might have had a period of extreme tomboyishness, and of a distant father. These were factors contributing to the creation of trans-sexuality, especially male to female. For female-to-male transsexuals, Stoller's speculations can be rendered as "too much father and too little mother masculinizes girls" (pp. 223–244). Stoller stated explicitly that female transsexualism is not the same condition as male transsexualism, stressing that female and male transsexualism are clinically, dynamically, and etiologically different (pp. 223–244).

After Stoller, many psychoanalytic theories of gender identity development blamed gender trouble on identifications with the "wrong" parent (Coates, Friedman, & Wolfe, 1991; Stoller, 1975; Lothstein, 1992.) And most psychoanalysts proceeded to view transgender expressions as an indicator of underlying pathology—be it a precursor of transvestism or homosexuality (Limentani, 1979), borderline disorders (Green, 1986), narcissistic disorders (Oppenheimer, 1991; Chiland, 2003), or psychosis (Socarides, 1970). Understandably, feeling relegated to the realm of pathology and abjection, transpeople rejected psychoanalysis. Ethel Spector Person & Lionel Oversey (1974/1999) have discussed in their now classic text the reasons behind the unwillingness of transsexual patients to participate in treatment. They concluded that it was in great part created by the judgmental stance of those conducting the treatment. Nearly all of the patients they interviewed described their experiences of therapy in terms ranging "from useless to catastrophic" (p. 143). In most cases, the intense negativism resulted from the clinician's propensity to judge the patients as psychotic and to dismiss the transsexual wish as delusional.

Transgender and psychoanalysis

Taking up recent theorizations in the transgender field, Gayle Salamon (2010) has eloquently called for a reappraisal of psychoanalytic discourse, putting forward a sophisticated approximation of psychoanalysis, phenomenology, and transgender studies in her book *Assuming a Body: Transgender and the Rhetorics of Materiality*. Similarly, Shanna Carlson (2010) has proposed a collaboration between discourses, observing that Lacanian psychoanalysis can offer "a richly malleable framework for thinking through matters of sex, subjectivity, desire, and sexuality" and that "integration of the two domains can only ever be a scene of fruitful contestation" (p. 69). I too have argued elsewhere (Gherovici, 2010, 2011) for a productive confrontation between psychoanalysis and transgender discourses and have shown how transgender people are actually changing the clinical praxis, advancing new ideas for the clinic that can be expanded to social and intellectual contexts.

One wishes that psychoanalysts would have by now abandoned the moralistic and stigmatizing attitudes of previous generations of clinicians who, puzzled by the transgender phenomenon, could barely disguise in their disparaging comments their fear and contempt. Candidly, Leslie Lothstein (1977) wrote a paper advising analysts on how to manage the negative counter-transference he anticipated they would experience with transsexual patients. This situation seems to confirm Lacan's (2006) observation that "there is no other resistance to psychoanalysis than the analyst's" (p. 497). Nonetheless, several psychoanalysts have worked with transgender patients raising interesting clinical questions, such as Collete Chiland (2003), Danielle Quinodoz (1998), Michael Eigen (1996), and Ruth Stein (1995). The number of people raising such questions is quite small, which is remarkable since transgender people appear more and more visible in today's society. According to Stephen Whittle (2006) "trans identities were one of the most written about subjects in the late twentieth century" (p. xi). Psychoanalysts have a lot of catching up to do.

In 2005, Shari Thurer, a psychoanalytically trained psychologist practicing in Boston, tried to wake up her colleagues whom she described as "arrested in moth-eaten bias—the conviction that there are two, and only two, normal versions of gender. . ." announcing that "sexuality has changed—all sorts of deviations have been 'outed'—but theories haven't caught up" (p. xi). While she accuses psychological theorists and practitioners of displaying archaic prejudices, Thurer (2005) praises theorists of sexuality—especially French cultural theorists "who leapfrog 180 degrees away from hierarchical thinking, who view sexuality as okay"—but suggests that despite all their political correctness seem to "lack common sense and are insensitive to people in pain" (p. xi). An example of the cross-pollination that she hopes for might come from the other side of the Atlantic. Giovanna Ambrosio (2009), an Italian classically trained psychoanalyst, assumes that analysts already work with gender nonconformist analysands but may not write about it. She acknowledges that "we are behind the times compared with the growing amount of medical, political-sociological, cultural, and mass media attention paid to this theme" (p.xvi). She invites her colleagues to pay more attention to the links between psychoanalytic theory and clinical experience even when that implies looking at "shaded areas" of sexuality (by which she meant transgenderism) (p. xiii).

Casting light into the dusty corners of our assumptions about sex, gender, and identity, one would hope that psychoanalysts will increasingly refuse to buy into sweeping generalizations and negative stereotypes. We should be able to break out of pointless debates between the foundations of sex and gender, the age-old debate of nature versus nurture, of biological essentialism versus social constructivism.

84 Patricia Gherovici

Charles Shepherdson (2000) relies on the work of Lacanian psychoanalyst Catherine Millot to contend that the body cannot be reduced to neither "a natural fact nor a cultural construction" (p. 94). Shepherdson's choice of author to support this claim may elicit a cry of alarm—Kate Bornstein has accused Millot of being a gender terrorist: "Gender terrorists are those who, like Ms. Millot, bang their heads against a gender system which is real and natural; and who then use gender to terrorize the rest of us. These are the real terrorists: the Gender Defenders" (Bornstein, 1994, p, 236).

Is Bornstein's accusation justified? Millot's interpretation of transsexuality is classic: her book *Horsexe* focuses on the motivations behind the demand for a sex change to determine which subjects may benefit from sex reassignment surgery and which may not. She contends that the demand for surgery needs to be interpreted before being accepted. No predetermined norm, she suggests, could generalize the particulars of a subjective motivation: "The feeling of being a woman trapped inside a man's body (or vice-versa) admits radically different interpretations, depending on the context. In the same way the demand for sex-change . . . may also emanate from a woman hypochondriac (this has been encountered) who claims to be a transsexual in order to have her breasts removed because she is afraid she may be affected with cancer, or from a hysteric who sacrifices herself to the power drive of the doctor willing to perform the operation" (Millot 1990, p. 26).

Millot argues that sex-change discourse lands transgender individuals in the land of the Lacanian Real, a place of unbearable fullness and plenitude that could not be seen or imagined, a place beyond sexual difference where gender would not be simply questioned or subverted but completely transcended. She claims that for those who identify with an "outside sex," any sex reassignment will be likely to fail since no anatomical transformation can grant a fantasized position of plenitude outside lack and desire. However, as Dean (2000) remarks, if reassignment surgery involves a fantasy about escaping sexual division altogether, "[t]here is a fundamental paradox, not to mention considerable pathos, in a male-to-female transsexual's undergoing orchidectomy— surgical removal of the testes—in order to elude castration" (p. 82). Millot contended that the identification "outsidesex" revealed an imaginary identification with the phallus, an identification that would be reflected in the preoccupation of transsexuals with their genitals, reiterating Lacan's 1971 observation that transsexuals "confuse the organ with the signifier,"[3] therefore the penis (an organ) is confused with the phallus (an instrument), that is, as a signifying tool that is operative only as an effect of language. Patrick Califia's (1997/2003) has rightly objected that "Millot seems obsessed with castration" and that she "sees sex-reassignment surgery in simplistic Freudian terms, as castration. She focuses on the loss of the penis, without taking into consideration what is gained in the process" (p.109). I too disagree with Millot's generalized assumption that most transsexuals live in the desert of the Real and therefore are psychotic. Instead, I argue for a depathologization of transgenderism and thus differ from the position taken by nearly all analysts. Transgenderism should not be systematically defined as pathology. If transgenderism is not pathological, then a sex change should not be considered either a treatment or a cure. My perspective follows Lacan's ethics to rethink sexual difference. This theory is a departure from the classical Freudian theory of the Oedipus complex and even from Lacan's first formulations that insisted on the symbolic order and the importance of father. It departs as well from a second period in Lacan's work when he would put the emphasis on the theory of fantasy and the object cause of desire. Lacan modified his whole position a last time in the mid-1970s when he elaborated a new conception of sexuality, just before discussing Joyce's writings and that can be somehow generalized.

My recent work exploring trans desire has revealed to me that contrary to Millot's assumption, transgender individuals are not "outsidesex" but obsessed with sexual difference. Furthermore, more often than not gender transition is not a wish to go beyond the gender binary but a desire to overcome the limits of mortal existence. What Millot calls "horsexe" and Jay Prosser calls "uninhabitable" is in fact the experience of a body that feels more dead than alive. Gayle Salamon criticizes Prosser description of transsexual's relation to their "fleshy materiality" as inhabiting the "unimpeachable real" noting that such a position relegates transsexual bodies to a place outside language, meaning, relation and desire, a site of abjection and death from which is impossible to theorize subjectivity, cis or trans (pp. 40–41). My clinical experience has taught me that the transgender body is often experienced as a deadly enclosure. What most analysands insisted on was not so much on losing or having a new body part but on finding a strategy to affirm the livability of their own new embodiment, so as to give new meaning to the materiality of their bodies; they want to find a new way of being.

Today I look at transgenderism differently from how I did in the past. Like many Lacanian psychoanalysts, I had paid too much attention to the conundrum of sex and gender, not realizing that the transgender request was directly aimed at the border between life and death. Both sex-change pioneers Eugen Steinach and Harry Benjamin developed an interest in sex hormones as part of their medical research to prolong human life. They performed great numbers of "rejuvenation" surgeries in a quest for immortality. Freud had a rejuvenation "Steinach operation," in an attempt at slowing the progress of his cancer of the jaw, but as he said in *Beyond the Pleasure Principle*, he was aware that cancers are caused by pesky cells that stubbornly refuse to die. This complex knotting of then recently discovered hormones, undying cells, and the ancient wish for an immortal life somehow reappears in the request of many of the analysands who identify as trans. The triumph experienced in numerous cases, following the at times grueling process of gender transition, can be condensed in the affirmation: "I exist." This "existence" seems to have been given to them as supernumerary, an excess beyond the dichotomy of gender. While I continue to challenge the pathologization historically enforced by psychoanalysis, I propose a clinical stance based on an ethics of desire that integrates death into the very core of being.

Notes

1 Parts of this chapter appeared first in P. Gherovici (2017) *Transgender Psychoanalysis: A Lacanian Perspective on Sexual Difference*, New York: Routledge. Reprinted by permission of Taylor & Francis, LLC.

2 See Kestenberg (1971).
3 "*Le transsexuel souhaite réaliser La femme en tant que toute, et comme il veut se libérer de l'erreur commune qui est de confondre l'organe avec le signifiant, il s'adresse au chirurgien pour forcer le passage du Réel*" [Transsexuals wish to realize Woman as Whole, and because they want to free themselves from the common mistake that consists in taking an organ for a signifier, they go and see a surgeon in order to force a breakthrough to the Real) (Lacan, 1971).

References

Ambrosio, G. (Ed.) (2009). *Transvestism, transsexualism in the psychoanalytic dimension*. New York and London: Karnac.
Benjamin, H. (1954). Transvestism and transsexualism as psycho-somatic and somato-psychic syndromes. *American Journal of Psychotherapy*, 8(2), 219–230.
Benjamin, H. (2006). Transvestism and transsexualism as psycho-somatic and somato-psychic syndromes. In S. Stryker & S. Whittle (Eds.), *Transgender studies reader*, 45–52. New York: Routledge.
Bornstein, K. (1994). *Gender outlaw: On men, women, and the rest of us*. New York: Routledge.
Bullough, V. (1994). *Science in the bedroom: A history of sex research*. New York: Basic Books.
Bullough, V. (2000). Transgenderism and the concept of gender. *The International Journal of Transgenderism*, 4(3). Retrieved from: www.atria.nl/ezines/web/IJT/9703/numbers/symposion/bullough.htm.
Bullough, V. & Bullough, B. (1993). *Cross dressing, sex, and gender*. Philadelphia: University of Pennsylvania Press.
Califia, P. (1997/2003). *Sex changes: The politics of transgenderism*. San Francisco, CA: Cleis Press.
Carlson, S. (2010). Transgender subjectivity and the logic of sexual difference. *differences*, 21(2), 46–72.
Cauldwell, D. O. (1947). *Effects of castration on men and women*. Girard, KS: Haldeman-Julius.
Cauldwell, D. O. (1950). *Questions and answers on the sex life and sexual problems of trans-sexuals*. Girard, KS: Haldeman-Julius.
Cauldwell, D. O. (1951). *Sex transmutation: Can one's sex be changed?* Girard, KS: Haldeman-Julius.
Cauldwell, D. O. (1955). Is "sex change" ethical? *Sexology*, 22, 108–112.
Cauldwell, D. O. (Ed.) (1956). *Transvestism: Men in female dress*. New York: Sexology Corporation.
Cauldwell, D.O. (2006). Psychopathia transexualis. In S. Stryker & S. Whittle (Eds.), *Transgender studies reader* (pp. 40–44). New York: Routledge. (Original work published in 1949, Psychopathia transexualis. *Sexology*, 16, 274–280.)
Chiland, C. (2003). *Transsexualism: Illusion and Reality* (P. Slotkin, Trans.). Middletown, CT: Wesleyan University Press.
Coates, S., Friedman, R. C., & Wolfe, S. (1991). The etiology of boyhood gender identity disorder: A model for integrating temperament, development, and psychodynamics. *Psychoanalytic Dialogues*, 1(4), 481–523.
Dean, T. (2000). *Beyond Sexuality*. Chicago: University of Chicago Press.
Dean, T. & Lane, C. (Eds.) (2001). *Homosexuality and Psychoanalysis*. Chicago: University of Chicago Press.
Eigen, M. (1996). *Psychic deadness*. Northvale, NJ: Jason Aronson.

Ekins R. & King D. (2001a). Pioneers of transgendering: The popular sexology of David O. Cauldwell. *The International Journal of Transgenderism*, 5(2). Retrieved from: www.symposion.com/ijt/cauldwell/cauldwell_01.htm

Ekins R. & King D. (2001b). Special Issue on David O. Cauldwell. Classic Reprints Series. *The International Journal of Transgenderism*, 5(2). Retrieved from: www.wpath.org/journal/ www.iiav.nl/ezines/web/IJT/97-03/numbers/symposion/ index-2.htm

Falzeder, E. (Ed.) (2002). *The Complete Correspondence of Sigmund Freud and Karl Abraham, 1907–1925*. London: Karnac Books.

Foucault, M. (1990). *The History of Sexuality. Volume I: An Introduction*. (R. Hurley, Trans.). New York: Vintage Books.

Freud, S. (1953). Three Essays on the Theory of Sexuality (1905). In *The Standard Edition of the Complete Psychological Works of Sigmund Freud*, Vol. 7. James Strachey (Ed., Trans.), 123–146. London: Hogarth Press.

Gay, P. (1998). *Freud: A Life of Our Times*. New York: W.W. Norton & Co.

Gherovici, P. (2017). *Transgender Psychoanalysis: A Lacanian Perspective on Sexual Difference*. New York: Routledge.

Green, A. (1986). *On Private Madness*. London: Hogarth Press.

Gutheil, E. ([1930] 1971). An analysis of a case of transvestism. In *Sexual Aberrations: The Phenomenon of Fetishism in Relation to Sex*. W. Stekel (Ed.). (S. Parker., Trans.). New York: Liveright Publishing Co.

Hamburger, C., Stürup, G., & Dahl-Iversen, E. (1953). Travestism: Hormonal psychiatric and surgical treatment. *Journal of the American Medical Association*, 15, 391–396.

Hausman, B. (1995). *Changing sex: Transsexualism, technology, and the idea of gender*. Durham, NC: Duke University Press.

Hirschfeld, M. (1910/1991). *Transvestites: The erotic drive to cross dress*. (M. A. Lombardi-Nash, Trans.) New York: Prometheus Books.

Kestenberg, J. S. (1971). A developmental approach to disturbances of sex-specific identity. *International Journal of Psycho-Analysis*, 52, 99–102.

Kinsey, A. (1953). *Sexual behavior in the human female*. Philadelphia: Saunders.

Krafft-Ebing, R. von (1886/1965). *Psychopathia sexualis*. (H. Wedeck, Trans.). New York: G. P. Putnam.

Lacan, J. (1971). Le séminaire XIX . . . Ou pire. Le savoir du psychanalyste (Seminar XIX . . . Or worse. The Knowledge of the Psychoanalyst) session of December 8, 1971, unpublished papers. Retrieved from: gaogoa.free.fr/Seminaires_HTML/19-OP/OP08121971.htm

Lacan, J. (2006). *Écrits: The first complete edition in English*. Translated by B. Fink. New York: Norton.

Limentani, A. (1979). The significance of transsexualism in relation to some basic psychoanalytic concepts. *International Review of Psychoanalysis*, 6, 139–153.

Lothstein, L. (1977). Countertransference reactions to gender dysphoric patients: Implications for psychotherapy. *Psychotherapy: Theory, research and practice*, 14 (1) 21–31.

Lothstein, L. (1992). Clinical management of gender dysphoria in young boys: Genital mutilation and DSM implications. In W. Bockting & E. Coleman (Eds.) *Gender dysphoria: Interdisciplinary approaches in clinical management* (pp. 87–106). New York: Haworth Press.

Lukianowicz, N. (1959). Survey of various aspects of transvestism in light of our present knowledge. *Journal of Nervous and Mental Disease*, 128, 36–64.

Meyerowitz, J. (1998). Sex change and the popular press: historical notes on transsexuality in the United States, 1930–1955. *GLQ*, 4, 159–187.

Meyerowitz, J. (2002/2004). *How sex changed: A history of transsexuality in the United States*. Cambridge, MA: Harvard University Press.

Millot, C. (1990). *Horsexe: Essays on transsexualism* (K. Hylton, Trans.). New York: Autonomedia.

Money, J. (1955). Hermaphroditism, gender and precocity in hyper-adrenocorticism: Psychologic findings. *Bulletin of the Johns Hopkins Hospital*, 96, 253–254.

Oppenheimer, A. (1991). The wish for a sex change: A challenge to psychoanalysis? *International Journal of Psycho-Analysis*, 72, 221–231.

Person, E. & Ovesey, L. (1978). Transvestism: New perspectives. *Journal of the Academy of Psychoanalysis*, 6, 304–322.

Prosser, J. (1998). *Second skins: The body narratives of transsexuality*. New York: Columbia University Press.

Quinodoz, D. (February 1998). A fe/male transsexual patient in psychoanalysis. *International Journal of Psychoanalysis*, 79, 95–111.

Salamon, G. (2010). *Assuming a body: Transgender and rhetorics of materiality*. New York: Columbia University Press.

Socarides, C. (1970). A psychoanalytic study of the desire for sexual transformation ('transsexualism'): The plaster-of-Paris man. *International Journal of Psychoanalysis*, 51(3), 341–349.

Stein, R. (1995). Analysis of a case of transsexualism. *Psychoanalytic Dialogues*, 5, 257–289.

Stein, R. (1998). The enigmatic dimension of sexual experience: The "otherness" of sexuality and primal seduction. *Psychoanalytic Quarterly*, 67, 594–625.

Stekel, W. (Ed.) (1930/1971). *Sexual Aberrations: The Phenomenon of Fetishism in Relation to Sex* (S. Parker, Trans.). New York: Liveright Publishing Co.

Stoller, R. (1975). Bisexuality: The 'bedrock' of masculinity and femininity. In *The Transsexual Experiment, Volume Two of Sex and Gender* (pp. 7–18). London: Hogarth Press.

Stryker, S. (2006). (De)subjugated knowledges: An introduction to transgender studies. In S. Stryker & S. Whittle (Eds.), *Transgender studies reader* (pp. 1–17). New York: Routledge.

Thurer, S. (2005). *The end of gender: A psychological autopsy*. New York: Routledge.

Whittle, S. (2006). Foreword. In S. Stryker & S. Whittle (Eds.), *Transgender studies reader* (pp. xi–xvi). New York: Routledge.

6
PRINCIPLES FOR PSYCHOANALYTIC WORK WITH TRANS CLIENTS

Sheila L. Cavanagh

Transgender[1] (trans★) studies have grown exponentially in North American cultural studies over the course of the last decade. Trans★ studies centralize and validate trans★ experience. They turn a critical gaze onto institutional sites and practices that objectify transpeople and authorize transphobia. Trans★ studies work in the field of psychoanalysis focuses on theories and clinical practices that exclude and/or construct transpeople as abnormal. In Lacanian psychoanalysis, trans★ studies scholars have been legitimately critical of a tendency to reduce transsexuality to psychosis (Adams, 1996; Chiland, 2000; Fiorini & Vainer, 2003; Morel, 2011; Shepherdson, 2000). Due in no small part to trans★ community health advocacy, the fifth edition of the DSM changed 'Gender Identity Disorder' (GID) to 'Gender Dysphoria' in an effort to de-stigmatize transsexuality. The diagnosis is no longer listed as a sexual disorder. The change in the language of diagnosis goes some way to redress the medicalization of transsubjectivity in psychiatry and the mental health professions. But considerable more work needs to be done to cultivate trans-positive mental healthcare in psychoanalytic circles.

In psychoanalytic theory and practice we must embark on a wholesale deconstruction of what I call the psychotic thesis originally set in motion by Catherine Millot (1990) in *Horsexe*. Millot argues in her book that transsexuality is psychotic and even now, almost thirty years later, has not revised her claim. In this chapter, I hope to establish a clinical distinction between transsubjectivity and what Jacques Lacan (1993) calls the push-toward Woman in psychosis (as a clinical structure). The distinction I make is intended to support the move to depathologize trans★ subjectivity in Lacanian psychoanalysis.

Not only does the psychotic thesis negate the authenticity and viability of trans★ (as a sexual position in its own rite), but it is usually accompanied by cautionary warnings about surgically and hormone therapies, none of which are supported by clinical evidence. Most objectionable, from a transpositive mental healthcare perspective, is the framing of gender affirming surgeries as mutations (Chiland, 2009; Coates, 2009; Morel, 2011; Stein, 1995). Clinical evidence in the North American context (and I suspect internationally) does not support the claim that trans★ is indicative of psychosis. In fact, researchers are increasingly documenting the positive effects of medically assisted transsexual transitions (Ainsworth & Spiegel, 2010), hormone blocking protocols for trans★ youth (Smith et al., 2001), and hormone therapy. Medical intervention when desired by the patient can be psychologically beneficial and palliative, even salubrious. It must also be stressed that "regret" in the case of sex reassignment surgeries is extremely low (Carroll, 1999; Kuiper & Cohen-Kettenis, 1989; Johansson et al., 2009; Rachlin, 2002) and this has, in the Canadian context, been amply demonstrated by the Trans Pulse survey of 433 trans★ people living in Ontario ("Trans PULSE Survey," n.d.).

I thus begin from the premise, originally put forward by Lacanian psychoanalyst Patricia Gherovici (2010), that transsubjectivity can be, and usually is, a sub-set of neurosis, a statistically common structure in which there is an operative paternal metaphor. A paternal metaphor, as I will explain below, interrupts the dyad between the developing-subject (as toddler) and the m/Other (who may also be a father). The paternal function enables metaphor and metonymy in language. Transpeople span a wide gender spectrum. Moreover, they do not occupy any one single sexual position or psychic structure. We all differ in our experience of the symptom and in relation to what Lacan calls the desire of the Other. It is the analyst's job to listen without presumption and to keep countertransferences in check. To the extent that analysts hold prefabricated ideas about what it means to be trans★ they will not be able to hear the analysand's symptom in its own unique configuration.

Let us remember that there are many ways to negotiate what Lacan calls the conundrum of sexual difference. No one structure (neurosis, psychosis or perversion) is a panacea. In principle, there may be ways to wrest psychosis from deviance and pathology. Neurotic patients can have more difficulties with anxiety and depression than psychotic patients. My intention is not to support a moral hierarchy in the psychoanalytic clinic. Nor is it to advance a neurocentric position which values the neurotic structure over and above psychosis (or perversion for that matter). Rather, my intention is to build upon the contemporary Lacanian scholarship in the North American context (Carlson, 2010; Cavanagh, 2016; Elliot, 2001; Elliot & Roen, 1998; Gherovici, 2010; Gozlan, 2014) that views transsubjectivity as one, among other, therapeutically sound ways to negotiate what Lacan calls the aporia of sexual difference. Certainly, there are trans★ clients who are, by Lacanian standards, psychotic and their trans★ status cannot be reduced to the push-toward-Woman. In other words, trans★ identifications are not always symptomatic.

I provisionally abide by Lacan's definition of psychosis as a structure whereby there is a missing paternal metaphor. But having said this, I also believe, as evidenced in the clinic of the everyday, that there is more overlap between the three Lacanian structures (neurotic, perverse, and psychotic) than is usually acknowledged. We must also question the Lacanian presumption that sexual positioning—as 'man' or 'Woman'—is mutually exclusive. Although Lacan insists there are only two sexual positions, only two ways to deal with the phallic premise, there is room to revisit these formulations and transpeople invite us to do so.

While psychoanalysis is well equipped with theoretical tools and analysts are well trained in clinical practice, ethics, technique, and so forth, they are, curiously, unequipped to deal with transsubjectivity. Lacanian practitioners have largely capitulated to the psychotic thesis: the belief that transsexuals are, by definition, psychotic. The psychotic diagnostic, as it is routinely applied to trans-patients, smacks of transphobia and interferes with needed medical healthcare delivery. The psychotic thesis is not always a legitimate diagnostic. When routinely applied to trans* patients it becomes evident that it is, actually, a refusal to deal with trans* sexual difference. Analysts must acknowledge and account for their anti-trans* sentiments in order to work with trans* clients.

Consider, for instance, Eric Laurent, a Parisian analyst affiliated with the New Lacanian School in France, who claims that transsexual women (whom he calls transsexual men) are psychotic without exception (Stevens, 2007, p. 212). Simona Argentieri (2009), yet another Lacanian analyst, reads transsexualities in terms of 'disorder,' 'pathology,' and perversion. Joël Dor, also a Parisian Lacanian psychoanalyst, locates transsexuality between the perverse and psychotic structure (2001, pp. 177–178). In *Sexual Ambiguities*, a book about sexuation, Geneviève Morel (2011) contends that the 'demand' for transsexual surgery is counter to the psychoanalytic aim. According to Morel (2011), the availability of a scientific solution (surgery) to the symptom of transsexuality offers the client an unhelpful and detrimental means to bypass the analytic process. The fact that most transpeople do not suffer from verbal hallucinations and fair better after sexual reassignment surgery (SRS) and/or hormone therapy *when they want it* (and let us remember that not all transpeople want medical intervention to support their transitions) does not seem to factor into her prognosis.

If Lacanian psychoanalysts are going to approach the clinic of transgender in responsible ways, they must acknowledge that Lacan's writing on 'transsexualist jouissance' was at a nascent stage when he died. It is not an established fact that Lacan viewed transsexuality as a tell-tale sign of psychosis (Gherovici, 2010). Although there can be, as illustrated in the case of Daniel Paul Schreber, a push-toward-Woman in psychosis, Lacan wondered if this 'transsexualist jouissance' was indeed a psychotic mechanism (Gherovici, 2010, p. 175). The query should give us pause. Lacan also remarks that "transsexualist practice [is] not at all unworthy of being related to 'perversion'" (Lacan, 2006, p. 474).

What did Lacan say about psychosis?

Lacan's most comprehensive discussion of psychosis is found in his 1955–1956 Seminar titled *The Psychoses*. What the psychotic reveals "in his discourse [is] what it [psychoanalysis] usually discovers as the discourse of the unconscious" (Lacan, 1993, p. 132). Psychosis is, for Lacan, a structure distinct from neurosis and perversion. It involves a unique problem of language. For the psychotic there is a hole in the Symbolic. Something escapes the signifier. While there is always something in excess of the signifier, the psychotic experiences a return of what escapes symbolization from without as a verbal hallucination. Schreber, for instance, had no signifier for 'Woman.' It thus returned from without and he experienced the signifier as invasive. A psychotic may experience a barrage of unmediated signifiers felt to be persecutory. The psychotic subject is inundated with meanings that do not refer to anything in particular. This is the character of verbal hallucinations.

Lacan tells us that neurotics repress an element of being that goes un-symbolized. Psychotics, by contrast, foreclose upon what is un-symbolized. Lacan writes that "something primordial regarding the subject's being does not enter into symbolization and is not repressed, but rejected" (Lacan, 1993, p. 81). The foreclosure of a signifier is indicative of the psychotic structure. While we can talk about the return of the repressed in neurosis as, for example, a symptom (like a nervous tick), the return of the signifier foreclosed in psychotics is far more serious and destabilizing. Lacan offers the following distinction between repression in neurosis and foreclosure in psychosis: "If the neurotic inhabits language, the psychotic is inhabited, possessed, by language" (1993, p. 25). He further explains that "whatever is refused in the symbolic order, in the sense of *Verwerfung*, reappears in the real" (1993, p. 13). The rejected signifier returns in the Real and morphs into something torrential. The signifier returns as hallucinatory experience, the psychotic hears voices. The hallucinatory activity is an attempt to palliate a missing signifier. Psychotic fantasies are attempts to patch a hole which Lacan also calls a "fault, a point of rupture, in the structure of the external world" (1993, p. 45). Although it must be remembered that some degree of hallucinatory activity is, as Bruce Fink (2004) reminds us, also characteristic of neurosis and related to the structure of desire in *all* subjects, it takes on a proportionately extreme form in psychosis.

Psychotic delusions including, for example, the push-toward-Woman are attempts to knot the signifier otherwise foreclosed. Without a three-way knot between the Symbolic, the Imaginary, and the Real, the subject cannot separate or achieve a gap between the 'I' and the signifier. The foreclosed signifier threatens the subject with Real annihilation. The desire of the Other is unmediated and terrifying. Lacking a signifier as a defense against the Other, the psychotic over-relies on the Imaginary register. Many Lacanian practitioners believe that when working with a psychotic patient, it is important to strengthen the function and capacities of the Imaginary. It is one of few psychical tools psychotics have to protect themselves against a barrage of unmediated signifiers. To the extent that gender (as Imaginary) is tied to sex (as Real) for neurotics, no amount of 'reparative' or 'conversion' therapy can alter the erotogenic components of the bodily schemata. It can only cause anxiety and distress. What psychoanalysts call sexual identification does not change because it is not a superficial construct—it is a psychically invested relation to language that enables *being* in relation to the desire of the Other. But unlike the neurotic, whose Symbolic world is knotted to the Imaginary and the Real, the psychotic can experience extreme bodily fragmentation.

The Name-of-the-Father

A psychotic structure indicates a lack of phallic meaning in the Imaginary. In other words, the Name-of-the-Father is inoperative. This is not about the absence of an actual biological father but an absence of the paternal metaphor. The Name-of-the-Father is, for Lacan, the fundamental signifier. "For psychosis to be triggered, the Name-of-the-Father—*verworfen*, foreclosed, that is, never having come to the place of the Other—must be summoned to that place in symbolic opposition to the subject" (2006, p. 481). A signifier of paternity is, in the Lacanian frame, needed to triangulate the mother–child dyad. Without the Name-of-the-Father, a hole opens up in the signified that "sets off a cascade of reworkings of the signifier from which the growing disaster of the imaginary proceeds, until the level is reached at which signifier and signified stabilize in a delusional metaphor" (Lacan, 2006, p. 481). To put this in another way, there is a hole in the Symbolic register of the subject. Something statistically atypical occurs during the Oedipal stage that prevents the installation of the Name-of-the-Father (as paternal function). The Name-of-the-Father "redoubles in the Other's place the very signifier of the symbolic ternary, insofar as it constitutes the law of the signifier" (p. 481). The paternal metaphor can be anything that introduces others and Otherness into the primary dyad. As such it is the "guarantor of the existence of a cultural order that constitutes discourse and society" (Aulagnier, 1975, p. 75). It is helpful to remember that, for Lacan, the maternal function introduces the child to its first Other while the paternal function introduces it to otherness.

According to Lacan, psychotics do not experience a gap between themselves and the Other because of this missing paternal function. The uninterrupted dyad prevents the subject from being able to use simile, allegory, and substitution in language. As such, psychotics are literal and cannot play with language. More worrisome is the fact that the Other cannot be interrupted. To make matters more difficult, the subject is not bequeathed an identity because the Name-of-the-Father is missing. As a result, the subject is not tied to the Symbolic (where language, signs, and symbols function). The body-image does not settle into a livable form and there is what Lacan calls a "lethal gap of the mirror stage" (Lacan, 2006, p. 476).

In her discussion of the Name-of-the-Father and the push-toward-Woman in Lacanian psychoanalysis, Patricia Gherovici (2010) explains that psychotics may experience feminization (not as gender identity) but as Real jouissance (p. 176). The unbarred jouissance of the Other takes over the psychotic's body. Involuntary feminization is a means to stabilize the signifier so that the subject can forge an identity. The push-toward-Woman works like the paternal metaphor. It is an attempt to stabilize jouissance.

The distinction I propose between the push-toward-Woman in psychosis and transsubjectivity is based, in part, on the fact that Lacan does notice a distinction between Schreber's psychosis and other analysands who would, by contemporary standards, be classified as trans★. He observes that Schreber's feminization does not involve an actual wish for a sex change. Lacan writes: "In no way has President

Schreber ever integrated any type of feminine form" (1993, p. 85). Rather his feminization is, as noted earlier, involuntary and imposed from without. For Lacan, Schreber's turn toward 'Woman' is not about desire but is, rather, a means to exist in relation to a foreclosed signifier. Schreber's struggle is not about sexual positioning (as it is for the neurotic), it is about *being* (or existence) itself. Schreber's fantasy (or delusion) is, in other words, an attempt to install a signifier—a paternal function—otherwise foreclosed.

Horsexe

As already mentioned, the psychotic thesis is based on the idea that transsexuality is psychotic. Millot claims that the transsexual symptom is analogous to the act of writing for James Joyce: transsexuality, like the act of writing, offsets psychosis. More specifically, Millot argues that the "transsexual symptom [in transsexual women] . . . corresponds to an attempt to palliate the absence of the Name-of-the-Father, that is, to define an outer limit, a point of arrest, and to achieve a suspension of the phallic function" (1990, p. 42). In his seminar on the psychoses, Lacan (1955–1956/1993) defines the Name-of-the-Father as a 'fundamental' signifier which enacts an Oedipal prohibition—a No (or limit to jouissance)—and, ultimately, enables the subject to assume a sexual position. Without an operative paternal metaphor, a subject cannot become a 'man' or 'Woman.' In neurotics, the signifier for the Name-of-the-Father is substituted for the desire of the Other.

For Lacan, sexual positioning is contingent upon how one experiences jouissance in relation to the Other. As Millot (1990) explains, the "subject's capacity to situate himself as man or woman relative to the phallus depends on the symbolization of the paternal function" (p. 35). Without a Symbolic anchor (triangulation), psychotics do not become sexuated subjects. 'Woman' (as signifier) is sometimes used, by psychotics, to impose a limit. The push-toward-Woman (feminization) is an attempt to establish a cut or limit to the Other's jouissance at the level of the signifier. But this limit is, according to Millot, bound to give way. It is not a Borromean knot, but a slip-knot. While more clinical work is needed to understand how the signifier 'Women' works for psychotics, it is necessary to consider the limitations to Millot's thesis with respect to trans* subjects.

As I will explain in what follows, the problem with Millot's thesis is that she universalizes a metonymic equation between transsexuality and psychosis inadvertently set up by Lacan. Having said this, there are important analytic insights to be taken from her work. Notably, she does not view Schreber—who does not actually request a sex change —*as* a transsexual. Schreber experiences the push-toward-Woman as involuntary and as a "scandalous violation, contrary to the order of things" (Millot, 1990, p. 41). She also, correctly in my view, observes that "pure transsexuality does not involve psychotic symptoms in the psychiatric sense" (Millot, 1990, p. 41). Although I would not propose a taxonomy measuring transsubjectivity in terms of purity, Millot does observe that transsexuality does not usually coincide with psychosis. Millot also writes about transsexual *symptoms* in terms of neurosis, hysteria in particular, but reserves this positioning only for transsexual men (whom she calls female transsexuals). Millot (1990) writes that the "transsexual symptom ranges from clearly psychotic . . . to those of the hysteric type" (p. 115). Additionally, Millot contends that because hysterics are undecided about sex they can be influenced to transition by a third party (1990, p. 116). Referring to transsexual men, she writes: "The man's side is chosen for want of knowing how to place oneself on the woman's side" (Millot, 1990, p. 117). Millot further notes that of the transsexual men she knows, none have psychotic symptoms (p. 117). While I take issue with the way transmasculinity is portrayed as easily influenced by a third party, it is productive, as Shanna Carlson (2010) and Patricia Gherovici (2010) suggest, to think about transgender in relation to hysteria (a neurotic structure).

For Millot, transsexual women have a "commitment to femininity" (1990, p. 41). When Millot notes that there may be no 'psychotic symptoms' in transsexuality and that what she calls the 'transsexual symptom' can also be of the 'hysterical type' she is referring to transsexual men. She observes that transmasculinity may be a way to "escape the requirement of being the object of the Other's *jouissance*" (p. 140). Although I reject Millot's distinction between transsexual men and transsexual women based as it is on natal sex, as opposed to sexual positioning, Millot may not be entirely wrong to read transsexuality as a way to impose a limit to the Other's jouissance. Certainly, Gozlan (2014) has suggested that transsubjectivity can be a way to mitigate the jouissance of the Other as it envelopes the body of the child-subject. In relational psychoanalysis, a comparable observation is made with respect to the role of a parental other in "colonizing" the subject's body-image (Lemma, 2013; Suchet, 2011). The question of psychic structure, in Millot's work, seems to hinge on the fact of natal sex and gender identity as opposed to sexual positioning. If she is to claim, as she does, that female transsexuals and male transsexuals are structurally distinct, how is it that she, as a Lacanian, can evoke natal sex when biology, as all Lacanians agree, has nothing to do with sexual positioning? In this way, her study reflects sociological and demographic bias and does not follow Lacan's analytic of sexuation.

Nevertheless, Millot reads transsexual women and transsexual men as two distinct groups who are also, paradoxically, quite similar in regard to "their relationship to the phallus, and in their identification with its incarnation of outsidesex, and even outside-body" (1990, p. 140). Both groups identify with the phallus and try to escape "being the object of the Other's jouissance" (p. 140). The difference, for Millot, is with respect to what the wish to transition reveals. It is either a "delusion of bodily transformation" (p. 115) indicative of psychosis, or a hysterical demand caused by indecision about one's sexed position. Despite this possible kinship between hysterics and trans* subjects first identified by Millot (1990), analytic attention in most Lacanian circles has, unfortunately, focused on the supposed 'psychotic' character of transsexuality.

Following the psychotic thesis, many contemporary Lacanians practitioners believe that transsubjects seek a perfect jouissance. A perfect union with the Other is, as all Lacanian analysts agree, impossible. We are all cut by the signifier and must negotiate loss along with the turbulent desire of the Other. Although many transpeople are hopeful about what may be gained by transitioning this, in and of itself, does not reflect a fantasy of a perfect union with the Other. It is not true that transpeople revere the power of medical doctors to make them the sex they wish to be. Although I am not a clinician, I have yet to meet a transsexual who views their doctor as God. Nor have I met a transperson who has not thought long and hard about exactly the kind of medical assistance they want (or do not want). Certainly, anecdotal evidence suggests that transpeople are under no illusions about the repercussions and limitations to existing surgical interventions. A 'perfect' synthesis between sexual morphology and gender are widely acknowledged to be impossible. I have seen playful attempts to embody what Lacanians call phallic totality in trans★ art, writing, and cultural production (wishes to be the ultimate man or 'Woman') but they are always satires, parodies, and performed in jest.

Lacanian clinicians are routinely encouraged to isolate the character of the 'demand' for a sex change. For example, Gherovici (2010), who has done much to depathologize trans★ in Lacanian psychoanalysis, advises analysts to establish whether the demand for SRS is functioning at the level of the signifier or, rather, at the level of the Real. If it is functioning at the level of the signifier a medically assisted transition can palliate the traumatic jouissance of the patient. If it is not, a medically assisted transition involving SRS can be, according to Gherovici, mortifying and devastating to the functioning of desire and jouissance. Although we should not reject the possibility that some patients may 'regret' surgeries or that some patients may experience surgery as destabilizing, I have not seen evidence that this is, in fact, a significant risk (although I have seen evidence to the contrary). While Gherovici is, in my reading, developing an important analytic distinction between the needs of neurotic patients and psychotic patients, I question whether a psychoanalyst can know or, ultimately, should decide whether a subject-client would benefit from a medically assisted transition. In my view, this decision should be up to the client to decide for themselves.

There are, in my view, too many cisgender analysts presuming to know what transpeople want. Millot, for example, contends that transsexual women want to be The Woman as opposed to *a* woman in general. In her formulation, transsexual women want to be 'All women' as opposed to *one* woman (not-all). Transsexual men, it follows, want to be "like everyone else, that is, men" (Millot, 1990, p. 105). For transsexual men, "identification with the male presupposes an active role for the father, and the existence of forces that thwart the subject's initial femininity" (p. 106). I am highly skeptical about the distinction Millot makes because in the clinic of the everyday we see transsexual women who want to be read as ordinary woman (not The Woman that men lack). Similarly, we see transsexual men who want to be read as *the* phallic-man. Some transsexual women *may* aspire to be The Women but this is not true for all transsexual woman. The same can be said for transsexual men. Some transsexual men may want to be ordinary, unexceptional men. Gender does not indicate sexual positioning in Lacanian terms. Nor does it indicate a wish for a perfect jouissance. I am in agreement with Phillipe Van Haute and Tomas Geyskens (2012) that Lacan's sexuation formulas do not "determine two kinds of subjects [man or Woman], but they express a field of tension in which each subject moves" (p. 151).

Yet another problem with Millot's (1990) formulation is that she reads transsexual embodiment as superficial and reducible to costume. She writes: "For transsexuals a book may be read by its cover, and the bodily frame is thought of as another article of clothing, to be retouched at will" (p. 116). The characterization of transsexual embodiment as one-dimensional and perfunctory is notably at odds with her earlier, more analytically sound, discussion about transsexuality being palliative in nature.[2]

Millot is opposed to SRS because she believes transsexuals confuse the organ and the signifier. "Their passion and their folly consists in believing that, by ridding themselves of the organ, they can also be rid of the signifier which, because it sexuates them also divides them" (Millot, 1990, p. 143). Like Millot, Morel (2011) claims the "madness here lies in choosing the wrong target: the organ instead of the signifier" (p. 187). Even a cursory review of trans* studies literature reveals a sophisticated understanding of the distinction between the penis (organ) and the phallus (signifier) and the way they function in the Symbolic.

While those following Millot's psychotic thesis believe that clients have to choose between surgery and analysis, clinical evidence increasingly demonstrates that this is a false choice. Psychoanalysts who work ethically and effectively with trans-clients in the relational paradigm underscore the vitally important role of language, mentalization, and mirroring in the postsurgical transition period (Hansbury, 2011; Lemma, 2012; Saketopoulou, 2014). Analysts are, increasingly, writing about how medical intervention can enable analytical work that was, prior to surgery, not possible. Speaking with great analytic integrity and self-reflexivity, Melanie Suchet (2011), a relational psychoanalyst, acknowledges her own analytic discomfort with her client's transsubjectivity and concordant discomfort with SRS due to the way she was taught to believe that transsexuals "attempt to gain untenable fantasy of psychic redemption through physical transformation" (pp. 177–178). After her work with a trans* clients she now believes that "for some, it is necessary to feel the scalpel, to imagine literally excising the trace of the other, cutting the body . . . excising the hated other, and demarcating a new body, emerging into a new space of corporeality, into a new sense of self that is habitable" (Suchet, 2011, p. 183).

Often, it is the analyst, not the client, who takes the desire for surgery too literally and views it as separable from the analytic process. In so doing, analysts forget the vital role of fantasy, desire, and discourse in the medically assisted transition. Unlike the analyst, trans* clients know the surgical cut does not operate alone. Gender pronouns, name changes, and analytic work (in whatever form it may take) are widely known to support a transition. Transpeople intuitively understand how the Imaginary and Symbolic coordinates of the body touch upon the Real. Gender affirming surgeries are not (only) about flesh (as Real), but mentalization and mirroring (in the Imaginary) and significance (in the Symbolic).

That transitions are significantly helped along by language is grounded in Lacanian theory. I recommend that analysts attend to Lacan's writing on what he calls "pronominal embodiment" (1993, p. 261). Pronominal embodiment indexes the importance of the signifier, as mode of address, in stabilizing the subject. Gender pronouns are like Lacanian quilting points whereby one is inducted into language. The quickest way to thwart analytic work with transpatients is to use legally assigned, as opposed to chosen, names and pronouns. This is not a question of participating in the "delusion of the client" (as one Lacanian analyst complained to me), but of respecting names and gender pronouns consistent with gender identity. Lacanian analysts must not focus on the so-called 'reality' of the situation as they see it. This 'reality' belongs to the analyst. When the analyst's reality enters into the clinical picture it becomes a countertransference and, thus, an obstacle to therapeutic work. Desire and jouissance are Real problems that have little to do reality in the Lacanian clinic.

Patricia Gherovici (2010) offers an important Lacanian alternative to Millot's psychotic thesis. She suggests that transsexuality responds to the inability of the Symbolic to write the sexual impasse. This is one of Gherovici's (2010) major insights. As she suggests, transsexuality may be about a "refusal to accept a discourse that is built on an error, that of taking the phallus for a signifier of sexual difference" (2010, p. 195). In other words, transpeople know that one signifier cannot write two sexes. But more than this, transsubjects animate the impasse and, in so doing, write the Symbolic error *as an error*. To the extent that the Lacanian Woman does not exist, it may be fair to suggest that transsubjectivity, regardless of gender identity, responds to what cannot be written, at least not fully, in the Lacanian Symbolic. In other words, transsubjectivity may be a novel way to write the Woman who does not exist. If follows that trans★ is not pathological; it is epistemological reckoning with the phallic signifier. Trans★ is an aesthetic and epistemologically significant position: it makes visible what lies outside the socio-Symbolic. As opposed to the 'symptom' of transsexuality, I suggest we consider the *insignia* of transsexuality.

Much like the hysteric, there is a desire to reckon with the Master discourse of sex in transubjectivities. In my view, trans★ is not unlike a feminist protest (regardless of the politics of particular transpeople). Moreover, transssubjectivity demonstrates that natal sex and gender identity have nothing to do with sexual difference. Transmen can have a penis, a signifier of lack, and transwomen can 'be' the phallus with and without a penis. Trans★ interrupts the normative uses of Lacanian psychoanalysis insofar as sexual identification is concerned.

The last challenge I make to the psychotic thesis is with respect to the said over-identification with the Other. Millot (1990), Shepherdson (2000), and Morel (2011) have all written that transsexuality involves a totalistic identification with the Other. This over-identification is said to come at the cost of desire. For example, Shepherdson writes that the transsexual demand is one "in which desire is lost, a demand that the subject appears to make, but which has come from the Other, and with which the subject has complied" (2000, p. 104). According to this logic, the 'demand' for surgery comes from an omnipotent and sometimes tyrannical Other. As such, surgeries should be refused. While this *may* be the case for psychotics, it is not the case for neurotics. For the vast majority of trans★ people who are neurotic, desire *is* the desire of the Other. It cannot be otherwise. For all neurotics, regardless of trans★ status, our desire is the desire of the Other. But we have efficacy, we can speak and act. We are, in Lacanian terms, supposed by the act of saying. This is why transsexual autobiographies and memoirs are so important. We must prioritize patient desire (and discourse), but in so doing we must not conclude that desire can ever exist outside the orbit of the Other.

While I support the psychoanalytic attempt to engage patient desire, I do not believe that medically assisted transitions are at odds with the psychoanalytic cure as theorized by Lacan. Trans★ *is* a viable sexual position that works creatively with the sexual impasse. While the verdict is still out on whether transubjectivity is a Feminine solution or, perhaps, a third solution, akin to hysteria, it is a solution nevertheless. Chris Coffman (2012) argues that sexual difference is a fundamental fantasy beholden to cis-heteronormativity that Lacanians must traverse to hear new permutations of desire, some of which I contend are trans★.

Notes

1 In this chapter, I use transgender (or trans★) as an umbrella term inclusive of those who experience a lack of correspondence between their gender and their sex assignment at birth. I use 'transsexuality' (as opposed to trans★) when (a) referring to the psychoanalytic literature that employs the term 'transsexual' for consistency and (b) to refer to those who access SRS and/or hormone therapies.
2 The economic obstacles to accessing medical intervention is at odds with the way surgeries are framed as an 'easy solution' to the impasse of sexual difference. Given the steadfast commitment required to access medical support for transitions in the vast majority of cases, SRS cannot be understood as a passive response to the demand of the Other.

References

Adams, P. (1996). *The emptiness of the image: Psychoanalysis and sexual differences*. New York: Routledge.
Ainsworth, T. A., & Spiegel, J. H. (2010). Quality of life of individuals with and without facial feminization surgery or gender reassignment surgery. *Quality of Life Research*, *19*(7), 1019–1024. doi.org/10.1007/s11136-010-9668-7
Argentieri, S. (2009). Transvestism, transsexualism, transgender: Identification and imitation. In G. Ambrosio (Ed.), *Transvestism, transsexualism in the psychoanalytic dimension* (pp. 1–40). London: Karnac Books.
Aulagnier, Piera. (1975). *La Violence de L'interprétation: Du Pictogramme à L'énoncé*. Paris: Presses Universitaires de France.
Carlson, S. T. (2010). Transgender subjectivity and the logic of sexual difference. *differences: A Journal of Feminist Cultural Studies*, *21*(2), 46–72.
Carroll, R. A. (1999). Outcomes of treatment for gender dysphoria. *Journal of Sex Education and Therapy*, *24*(3), 128–136. doi.org/10.1080/01614576.1999.11074292
Cavanagh, S. L. (2016). Transsexuality as sinthome: Bracha L. Ettinger and the Other (Feminine) sexual difference. *Studies in Gender and Sexuality*, *17*(1), 27–44. doi.org/10.1080/15240657.2016.1135681
Chiland, C. (2000). The psychoanalyst and the transsexual patient. *The International Journal of Psychoanalysis*, *81*(1), 21–35.

Chiland, C. (2009). Some thoughts on transsexualism, transvestitism, transgender and identification. In G. Ambrosio (Ed.), *Transvestitism, transsexualism in the psychoanalytic dimension* (pp. 41–54). London: Karnac Books.

Coates, S. (2009). Developmental research on childhood gender identity disorder. In P. Fonagy, R. Krause, & M. Leuzinger-Bohleber (Eds.), *Identity, gender, and sexuality: 150 years after Freud* (pp. 103–131). London: Karnac Books.

Coffman, C. (2012). Queering Žižek. *Postmodern Culture*, 23(1). doi.org/10.1353/pmc.2013.0024

Dor, J. (2001). *Structure and perversions: The Lacanian clinical field*. New York: Other Press.

Elliot, P. (2001). A psychoanalytic reading of transsexual embodiment. *Studies in Gender and Sexuality*, 2(4), 295–325. doi.org/10.1080/15240650209349180

Elliot, P., & Roen, K. (1998). Transgenderism and the question of embodiment: Promising queer politics? *GLQ: A Journal of Lesbian and Gay Studies*, 4(2), 231–261.

Fiorini, L., & Vainer, A. (2003). The sexed body and the real—its meaning in transsexualism. In A. M. Alizade (Ed.), *Masculine scenarios* (pp. 101–108). New York: Karnac Books.

Fink, B. (2004). *Lacan to the letter: Reading Ecrits closely*. Minneapolis, MN: University of Minnesota Press.

Gherovici, P. (2010). *Please select your gender: From the invention of hysteria to the democratizing of transgenderism*. New York: Routledge.

Gozlan, O. (2014). *Transsexuality and the art of transitioning: A Lacanian approach*. New York: Routledge.

Hansbury, G. (2011). King Kong & Goldilocks: Imagining transmasculinities through the trans–trans dyad. *Psychoanalytic Dialogues*, 21(2), 210–220. doi.org/10.1080/10481885.2011.562846

Johansson, A. Sundbom, E., Höyerback, T., & Bodlund, O. (2009). A five-year follow-up study of Swedish adults with gender identity disorder. *Archives of Sexual Behavior*, 39(6), 1429–1437.

Kuiper, A. J., & Cohen-Kettenis, P. T. (1998). Gender role reversal among postoperative transsexuals. *International Journal of Transgenderism*, 2(3). Retrieved from: www.researchgate.net/publication/270273121_Gender_Role_Reversal_among_Postoperative_Transsexuals

Lacan, J. (1993). *The seminar of Jacques Lacan: Book III, the psychoses 1955–1956*. (J.-A. Miller, & R. Grigg, Trans.). New York: W.W Norton & Company.

Lacan, J. (2006). *Écrits: The first complete edition in English* (B. Fink, Trans.). New York: W.W. Norton & Company.

Lemma, A. (2012). Research off the couch: Re-visiting the transsexual conundrum. *Psychoanalytic Psychotherapy*, 26(4), 263–281.

Lemma, A. (2013). The body one has and the body one is: Understanding the transsexual's need to be seen. *The International Journal of Psychoanalysis*, 94(2), 277–292. doi.org/10.1111/j.1745-8315.2012.00663.x

Millot, C. (1990). *Horsexe: Essays on transsexuality*. New York: Autonomedia.

Morel, G. (2011). *Sexual ambiguities: Sexuation and psychosis*. London: Karnac Books.

Rachlin, K. (2002). Transgender individuals' experiences of psychotherapy. *International Journal of Transgenderism*, 6(1). Retrieved from: www.wpath.org/journal/www.iiav.nl/ezines/web/IJT/97-03/numbers/symposion/ijtvo06no01_03.htm

Saketopoulou, A. (2014). Mourning the body as bedrock: Developmental considerations in treating transsexual patients analytically. *Journal of the American Psychoanalytic Association*, 62(5), 773–806. doi. 10.1177/0003065114553102

Schilder, P. (1950). *The image and appearance of the human body: Studies in the constructive energies of the psyche*. New York: International Universities Press.

Shepherdson, C. (2000). *Vital signs: Nature, culture, psychoanalysis.* London: Routledge.

Smith, Y. L. S., Van Goozen, S. H. M., & Cohen-Kettenis, P. T. (2001). Adolescents with gender identity disorder who were accepted or rejected for sex reassignment surgery: A prospective follow-up study. *Journal of the American Academy of Child & Adolescent Psychiatry,* 40(4), 472–481. doi.org/10.1097/00004583-200104000-00017

Soler, C. (2016). *Lacanian affects: The function of affect in Lacan's work* (B. Fink, Trans.). New York: Routledge.

Stein, R. (1995). Analysis of a case of transsexualism. *Psychoanalytic Dialogues,* 5(2), 257–89.

Stevens, A. (2007). Love and sex beyond identifications. *The Later Lacan: An Introduction,* 211–221. Albany, NY: State University of New York Press

Suchet, M. (2011). Crossing over. *Psychoanalytic Dialogues,* 21(2), 172–191. doi.org/10.1080/10481885.2011.562842

Trans PULSE Survey. (n.d.). Retrieved March 23, 2017, from http://transpulseproject.ca/resources/trans-pulse-survey/

Van Haute, P., & Geyskens, T. (2012). *A Non-oedipal psychoanalysis? A Clinical anthropology of hysteria in the works of Freud and Lacan.* Leuven: Leuven University Press.

7

REALITIES AND MYTHS

The gender affirmative model of care for children and youth

Diane Ehrensaft

Major mental health treatment models for gender-nonconforming children and youth

As of the second decade of the twenty-first century, three major treatment models are available for addressing the needs of gender-nonconforming children and their families, with a lively controversy surrounding them. Before delineating the three models and addressing the nature of the controversy, let us start with a typical referral that may come the way of any mental health gender specialist, regardless of their orientation:

> Hi Dr., I came across your information while I was researching for my son. He recently just turned four and wants to be a girl and is only drawn to girl toys/clothes for the past two years. We have not spoken with a professional doctor. But wanted to reach out early and find ways we as parents can support him.
> Please let me know if you could help. Thank you!

For a moment, let us dial back a generation. If this child's name was Kyle and the same query came to a mental health professional participating in Dr. Richard Green's clinic at UCLA, the treatment recommended and then implemented could very well have looked like this:

> When he was five, Kyle entered a behavior modification program . . . in a laboratory setting and at home. At home, a token reinforcement program was instituted. Kyle received blue tokens for "desirable" behaviors, such as play with boys' toys or with boys, and red ones for undesirable behaviors, such as doll play, "feminine" gestures, or playing with girls. Blue tokens

were redeemable for treats, such as ice cream. Red tokens resulted in a loss of blue tokens, periods of isolation, or spanking by father. The treatment program lasted ten months.

R. Green, 1987, p. 295

Setting a precedent for other clinicians of the time treating children who presented as gender-nonconforming, Kyle's treatment at the UCLA program is emblematic of the model implemented during this era, with the goal of helping children accept the sex assigned to them at birth and adopt the culturally defined appropriate gender behaviors that would match that sex assignment. Underlying the treatment was the intent of warding off a homosexual outcome for young effeminate boys.

What would be done today with a young child who presents as gender-nonconforming, be it a boy who likes to wear dresses, the boy who says "You've got it wrong, I'm a girl," or any child who defies social expectations regarding either their gender identity or gender expressions? It depends who you ask. Let us start with what I will label the "live in your own skin" model, as shaped by the work of Drs. Susan Bradley and Ken Zucker at the Center for Alcoholism and Mental Health gender clinic in Toronto (Zucker & Bradley, 1995). In this model it is assumed that a young child has a malleable gender brain, so to speak, and that a treatment goal would be to facilitate a child accepting the gender identity that matches the sex assigned to that child at birth. The rationale behind this goal is that being transgender is a harder way to live your life, so why not offer the child an easier life, with no harm done, given the plasticity of the young child's gender brain. In a 2015 interview with the *National Post*, Dr. Zucker explained the "learning to live in your own skin" approach this way: "You are lowering the odds that as such a [gender-nonconforming] kid gets older, he or she will move into adolescence feeling so uncomfortable about their gender identity that they think that it would be better to live as the other gender and require treatment with hormones and sex-reassignment surgery" (Cross, 2015). In addition to presuming gender identity malleability in young children, the model also assumes that parents' own conflicts or issues about gender likely contribute to a young child's gender dysphoria. With the parents' consent, and only with their consent, the "live in your own skin" model would employ a combination of behavior modification, ecological interventions, and family system re-structuring to facilitate the child arriving at a place of accepting the gender matching their sex assigned at birth. Practices could include taking away cross-gender toys at home and replacing them with "gender-appropriate" toys, altering children's playmate choices to include more same-sex contacts, enrolling the children in "gender-appropriate" activities, encouraging the like-sex parent to become more actively involved and the opposite-sex parent to step back in relationship to the child, and offering psychotherapy to both the child and parents, with the treatment of the child aimed at exploring the child's gender and solidifying a live in your own skin outcome, and the treatment with the parents aimed at investigating conflicts or psychological issues stemming from or contributing to the child's gender dysphoria. If by the arrival of puberty a child is still exhibiting cross-gender identifications and expressing a cross-gender identity, that child should be supported in transitioning to the affirmed gender, including receiving puberty blockers and hormones, once it is assessed through clinical interviews and psychometric testing that the affirmed gender identity is authentic, for 1) it is now too late to intervene in facilitating a child living in their own skin, as the sensitive period of malleable brain development of gender has closed, and 2) this child can by the arrival of puberty be counted among the persisters who consistently express a cross-gender identity that will most likely remain stable into adulthood. So in this model, the parent reaching out for support of her four-year-old son might be encouraged to engage in the treatment program outlined above, with the goal of helping her child accept that he is a boy, not a girl.

Now let us move to the second model for treating gender-nonconforming children. This would be the "watchful waiting" model designed by the members of the interdisciplinary team at the Amsterdam Center of Expertise on Gender Dysphoria, VU University Medical Center, under the leadership of Dr. Peggy Cohen-Kettenis. Borrowing from a medical intervention (GnRH agonists) already in use for children exhibiting precocious puberty, their team is responsible for introducing the use of puberty blockers for gender purposes, to put a pause on pubertal growth and allow more time for a youth to explore their gender and consolidate their adolescent gender identity, with the future possibility of hormone replacement therapy (also referred to as cross-sex hormones) to align their bodies with their affirmed gender identity. In their model a young child's demonstration of gender nonconformity, be it in identity, expressions, or both, is not to be manipulated in any way, but observed over time. As in the live in your own skin model, if a child's cross-gender identifications and affirmations are persistent over time, interventions are made available for a child to consolidate a transgender identity, if that is assessed as in the best interests of the child—through social transitions, puberty blockers, and later hormones and possible gender affirming surgeries. No attempts are made to alter either a child's gender identity or expressions; yet it is postulated in this model that it would be better to hold off until puberty on any social transitions of a child from one gender to another, and instead give them safe spaces to fully express their gender as they prefer before facilitating any gender transitions (Cohen-Kettenis & Friedemann, 2003). The rationale for holding off on any social transitions is not to ward off a transgender identity but rather that: 1) it would be advantageous that a child experience the first stages of physical puberty for that child to best make a determination of the gender that feels most authentic to them; 2) given developmental stages of childhood, facilitating a social transition from one gender to another at a young age may create a form of cognitive constriction—the child may be prematurely blocked from considering any other possibilities once moved into a cross-gender status and socially constricted from further childhood gender exploration because now they know the cross-gender identity is what everyone has come to expect from them; 3) socially transitioning a child at a very young age may preclude the child from maintaining a realistic understanding of their body and historical status—as a penis-bodied (once a boy) or vagina-bodied (once a girl) person. In informing their practices, this model, like the live in your own skin model, relies on the data gathered about persisters and desisters, both at their own clinic in the Netherlands and in other international studies, particularly those conducted at the CAMH gender program in Toronto. Specifically in the watchful waiting model, since the vast majority of children desist in their gender dysphoria by adolescence, best practices would be to wait and see if the child persists into adolescence before making any significant changes in a child's gender identity.

During the pre-adolescent waiting period, the children are followed carefully by the clinic team in the watchful waiting model, with the support of outside therapists in the community (which is required before a child can receive medical services), to assure that the children are growing well and getting their emotional needs met, and in preparation for later transitioning and medical interventions if the child proves to be a good candidate. Like in the living in your own skin model, the children going through the program also receive a full battery of psychological tests, documenting not only their gender status but also their cognitive-social-emotional functioning. Some of these instruments are delivered to the children directly, some to their parents or teachers. If the mother asking for help with her four-year-old were to attend the Amsterdam clinic with her child, the team might do an assessment and advise that the four-year-old be followed over time, with the understanding that if her son's declarations of wanting to be a girl persisted over time and if he continued to be drawn only to girl toys and activities, consideration of puberty blockers to buy more time to explore gender could certainly happen later, but for now it would be best to let her son continue to be a son free to explore whatever activities he enjoyed, with no corrections on his expressed desire to be a girl.

Briefly, the live in your own skin model is now banned by statute in numerous states and municipalities in the U.S. and in one province in Canada (Ontario), stipulating that mental health professionals are not to engage in practices that attempt to alter the gender expressions or gender identity of a minor. In 2015, after an external review, the CAMH gender clinic was closed, with the assessment that its practices fell below the prevailing standards of care for gender-nonconforming children because of the implementation of interventions that attempted to change a child's gender, a practice that was not only banned in the province of Ontario but declared unethical and potentially harmful by major health organizations internationally, including the World Professional Association for Transgender Health, the American Psychological Association, and the American Psychiatric Association. A Canadian study conducted by Wallace & Russell assessed that in the living in your own skin model "there appears to be an enhanced risk of fostering proneness to shame, a shame-based identity and vulnerability to depression" (Wallace & Russell, 2013, p. 120).

The watchful waiting model is a highly respected model of care worldwide, offering careful and cautious procedures; but it has run into a snag: many contemporary families in the Netherlands are not content to hold their children back from social transitions until puberty, and have, through both local and international support networks of parents and professionals, proceeded to facilitate their children's social transitions without awaiting clinic approval or waiting until puberty arrives. Parents do this not because they are impatient or cave to their children's demands, but because evidence is accruing that young children thrive when given a green light to live in the gender that is most authentic (Olson et al., 2015), and are at risk for symptomatic behaviors if prevented from doing so.

This brings us to the third model of care, the "listen and act" model, which is now commonly known as the gender affirmative model (cf. Hidalgo et al., 2013). This model is closely aligned with the watchful waiting model but in opposition to the live in your own skin model. Where listen and act parts ways with watchful waiting is in the waiting part. Since this is the model that will be highlighted in this chapter, let us begin with a full description of both the theory that informs and the practices that are followed in the model.

The listen and act gender affirmative model is defined as a method of therapeutic support that includes listening to the children, allowing them to speak for themselves about their self-experienced gender identity and expressions, and providing support for them to evolve into their authentic gender selves, which might include social transition from one gender to another and/or evolving gender-nonconforming expressions and presentations, as well as later gender-affirming medical interventions (puberty blockers, cross-sex hormones, surgeries). A particular set of premises informs the model:

- Gender variations are not disorders.
- Gender presentations are diverse and varied across cultures, requiring cultural sensitivity.
- Gender involves an interweaving, over time, of biology, development and socialization, and culture and social context.
- Gender may be fluid; it is not necessarily binary.
- If present, individual pathology is often secondary to negative interpersonal and cultural reactions to a child.
- Gender pathology lies more in the culture than in the child.

Hidalgo et al., 2013

The developmental theory underlying these premises is that gender is an unfolding process occurring over the course of a lifetime. This applies to both gender identity and gender expressions, although it is posited that gender identity is a relatively more stable and consistent construct compared to gender expressions. The theory does not assume, however, as traditional gender theory does, that in normative development gender identity is fixed at age six, associated with a child's evolving understanding that their own gender is a stable, immutable category and there are no "backsies" on one's established gender (cf. Tyson, 1982, for a full description of this traditional developmental theory of gender). In contrast, in the gender affirmative model, if a child affirms a cross-gender identity and later changes their mind and desires to return to the gender matching the sex assigned on their birth certificate or desires yet an additional social transition over time, this is not seen as a potential problem, as long as this progression over time is an organic unfolding rather than an indication of a chaotic inner core and as long as there are social supports in place for those subsequent transitions.

The theory also separates out gender development from sexual identity development, perceiving them as two independent developmental tracks, albeit ones that can cross or connect over the course of a person's life. Within the gender affirmative model, gender health is defined as a youth's opportunity to live in the gender that feels most real and/or comfortable, or, alternatively, a youth's ability to express gender with freedom from restriction, aspersion, or rejection (Ehrensaft, 2016). When considering a child's gender status, attention is paid to both gender identity—Who I know myself to be as male, female, or other, and gender expressions—How I do my gender, the clothes I wear, the toys I choose to play with, the friends I connect to, the activities I am drawn to, and so forth, mindful that a child's gender identity may tell us something very different about the child than a child's gender expressions.

With the intent of enhancing gender health in children and youth, the gender affirmative model has four major treatment goals:

- facilitating an authentic gender self;
- alleviating gender stress or distress;
- building gender resilience;
- securing social supports.

The caveat here is that no assumption is made that every child who is exhibiting a gender-nonconforming presentation is in need of mental health treatment. Recall that one of the underlying premises of the gender affirmative model is that pathology more likely resides in the social context, rather than within the child. This leads to a treatment model in which interventions may be targeted at the surrounding environment, rather than the child's individual psyche, calling on clinicians to step out of their offices and into the community, intervening on behalf of the child with schools, social and religious institutions, and policy-making bodies to remove the pathology impinging on the child. That social pathology might take the form of transphobic attitudes and responses, gender policing, bullying and harassment, more subtle chronic microaggressions (Wing Sue, 2010), as when a teacher continues to use improper gender pronouns, despite the child's and family's persistent request to act in accordance to the child's affirmed gender identity. A corollary to the "stepping out into the community" practice is the employment of parent consultations in lieu of individual psychotherapy (Ehrensaft, 2011, 2012; Malpas, 2011). Often, it is not the child but the parents who need our services: to make sense of their child's gender, work through any extant conflicts and anxieties about their child's gender, and move toward acceptance of their child. Like their child, parents too may need help in developing or strengthening their gender resilience, particularly in the face of a social environment that may blame them for their child's gender "transgressions." Working collaboratively with parents and family and strengthening of their gender resilience stands as a primary task within the listen and act model.

If individual treatment for the child is indicated, it would be for one of four reasons: 1) to assess a child's gender status; 2) to afford the child a "room of their own" to explore their gender; 3) to identify and attend to any co-occurring psychological issues; 4) to address and ameliorate a child's gender stress or distress; 5) to provide sustenance in the face of a non-accepting or rejecting social milieu, which might include family, school, religious institution, or community.

The role of the mental health professional is to 1) join with the child, the family, and allied professionals to learn about the child's authentic gender self and identify impediments to that self either developing or feeling free to express itself; 2) determine if a child's gender presentation is a symptom of some other problem in life or the child's gender core; 3) create a working alliance with the people who will be central in promoting the child's gender health: parents, guardians, siblings, grandparents, or other significant others; pediatricians or family physicians; pediatric endocrinologists; educators; attorneys; 4) develop a plan of next steps in facilitating a child living in their authentic gender self; 5) collaboratively implement those steps. Some professionals working in this model will call on psychometric or projective measures to gather information about the child; others will rely on observation, play, interviewing, and dialogue. Referring back to the premises outlined above that underlie the model, if assessment instruments are employed, every effort is made to use protocols that do not rely on binary measures of gender (e.g., Are you a boy or a girl?) and are not pathology-oriented, but instead assess strengths as well as weakness and differentiate between gender expressions and gender identity. To that end a subgroup of Mind the Gap, the mental health consortium of the San Francisco-based Child and Adolescent Gender Center, has designed a packet of assessment and interview protocols based on the gender affirmative model, available to those who have gender specialist background and receive training for use of the packet.

Whereas all members abiding by the gender affirmative model celebrated the removal of the gender identity disorder from the Diagnostic Statistical Manual and a replacement with gender dysphoria as the diagnostic category for children and adolescents, a debate remains as to whether there should be any gender diagnosis at all. In parallel to the removal of homosexuality as a diagnostic category with all the stigma that had been attached to it, the question is asked by many who adhere to the gender affirmative model: If gender diversity in children (or adults) is not a disease, why should there be a mental health diagnosis attached to it? Others argue that the gender dysphoria or other proposed childhood gender diagnoses (such as gender incongruence) target the stress or distress attached to gender nonconformity, not the gender conformity itself and allow children to be identified and receive the services they need. At the writing of this chapter, the debate is unresolved (cf. Drescher et al., 2016).

Finally, the basic therapeutic tenet of the model is quite simple and straightforward: When it comes to knowing a child's gender, it is not for us to tell, but for the children to say. So we listen, and learn. Once we have explored and gathered the information we need to assess a child's gender status, we are open to acting rather than waiting, which is the main feature that differentiates the gender affirmative model from the Dutch model of watchful waiting, and is certainly in opposition to the living in your own skin model. If, after careful consideration, it becomes clear that a young child is affirmed in their gender, informing us in word and action that the gender they know themselves to be is different than or opposite to the gender that would match the sex assigned to them at birth, we would support a social transition to allow that child to fully live in that gender, whether that child be three, seven, or seventeen years old. We would be governed by stages, rather than ages, and see no need to hold a young child back who has been insistent, consistent, and persistent in affirming their gender identity. In that respect, the gender affirmative model abides by the principle that if a cisgender child is expected to be fully cognizant of their gender identity by the age of six, as the developmental theories indicate, so, too, should a transgender child be recognized for that same cognitive-emotional capability. Once the child's gender comes into clear focus, which we posit can happen with a child of any age, we see no need to ask them to wait until puberty or beyond to claim that gender for themselves, and are instead alerted to the psychological harm that can be done, including heightened risk for generalized anxiety, social anxiety, oppositional behaviors, depression, and compromised school performance, if we enforce a child living in a gender that is inauthentic to them.

In the gender affirmative model, the mother of the four-year-old querying about her son's cross-gender interests would be invited into the consultation room, along with any other parenting figure involved, to report more about what she had been observing in her child's behaviors from infancy to the present; to determine whether her son is showing any signs of stress or distress about his interest in all things girl; to explore whether her child is simply being gender expansive in his gender interests or trying to communicate that his gender identity is not male, as they had assumed. If there was evidence of this little boy suffering from stress or distress, by parents' report, or if the parent(s) desired to get a clearer picture of their child's gender status, we would then invite them to bring their son in for some observation and play sessions. There would then be the opportunity to reflect, in collaboration with the parents or caregivers, on any evidence that this child was consistent in cross-gender declarations, as in "I'm a girl, not a boy" and these declarations were persistent over time and not attributable to any other problems in life. If that evidence made clear that this was a child who was communicating about a cross-gender identity rather than a desire to be gender expansive in his activities but firm in his male identity, and if the parents were supportive of their child's gender identity affirmations, we would not find it necessary to recommend to this mother that she wait until puberty to take action regarding her child's gender identity. Instead, we would consider a present social transition to the gender that was more authentic for this child, in this case female. This recommendation would be in accordance with our principles of gender health: allowing the child to live in the gender that feels most authentic—now. If, on the other hand, the child was happy as he was, if given the latitude to play with whatever he wanted and wear whatever he desired, as a boy, absent any gender policing, the recommendation to the mother might be to go home and enjoy her son, just the way he was; be on the ready to support him in the face of anyone who reacted negatively to his gender creativity; and call us in the future any time she (and parenting partner[s]) might want to consult further. Along with this recommendation would be a reminder that we can only know the cross-section of this child's gender as he presents it at age four. We all have to be cognizant that his gender may evolve into another configuration later in childhood, at which point we can do a new assessment.

Learning to read a child's gender communications

Gender is an interweaving of nature, nurture, and culture, over time, which means that a particular child's gender will have ingredients of all three major set of threads. Yet when it comes to self-knowledge about one's gender, the gender affirmative model asserts that gender awareness comes from within, rather than dictated from without, bringing us back to the basic tenet: If you want to know a child's gender, ask, don't tell. This means that we do not push children into one gender status or another but allow them to both discover and disclose their own. On the other hand, it does not mean that children dictate what is going to happen in solidifying and affirming their gender. Until the age of majority, and in some cases beyond, parents and caretakers, in consultation with professionals, will continue to be the ones making major decisions for their children. Ideally, they will do this in accordance with the primary goal of affording their child the opportunity to live in their authentic gender free from aspersion or rejection.

As previously stated, the gender affirmative model offers a simple and straightforward therapeutic guideline: It is not for the adults to tell, but for the children to say who they are. Yet this task is easier said than done: How are we to know what they are saying? It necessitates learning to find the children in translation. It necessitates learning to differentiate those who are grappling with, exploring, or declaring their gender identities from those who are simply challenging the social expectations for the presentation and expression of their gender selves, from those who are trying to tell us about both. Recall the other premise of the model: gender is not necessarily binary. A child's gender self may be multidimensional, on a spectrum, or even composed of infinite combinations and permutations. Think of the child as weaving a gender web, consisting of the three major cords of nature, nurture, and culture, woven together over time (Ehrensaft, 2011, 2012, 2016). More specifically, if we break those cords down into their component threads, a child's gender web will incorporate their chromosomes; hormones; hormone receptors; gonads/primary sex characteristics; secondary sex characteristics; brain; mind; socialization: family, school, community; culture: values, ethics, laws, theories, and practices. Like fingerprints, no two children's gender webs will be the same. Yet unlike fingerprints, a child's gender web is not immutable; it can change over the course of a child's lifetime. So put another way, our job as mental health professionals is to decipher a child's gender web, at the cross-section during which we are meeting up with that child. This is no short order.

To do so, we call on translation tools. Actually, those tools come in the form of the basic principles of child psychotherapy along with some specific techniques gleaned from psychoanalytic practices. That we can call on psychoanalytic techniques to guide the gender translations is in some way ironic, as the theories underlying these practices are often far from gender affirmative. Instead, they are steeped in a model that perceives gender nonconformity as a reflection of internal conflict best explored through intensive multiple-times-a-week sessions of psychoanalysis and simultaneous parent psychotherapy to treat the parents' conflicts that contribute to the child's gender dis-ease (which, it should be pointed out, is an important component of the live in your own skin model). Yet the psychoanalytic techniques themselves, when applied to deciphering a child's gender communications, are invaluable.

The first tool is listening, which includes suspending any expectations or judgments and remaining in a suspended state of not knowing until the child unfolds who they are. The listening is not only for words, but also for the messages that come from actions, as children are so often more of action than word when it comes to communicating, especially about gender, which can be a tender subject.

One caveat about listening, as taught to us in psychoanalytic training. Along with listening came waiting: Let the child bring the material to you, do not force it on the child. When facilitating gender explorations with a child, you might be waiting until hell freezes over before a child will voluntarily articulate their gender issues. In addition to the inchoate nature of our inner gender self-knowledge, often difficult to transfer accurately into words, children internalize as early as age three a sensibility that when it comes to transgressing socially prescribed gender norms, we don't talk about such things. So the golden rule of waiting for the child to bring their issues to the therapist rather than the therapist imposing them on the child will not hold up well with the gender-nonconforming child. The therapist may get far more traction by setting the tone for the child: This is a place where we can talk about gender and you can help me learn about yours. At the same time, if the child gives any indication that they do *not* want to talk about gender, it is important to step back and respect the child's timing.

The second tool is mirroring (Devor, 2004; Frank, 2001; Winnicott, 1967). I want to highlight this technique as essential to therapeutic work with gender-nonconforming children and youth. Metaphorically, we are moving from listening to seeing, from ears to eyes. To mirror is to reflect back to the child what the child is showing the therapist about who they are, as mediated by the therapist's own internal thoughts based on what the therapist is seeing. The more the therapist engages in this process, the more the child opens up.

Many children who are gender-nonconforming suffer from the chronic microaggressions (Wing Sue, 2010) that come in the form of "misgendering." Others, including parents, fail to see who the child really is, and offers a child only a distorted image of their gender. An example would be a child assigned male at birth who says, "I'm not a boy, I'm a girl. God got it wrong," and the parents' response is, "Well, you can't be a girl. You have a penis." If, as Diamond (2000) pointed out, gender comes from brain messages not from genitalia, now not only God, but the parents have gotten it wrong. As these distortions are so prevalent in the lives of gender-nonconforming children, the use of the mirroring technique often emerges as the most salient therapeutic technique in opening up further pathways for gender exploration and building gender confidence and resilience. In relational terms, to remain invisible or misperceived is a basic denial of self; to feel seen and mirrored is the core element in the affirmation of an authentic self, and an essential component of gender health.

Lastly, reference has already been made to the function of play as a central communication tool for children. This applies to all aspects of life, but particularly to communication of gender thoughts and feelings. The play can be in the form of drawings, manipulation of toy figures, puppet play, make-believe games, storytelling. One young transgender boy, before transition, came up with a creative tale about himself: Born on an alien planet, the little alien was transported light years away, where the little alien discovered a world where everyone was a girl and the only clothes available were pink and frilly, the only things to play with Barbies and pretend make-up kits. So the little alien was forced to live as a girl until someone realized she was not a girl at all, but an alien. The translation: alien = boy. The story was a poignant statement of this child's psychological experience of being a stranger in a strange land when perceived as a girl. The therapist's communication of this translation to the child proved invaluable.

Final task: dispelling myths

Because the gender affirmative model has emerged amidst a controversy about the best care for children who go against the gender grain, I would like to conclude by dispelling some prevalent myths about the gender affirmative model. The first myth is that gender affirmative practitioners are governed by trans-activist politics rather than scientifically sound principles, with a goal of pushing children toward a transgender outcome. To the contrary, there is every effort to be evidence-based, not politically driven, and the only good scientific outcome is one that is authentic for the child, and never one that would include irreversible medical interventions if those would not be in accordance with a child's true gender self. A related myth is that the model advocates medical interventions for very young children, including medications and surgery. There are absolutely no gender-affirmative medical interventions available to a child under the age of puberty. A third myth is that gender affirmative practitioners rubber stamp whatever the child tells them about their gender—after all, it is for the children to say, not for the adults to tell. Hopefully, that myth has been adequately dispelled in the above description of the careful listening, mirroring, and collaborative reflection with parents and any other allied professionals employed to bring a particular child's gender into focus. The last myth is that young children cannot possibly know their gender, and it is therefore irresponsible, if not abusive, to allow young children to do something as drastic as change from one gender to the other, especially since it is just a phase they are going through which will most likely dissipate over time. The reality is that it is rarely just a phase and children are quite capable of knowing their authentic gender at an early age. Further, if we take the time to differentiate gender identity from gender expressions, we will see that the so-called persisters and desisters of clinical research are as distinguishable from each other as apples are from oranges.

The reality, rather than the myth, of the gender affirmative model is this: We listen to the child, help the child discover the gender position that feels most authentic and develop a resilient ego rind (the "skin" we see the child living comfortably in) for that gender self. We do not equate "living comfortably in your own skin" with living uncomfortably with your assigned sex. No attempt is made to ward off a transgender or gender-nonconforming outcome if that is the child's authentic gender self. Therefore, to live comfortably in your own skin may include pre-pubertal social transitions, puberty blockers, and cross-sex hormones in adolescence. The critical variables for promoting gender health will be social acceptance and support for the child accompanied by the facilitation of the child's authentic gender self. The outcome: gender-healthy children.

References

Cohen-Kettenis, P., & Friedemann, P. (2003). *Transgenderism and intersexuality in childhood and adolescence*. Thousand Oaks, CA: Sage Publications.

Cross, J.M. (2015). Outcry prompts CAMH to review its controversial treatment of trans youth. *Metro News*, Toronto, March 18, 2015, http://metronews.ca/news/toronto/1315743/outcry-prompts-camh-to-review-its-controversial-treatment-of-trans-youth/

Devor, A. H. (2004). Witnessing and mirroring: A fourteen stage model of transsexual identity formation: *Journal of Gay & Lesbian Psychotherapy*, 8 (1–2): 41–67.

Diamond, M. (2000). Sex and gender: Same or different? *Feminism & Psychology*, 10: 46–54.

Drescher, J., Cohen-Kettenis, P.T., & Reed, G.M. (2016). Gender incongruence of childhood in the ICD-11: Controversies, proposal, and rationale. *Lancet Psychiatry*, 3: 297–304.

Ehrensaft, D. (2011). *Gender born, gender made: Raising healthy gender-nonconforming children*. New York: The Experiment.

Ehrensaft, D. (2012). From gender identity disorder to gender identity creativity: True gender self therapy. *Journal of Homosexuality*, 59: 337–356.

Ehrensaft, D. (2016). *The gender creative child: Pathways for nurturing and supporting children who live outside gender boxes*. New York: The Experiment.

Frank, M. M. (2001). On mirroring and mirror hunger. *Psychoanalysis & Contemporary Thought*, 24(1): 3–29.

Green, R. (1987). *The 'sissy boy' syndrome and the development of homosexuality*. New Haven, CT: Yale University Press.

Hidalgo, M.A., Ehrensaft, D., Tishelman, A.C., Clark, L.F., Garofalo, R., Rosenthal, S.M., Spack, N.P., & Olson, J. (2013). The gender affirmative model: What we know and what we aim to learn. *Human Development*, 56: 285–290.

Malpas, J. (2011). Between pink and blue: A multi-dimensional family approach to gender nonconforming children and their families. *Family Process*, 50(4): 453–470.

Olson, K.R., Durwood, L., DeMeules, M., & McLaughlin, K.A. (2015). Mental health of transgender children who are supported in their identities. *Pediatrics*, 137(3): 1–8. DOI: 10.1542/peds.2015-3223.

Tyson, Phyllis. (1982). A developmental line of gender identity, gender role, and choice of love object. *Journal of the American Psychoanalytic Association*, 30: 61–86.

Wallace, R., & Russell, H. (2013). Attachment and shame in gender-nonconforming children and their families: Toward a theoretical framework for evaluating clinical interventions. *International Journal of Transgenderism*, 14: 113–126.

Wing Sue, D. (2010). *Microaggressions in everyday life: Race, gender, and sexual orientation*. New York: Wiley

Winnicott, D. W. (1967). Mirror-role of the mother and family in child development. In P. Lomas (Ed.), *The predicament of the family: A psycho-analytical symposium*. London: Hogarth, 26-33.

Zucker, K., & Bradley, S.J. (1995). *Gender identity disorder and psychosexual problems in children and adolescents*. New York: The Guilford Press.

8

TRANSITION AND CHILDHOOD

Questioning the medical approaches[1]

Erik Schneider

> Flower to teeth
> Not even
> And neither to the gun
> It's in the prime of life
> That engrave the dreams
> In mine I'm not sleeping
> And they are imp
> I'm not a soldier
> And I fight for me
> My life luggage
> Is filled of rags
> Because I'm a girl
> That is dressed as a boy
> So sometimes I simply dream
> That they let me be who I am
> And that others don't judge me
>   Ludiane de Brocéliande[2]

We come into contact with binary gender/sex norms right after birth at the latest, and they accompany us throughout our lives. Various societal and individual concepts are intrinsic to them, in order to define what *sex/gender*[3] might actually mean (Voß in press). Physicians play a central role in the communication, propagation of, and adherence to those norms. They similarly claim the authority over defining in this context what is healthy or pathologic. The latter also entails, among other aspects, identifying the need for "clinical diagnostics" or "therapy." Medical recommendations, however, have shown arbitrariness when dealing with individuals who do not fit the concept of traditional binary sex/gender norms.[4] A lack of knowledge or familiarity on the physician's side (RADELUX II: 15, 17, 23) often leads to recommendations that are based on assumptions of (mental) disorders or pathologies whereas scholarship has not remotely proven their existence yet (Drescher et al. 2012). Even so, *transsexualism*,[5] *gender identity disorder in childhood*,[6] or *gender dysphoria* (see American Psychiatric Association 2013) are still diagnosed and recommendations are yet devised for the children's lives. So-called *conversion therapy* and other "normalizing treatments" are still conducted. When children undergo such treatments, they are sometimes subjected to controversial "open-ended psychotherapeutic interventions" like open-ended play psychotherapy (or simply talk therapy) (Zucker 2008; Zucker et al. 2012). Most recently, such treatments have been increasingly questioned and rejected, in part by referring to their potentially damaging effects (Alessandrin 2013: 49–58; Lev 2004: 315–347; Raj 2002; Schneider in press; Wallace & Russell 2013; Zinck & Pignatiello 2015). It is problematic, for instance, that prepubescent children are subjected to "diagnoses" and in certain cases "therapies" even if they are perfectly well. They often have to undergo such measures only to maintain the opportunity of having the healthcare system reimburse the possible costs of later hormonal treatments and/or surgeries as adolescents and adults. Those healthy prepubescent children do not have to be subjected to such medical treatment and do factually not require medical attention at all. There thus is no diagnostic or therapeutic need for such attention. It is their everyday life situation within the family and with the people around them that is paramount for these children. They are particularly faced with managing day-to-day (personal) everyday-life challenges at home, when entering school, and in elementary school itself. It raises the question if professionals, especially those in the field of medicine, should play a role for those children beyond the pediatric examinations in childhood and school—and if they should play a role, which one?

Terminology, definitions, and concepts

The process of assigning sex and gender in the medical professions is culturally fixated and typically follows normative standards based on the appearance of genitalia. Because the terms *biological sex* or *natal sex/gender* are usually employed, the cultural assignment and fixation remains invisible to the eye. The term *assigned sex/gender*[7] is thus used in this chapter instead of *biological sex* or *natal sex/gender*. Terms like *transgender* or *transsexual* aren't used to avoid a conflict with the self-determination of the children. Therefore, no definition is given.

This chapter discusses prepubescent children whose *assigned sex/gender* differs from their *sex/gender-related self-perception* and *-positioning*, respectively. The so-called *sex characteristics* of those children are "unambiguously" *female* or *male* from a medical standpoint. It should be added that, in order to do justice to their self-determination, these children are not grouped in this chapter under an umbrella term. They typically refer to themselves as *girls*, *boys*, or in a nonspecific way in this context. Using umbrella terms does not absolve one from inquiring after what the children wish to be called. They hold the only authority over any terminology referring to them. Using generic terms may also be considered an infringement of people's self-determination. For this very reason, children are attributed and referred to by their self-perceived sex/gender-specific terms in this chapter, not by assigned ones. Moreover, there factually does not exist a generally accepted term. None of the following, for instance, enjoys universal acceptance: *transgender, transsexuals,* or the abbreviation *trans*, gender independent, gender non-conforming, gender variant, gender creative children* (Ehrensaft 2011; Pullen et al. 2015; Pullen & Sansfaçon 2012). Anyhow, to grapple with an important part of the complex situation of children whose sex/gender assigned at birth differs from their sex/gender-related self-perception and -positioning this chapter remains on a descriptive level without using an umbrella term.

The term *gender identity* is equally and deliberately avoided in this chapter as the terms *gender* and *identity* are each based on different concepts which are also in part controversially debated. There is, further, no field in science that could explain conclusively, or even predict, how the so-called *sex/gender identity* develops for either the people who accept their assigned sex/gender or those who do not (Schneider in press). There are also no scientific criteria for distinguishing between a *normal* and a *pathological sex/gender identity* (Langer & Martin 2004; Schneider & Keins 2013).

The term *sex/gender variance* is also avoided. It is problematic, on the one hand, with an eye on the great variety of human identity, to differentiate between *sex/gender variant* and *non-sex/gender variant* people. The term is, on the other hand, closely connected to sex/gender stereotypes. In order to prevent any confusion of terminology, neither are children discussed in the scope of this chapter who perceive themselves as *intersex*[8]—or are perceived as such by others—nor *sexual*[9] or *romantic*[10] orientations.

Whereas having been rather unknown until recently, the phenomenon of the assigned sex/gender varying from the own sex/gender-related self-perception has attracted growing media attention (Bal 2015; Lorriaux 2015; Kleeman 2015; Padawer 2013). This holds particularly true with regard to younger children, namely those who have not yet reached puberty, or children who have not yet been sent to school (see Ehrensaft 2011; Schneider 2012; Schneider & Keins 2013). In addition, parents are becoming more perceptive and ask whether the phenomenon could exist in their child and seek support at parental groups and associations.[11]

The mother of Lucy, an eight-year-old girl, reports, for instance:

> Lucy was three years old when she expressed herself for the first time. She told us that she was not a boy but a girl. At the beginning, my former husband and I had seen it as child's talk. We said "No, you are a boy," but she did not let it go. She said she was a girl. She kept saying that, and when she was four years old she wanted me to "take off" her pee pee.[12]

Those children may express their sex/gender-related self-perception at the same age as children who accept for themselves the assigned sex/gender; that is, roughly at the age of two or three. As early as at that age—as at any other age in their lives—they are the only ones who are capable of reliably declaring themselves. There are, however, no reliable studies available which could quantify the number of such children. Olson et al. (2015) found that they are not at all confused in their sex/gender identity. They assert that "[their] results provide evidence that, early in development, transgender youth are statistically indistinguishable from cisgender children of the same gender identity." It seems worth testing whether and how those findings are translatable to children who accept the assigned sex/gender at one point but not at another, or to those who feel they belong to both sexes/genders, to none, or to another (see Brill & Pepper 2011). Little is yet known about these children because their parents rarely seek either professional support or the interchange with other parents. At whatever age, though: children will not immediately voice having become aware of their self-perception in relation to expectations of others that are based on the assigned sex/gender. It is not uncommon for some years to pass, before they will have acquired the necessary vocabulary and concepts to be capable of such self-expression (Kennedy 2013; Kennedy & Hellen 2010; McBride 2013: 20–23).

Within the medical professions, there is a highly controversial debate concerning at what age, or "maturity level," children are able of identifying their own *sex/gender-related self-perception* or *-positioning*. Equally discussed is how to deal best with children whose assigned sex/gender differs from their self-perception. It is debated in the psy★[13] disciplines in particular whether or not it is pathologic if children (and adults) do not accept their assigned sex/gender. Adolescents as well as adults sometimes have to endure lengthy psychiatric or psychologic diagnostic examinations and "therapies." This is done because the diagnoses as a call for action will ensure the healthcare system's coverage of potential costs for medical care such as hormonal treatments and/or sex reassignment surgery. Thus is the formal argument. Psy★, in contrast, have not yet proven even the existence of any pathology at all. The reason why prepubescent children should be subjected to such measures remains incomprehensible unless resorting to sex/gender stereotypes that are at the root of definitions used for said diagnoses.

A science-based consensus that rests firmly on standardized scholarly studies is also still missing (see, among others, Hidalgo et al. 2013). There are roughly three approaches identifiable in the medical professions (Schneider in press):

1. The *accepting* approach (also called *affirmative*): children are accepted and supported in a way that confirms to their currently expressed needs. It is based on the idea that attempting to change a person's sex/gender auto-determination is harmful (American Psychological Association: Factsheet).
2. The *normalizing* approach: observing the culture-based binary sex/gender norms are emphasized while downplaying the children's needs as they express them. The aim is to actively discourage from gender non-conforming behavior (Schneider 2013: 17, points 66/67).
3. The *wait and see* approach: parents are recommended not to react to the children's behavior which adults construe as differing from the children's assigned

sex/gender. The children's behavior is factually ignored, or the children are distracted from their so-called *gender non-conforming behavior*.

Regarding the attitude of some medical doctors it seems to be necessary to mention a fourth approach. Those professionals do not react when asked by parents how to deal with their children's behavior if it differs from the respective sex/gender norms. Their approach could be termed the "eschewing or avoiding" one.

Neither the "wait-and-see" approach nor the eschewing/avoiding approach should be considered as "neutral." They similarly disregard the expressed needs of the children. In addition and by implication, these approaches equally uphold sex/gender norms. It seems, in fact, reasonable to count these to the class of "normalizing" approaches. This further begs the question of which approach is ethically acceptable when dealing with children whose assigned sex/gender differs from their own sex/gender-related self-perception. How to react appropriately to these children's currently expressed needs? The United Nations' Convention on the Rights of the Child (United Nations 1989) offers some orientation, and it should be seen as governing societal and medical decisions.

Childhood and parenthood

When the assigned sex/gender of (very) young children differs from their sex/gender-related self-perception, some of the most frequently asked questions are: will it be permanent, and based on what criteria could this self-perception be considered lasting? These questions cannot be answered with complete certainty today. In fact, scholars have not yet succeeded in resolving them in a scientific way in order to establish prognostic factors. Is finding answers to them, however, even meaningful at all for these children and their parents? Parents are predominantly more interested in how to realize that their children may not develop according to traditional sex/gender norms in the first place.

First and foremost, we should note that there is a wide variety of expressions in verbal and non-verbal communication among children and also to adults. Some examples might be mentioned as they seem significant:

- Preferring clothing and/or games that are assigned to the so-called opposite sex. The mother of a trans★ boy mentions that: "it has always been apparent that Paul was different. In kindergarten he had preferred playing games for boys, his best friends had been (and still are) boys. *Spiderman, Cars, SpongeBob, Star Wars* were the flavor of the month; the color pink or Princess Lillifee [a German hyper-stereotypical "girly" cartoon character] almost made him vomit (Keins 2015: 11)."
- Resignifying[14] toys, as the mother of Karl, a six-year-old girl, remarks: "Karl rejected typical toys for boys (cars, knights, tools, soccer), or he 'disassociated' them. The other boys could not understand that." The knights, for instance, protect the princess, cars transport dolls and fairies.[15]

- The way to refer to themselves. Children, for example, who are assigned girls refer to themselves as *boys* and/or choose *male* first names which might be adopted by their siblings.[16]

Children might also reject their genitalia at a very young age, and may explicitly request them being removed,[17] or might be suicidal (Lüthi & Fuchs 2013; Schneider 2013: 12–13). Depressiveness or suicidality often occurs in the context of denying their sex/gender-related self-perception, societal rejection, or their experience with corrections and penalties (Ehrensaft 2012; McBride 2013: 52; RADELUX II 2012: 15). Psychological symptoms, including suicidality, often wane when children are then accepted with their *distinctiveness*[18] (Li & 2013).[19] It is an important source of resilience for children whose parent(s) back them by accepting the children's sex/gender self-positioning, and also by supporting them in exploring their *sex/gender self*.[20]

This is not to say that children are "urged" or "supported" to display a behavior that is considered "normal" for the assigned sex/gender but to encourage them in being themselves according to the felt sex/gender. Such backing is rather present in allowing those children to express themselves in utterances and behavior reflecting their unguarded self. Following the affirmative approach ensures that these children are enabled to endure and live through being bullied by other children, or being corrected or punished by adults. Evidence strongly suggests the positive influence of this approach (American Psychological Association 2015: 847). Experts increasingly highlight the need for the children under their care to have their sex/gender self-positioning accepted, as it is often expressed in first names they have chosen for themselves (Ehrensaft 2011; Hidalgo 2013; Menvielle 2012). Parents who do support their children may also be subjected to a third party's hostility (Ehrensaft 2011). Due to a lack of space, it is impossible to discuss in the context of this chapter the perspective of parents. Parents may experience being threatened with the removal of custody over their children, with claims of dangers and harm to the best interests of the child made by outsiders. Mothers may also have to face being diagnosed with suffering from *Munchhausen by proxy syndrome* (Keins 2015: 65–66).

Social transition: what?—when?—who has to decide?

The term *social transition* might be understood as changing the gender role from the assigned sex/gender to the felt one.[21] The specific point in time at which this transition should take place is particularly debated in the medical professions. As of today, there neither exists the one preponderant majority opinion, nor scientific findings that might offer reliable answers to those complex questions. The current discourse is rather marked by opinions of individuals or groups who all agree that ethical questions are raised in this context and that they do require a nuanced approach (Hidalgo 2013).

When trying to find answers to those questions, Article 3 of the United Nations' Convention on the Rights of the Child concerning the *child's best interest* has to be in the focus of considerations. Other rights of the UN Convention should be acknowledged as well. It is equally central to consider Article 8 on *identity*, Article 12 on the *respect for the views of the child*, and Article 18 on *responsibility for the best interest of the child*. A social transition in early childhood may reduce psychological conditions such as anxiety, depression, or suicidality (Ehrensaft 2012). The essence of this approach is the need to intervene in a hostile and rejecting environment, rather than individualizing the issue of cultural sex/gender norms (Hill et al. 2010; Menville 2012; Raj 2002).

Axiomatically speaking, not all minors go through a social transition. There are children who exclusively live within the role of their felt sex/gender and not in that of the assigned one. They neither hide their self, nor do they explicitly "come out."[22] They also do not undergo a social transition. Their distinctiveness is known in their family circle and their environment, and their friends—especially at the age of being toddlers—often accept the way they are and behave.[23] It is upon entering school that some children and their parents inquire about how to deal with the gender-based distinctiveness. A number of them opt for sending them to school without (initially) revealing any further details. Those parents register their children in the sex/gender the children perceive for themselves, and under the first names the children have chosen. In these cases, the children experience it as more fitting to live with their "secret" and the risk of being "detected." They do not wish to be exposed to rejection or possible subsequent bullying. Some of those children, however, often perceive this decision as a burden at a later point. They also often fear being accidentally outed (Ehrensaft 2013).[24] Some therefore may choose coming out after preparatory measures such as informing the school staff.

In the event of a coming-out it is essential to discuss beforehand how to proceed in respect to employing the chosen name on the school certificates, or in respect to spaces and activities that are segregated by sex/gender, such as restrooms, changing rooms, physical education in general and swimming lessons in particular (Augstein 2013). Informing the school staff insufficiently, or not at all, may lead to children having to fear being punished for choosing the restroom they feel appropriate for them.[25] Other families opt for an open approach, especially when the children's distinctiveness has been publically known in pre-school, and their school-mates are sent to the same primary school class.[26] Whatever the children's and their families' decision, it has to be respected. Parents are becoming more aware of the work of parental groups such as Trans-Kinder-Netz e.V. in Germany, SAIL NI (Support|Acceptence|Information|Learning) in Northern Ireland, or the parent group of Intersex & Transgender Luxembourg asbl. These organizations typically also offer information sessions for schools and an option for the exchange of experience among parents as well. Parents may thus get informed in advance about the advantages and disadvantages when looking for the right school for their children. Making their respective decision after being informed, the family's choice should be seen as a carefully considered one.

Today, many children and their parents often decide for themselves whether and when to undergo social transition, and do not turn to professionals in the medical fields for that. Involving psy★ thus does not seem to be necessary in this decision-making procedure. It might be advisable, however, if children and/or parents are unsure, to seek support. It also seems necessary if schools request a medical certificate before registering children both with the felt (perceived?) sex/gender and under the chosen first name. The latter, allowing the use of the chosen name only upon having in hand medical opinions, is often the case if school staff are not trained in dealing with these children. "there [is no provision in the German law] at all which might refer to [forms of address]. Everybody is thus free to address another person with the new first name. Even the children might introduce themselves with the new name [. . .] The student therefore should be registered and should have a record at the school according to the new identity." This, on the other hand, does not hold true for school certificates. The point of transition further has to be discussed with the children, based on the children's desire, and oriented toward their needs.

The mother of Lena, a nine-year-old child, reports her daughter's desperate statement:

> Look at me and you see that I am a girl[. I]t has to be enough that I say it, then especially. Why does nobody believe me? Why do I have to explain it? Why do I have to speak about my life[? Y]ou cannot explain when you realized it and in what way[!] It is just the way it is[. T]hose are stupid questions. Nobody will understand it anyway unless they are that way. The lawmaker must be a stupid man if he believes that transpeople have to do all of that to get what is right for them[:] identity card [in their own, chosen names], hormones, and surgery. When I am a woman with a vagina I am not trans anymore [, and] they have to leave me alone then. [She cried and said:] I will not take part in this, I won't see experts. Instead I will live as a girl then as long as this is possible, and if somebody calls me [a] "man" because of how I look I will kill myself[. I] will kill myself anyway if I have to become a man.[27]

It may come as a surprise that children confront these questions long before they reach puberty. Yet they are also typically confronted with having to meet with a psy★ at a young age although they are not ill. This might serve as a kind of hedging for the parents within the "system," because a "specialist" (psy★) ensures independent documentation. Moreover, in order to potentially qualify their children for deferring hormones when reaching puberty, some parents try to convince them to meet regularly with a psy★ so that they can present proof of long-term treatment if necessary. These children do not always accept this without objection. They will learn in this case that a positive vote of their psy★ might be their only chance to receive medication suppressing the physical changes of puberty which, in turn, might be a matter of life and death for them (Giordano 2008).

In conclusion, there is no indication so far that parents, together with their children, are incapable of managing the social transition and entering school, respectively, in an autonomous way as long as the children can rely on their parents.

Professionals and childhood: considering whose needs?

When seeking the help of professionals it is of essence to determine whose needs are addressed. It should be distinguished between needs that are expressed by the children, or psychological stress they may suffer from, and the need to address the adults' fears and apprehensions. The latter may refer to parents, professionals, or other adults. It is ethically questionable to introduce children to a psychiatrist/ psychologist only because they differ from traditional sex/gender norms that factually do not reflect reality. In other words, the individual does not diverge from the norm, but the norm diverges from reality. A further argument for psychiatric or psychological treatment of every prepubertal child mentioned by medical doctors is "the difficult way" of these children.[28] This approach introduces the impression that only psy★ treatment can solve the "problem" or support the child in an ideal way. This is another claim of medical doctors that has not been scientifically proven. Therefore, it is necessary to promptly and precisely name the actual question or problem focusing on the current needs of a child, if given. Generally asking for a psy★ treatment to all children can't be linked to individual needs of them.

An assigned sex/gender that differs from the children's self-perception and behavior is not pathologic as such, when, for instance, assigned boys *perceive or consider themselves as girls* and/or wear so-called *girls' clothes* and/or wish to play with *dolls and other stereotypically female attributed toys*. It thus seems imperative to document the children's psychological stress in order to justify a medical intervention. If this stress is not present, it is advisable to consider whether it is rather the parents' insecurity and/or psychological stress in regard to their children's gender distinctiveness that is to be addressed. The reasons for the children's psychological stress may be manifold but are frequently found in having their sex/gender-related self-perception or -positioning not accepted or even rejected. This might be the case, for instance, if children are forbidden to choose their own first names, to wear clothes or play with toys they consider appropriate but which may be attributed to the opposite gender. If the rejection or attempts of "normalization" come from the parents, it will especially put the children under substantial pressure, and weaken the bond with their parents (Hill & Menville 2009: 255–256). Cissexism,[29] transmisogyny,[30] and/or heterosexism[31] are often involved. Teasing and marginalization in school and the environment might also produce psychological stress, as could the physical characteristics of the assigned sex/gender. Children rather need to be heard, accepted, respected, and loved.

It is possible to intervene through informing and reassuring parents that sex/ gender diversity is but one aspect of the human being, and that it is not an illness if their children do not develop according to traditional sex/gender norms. Absolving them from a perceived guilt relieves the pressure for many parents. Children are supported by a relationship with their parents which they can rely on and on whose basis they are unquestionably accepted with their sex/gender distinctiveness. Apart from factual information about the variety of human perception and behavior, many parents profit from an exchange with other parents. It is therefore often helpful to provide contacts of the national, or nearest regional, parental group. De-dramatizing the social and other transitions and emphasizing the option of re-transition help children and parents alike. Parents decide which professional field is most suitable to answer their respective questions. Fundamentally speaking, professionals from the fields of pedagogics and social work are possibly as much qualified as those from the medical professions. If medical certificates are requested, for example for school documents and/or the exemption from swimming lessons, the pediatrician or family doctor might provide them. Professionals of the psy* disciplines may help if there are signs of psychosocial stress. Resolving conversations could contribute to more empathy for the children's needs, especially if the parents are divided over how to deal with their children and/or one or both press them into the assigned sex/gender role. Some parents then realize the harm that may be caused by correcting and punishing their children if those behave in a way that is atypical to their assigned sex/gender. If the questions of puberty and its possible suppression arise it is again the decision of the children and their parents on how to proceed. They are often referred to so-called multi-disciplinary teams in which a psy* is involved, and who may exceedingly influence making the decision over the further steps. Whether this is necessary in any case, however, remains a question.

There are conflicting interpretations and approaches in how to deal with scientific findings on the cause, development, and support of children whose assigned sex/gender does not correspond to their own sex/gender-related self-perception or -positioning (and/or their behavior). This includes the use of terms, definitions, and concepts. In light of differing opinions, it is suggested that professionals and parents resort to ethical recommendations for the practice and their daily lives, respectively: seeing the child's best interest as the basic principle. In particular the articles of the United Nations' Convention on the Rights of the Child: Article 8 concerning *identity*, Article 12 on *respect for the views of the child*, and Article 18 concerning the *responsibility for the best interest of the child* may provide some guidance. Such an approach involves two aspects: on the one hand, respecting the sex/gender-related self-perception and -positioning unconditionally, meaning without resting it on external conditions; and, on the other hand, being guided by the currently expressed needs of the children and their parents (Riley 2013) as long as the parents' needs are in accord with the rights of the child. On a concrete level, a children's rights perspective could translate into using the first names and personal pronouns the children consider appropriate and enabling them to dress and behave, including the use of the locker rooms according to their self and perception. Just like all other children they have to be protected from discrimination, and their equality has to be ensured especially in school.

An accepting parental approach to their children's distinctiveness will enable children to develop resilience for their future life, whereas rejecting or impeding this distinctiveness will lead to a high strain in their bonding and may affect it immensely in a negative way. A secure filial–parental bond suggests that parents are competent enough to manage their children's transition upon consultation with them and under consideration of their expressed needs. This holds true as long as nothing indicates otherwise. So-called *gender experts* might play a supplemental role if children and parents wish them to.

A children's rights-oriented approach suggests that professionals, especially psy★, motivate parents to accept their children as they are, and to support them in the development. Every course is individual, and every family has to find their own way. Avoiding umbrella terms like transgender, transsexual and so on, as well as using descriptions of the mentioned children, allows for the self-determination of each child in respect of its individuality and needs. Information and reports on how other families dealt in comparable situations might be supportive. Responsibility for the best interest of the child suggests a client-centered and family-supporting approach, as well as safe spaces that are free from discrimination. Regardless of the position psy★ seek to take in the inner-medical and societal debate concerning the topic of *sex/gender*, the question arises as to how meaningful sex/gender records are in general; that is making them permanent in the birth certificate, or documenting them at the registry's office, or reducing a child to this assignment. Nobody, neither parents nor professionals from the medical, pedagogical or social fields, can predict how children will develop. They cannot predict whether or not children will permanently or temporarily accept a binary sex/gender (or which), a static or fluid one, or what resulting needs may arise. While it is not at all clear whether there will ever be conclusive proof of pathology in children who do not develop according to fixed sex/gender norms, observing the respect for the views of the children suggests that psy★ approach all children in an unbiased way and contribute to solutions that are based on the children's needs and their rights. Such an approach suggests taking seriously their individuality as well as their ability to decide on their concerns regarding sex/gender-related topics.

Notes

1 Translated from the German by Anton Hieke.
2 This poem "Fleur" (p. 27, *Ma fille est un homme*. Suresnes: Les Editions du Net, 2015) is translated and reprinted from the original German with the kind permission of the author Ludiane de Brocéliande.
3 The German term *Geschlecht* does not distinguish between the cultural concepts of *biological sex* and the social one of *gender*.
4 German *Geschlechternormen*.
5 See World Health Organization (1990): International Statistical Classification of Diseases and Related Health Problems 10th Revision (ICD-10)-WHO Version for 2016. Chapter V. Mental and behavioural disorders (F00-F99), F.64.0. http://apps.who.int/classifications/icd10/browse/2016/en#/F60-F69 (accessed January 10, 2016).
6 See World Health Organization (1990): F.64.2, ibid.
7 In German *Zuweisungsgeschlecht*.
8 Intersex is understood as a set of anatomical conditions which do not confirm to the medical standard categories of "male/female." They may feature variations on the levels of chromosomes, hormones, gonads, genitals, etc. The complexity of intersex has not sufficiently been discussed for the psychological level.
9 See ANAGNORI: The group of people or genders to which a person may be sexually attracted, if at all. http://anagnori.tumblr.com/post/67669933207/words-and-concepts-used-in-asexual-communities (accessed February 1, 2016)

10 See ibid.
11 The chairperson of Trans-Kinder-Netz e.V. (TRAKINE), Kati Wiedner reports, for instance, that more than 120 parents have sought counseling with that organization since its inception in 2012. Trans-Kinder-Netz e.V. is an international organization of parents and relatives of underage trans*children, and is based in Berlin, Germany. Kati Wiedner, "Report of the CEO" (presented at the general meeting of Trans-Kinder-Netz e.V., September 18–20, 2015).
12 Trans-Kinder-Netz e.V. (2012): "*Bericht der Mutter eines 8-jährigen Transkindes* [Report of the mother of an eight-year-old-trans*child]," http://www.trans-kinder-netz.de/files/pdf/Bericht_einer_Mutter_eines_8_jaehrigen_Transmaedchens.pdf (accessed January 10, 2016).
13 Psy* is used as an umbrella term for the related fields of psychiatrists, psychologists, and psychotherapists. It is based on the use by Tom Reucher, a French psychologist.
14 It is important to consider that resignification of clothes, toys or other objects may play a central role in the behavior of most children. De- and/or re-gendering toys, like in Karl's case, is interpreted by adults as an early sign for a child's rejection of the assigned sex/gender. The reference to sex/gender stereotypes in toys and clothes in the behavior of children who are not linked to sex/gender deviance is broadly unexplored. Rather, the display of seemingly gendered behavior is evaluated by adults (parents as well as professionals) according to sex/gender norms. Further, every object can be gendered, de- and re-gendered according to culture perceptions, and others open for change.
15 Trans-Kinder-Netz e.V. (2012): "*Erinnerungen einer Mutter eines 6 jährigen Transmädchens* [Recollections of the Mother of a six-year-old trans*girl]," www.trans-kinder-netz.de/files/pdf/Mutter_von_Lisa.pdf (accessed January 10, 2016).
16 Report of parents at the meeting of the parental group of Intersex & Transgender Luxembourg on October 14, 2015.
17 According to one report, the girl said "The penis has to go; I don't want it anymore." Karl's mother mentions that "One evening, Karl was in the shower and tried to cut off his pee pee with a plastic knife from the toy shop. Karl [said] "I will grow a vagina then. There really is a fairy who can turn me into a real girl[.] I want to have long hair and a vagina[. T]hen I will always wear real girls' dresses ... I am sad when I see my pee pee, I don't want it, when will it go away?" See Trans-Kinder-Netz e.V. (2012): "*Erinnerungen einer Mutter eines 6 jährigen Transmädchens*." [I, Girl: The Recollections of the Mother of a 5½-year-old gender-variant child]. www.trans-kinder-netz.de/files/pdf/Mutter_von_Lisa.pdf (accessed January 10, 2016).
18 Distinctiveness, in German *Besonderheit*, is the term used by some children of the parental group of Trans-Kinder-Netz e.V.
19 Report of a father at a meeting of the parental group of Trans-Kinder-Netz e.V. in 2014.
20 This conclusion is drawn from parents reporting to the author that their children were initially being corrected. They realized just how much their children had suffered under that correction. Some children had displayed also signs of psychological stress as a result. When supporting the children, however, by accepting their distinctiveness, the children's discomforts often waned completely.
21 There are other forms of transitions in the fields of medicine and law besides social transitions. They are not discussed in the context of this article.
22 "Coming out" is understood as the process of people voluntarily making their distinctiveness known to others.
23 This conclusion is drawn from parents' reports to the author in the years 2014/15.
24 "Outing" is understood as the process of people having their distinctiveness made known to others by a third party either by accident or on purpose.
25 Trans-Kinder-Netz e.V. (2012): "*Bericht von Lenas Mutter* [Report of Lena's Mother]," www.trans-kinder-netz.de/files/pdf/Lenas_Mutter.pdf (accessed January 10, 2016).
26 Report of parents at the meeting of the parental group of Intersex & Transgender Luxembourg in 2015.

27 Reports shared with the author in 2015.
28 Witsch, Michael: Genderdysphoria – Geboren im falschen Körper [gender dysphoria – born in the wrong body], talk during the 5th National Day of Educaltional Health [5ième Journée Nationale de la Santé Scolaire], www.sante.public.lu/fr/espace-professionnel/exposes/journee-sante-scolaire/journee-sante-scolaire-2016/Journee-nationale-de-la-Sante-2016_Programme.pdf (accessed March 11, 2017).
29 Hostility and devaluation against people who do not fit into traditional sex/gender norms.
30 Hostility and devaluation against women assigned male at the time of their birth, who do not fit into traditional sex/gender norms.
31 Hostility and devaluation against people who do not fit into heterosexual norms.

References

Agence France Presse (2015a). Sweden adds gender-neutral pronoun to dictionary. *Guardian*. Retrieved from www.theguardian.com/world/2015/mar/24/sweden-adds-gender-neutral-pronoun-to-dictionary

Agence France Presse (2015b). Schwedische Sprache: Nicht Mann, nicht Frau, sondern "hen." *Spiegel online*. Retrieved from: www.spiegel.de/schulspiegel/ausland/schule-schweden-neues-geschlechtsneutrales-personalpronomen-a-1025479.html

Alessandrin, A. (2013). Transidentités: histoire d'une dépathologisation. In M. Y. Thomas, K. Espineira, & A. Alessandrin (ed.) *Observatoire des transidentités*. Paris: L'Harmattan.

American Psychiatric Association (2013). Gender dysphoria. In *Diagnostic and statistical manual of mental disorders*. 5th ed. Arlington, VA: American Psychiatric Association. Retrieved from: www.dsm5.org/documents/gender%20dysphoria%20fact%20sheet.pdf

American Psychological Association (2015). *Guidelines for psychological practice with transgender and gender nonconforming people*. Retrieved from: www.apa.org/practice/guidelines/transgender.pdf

American Psychological Association (Factsheet). *Gender diversity and transgender identity in children*. Retrieved from: www.apadivisions.org/division-44/resources/advocacy/transgender-children.pdf

Augstein, S. M. (2013). Zur Situation transsexueller Kinder in der Schule vor der offiziellen (gerichtlichen) Vornamensänderung. Retrieved from: www.trans-kinder-netz.de/pdf/Augstein%20Maerz%202013.pdf

Bal (2015). Fünfjähriges Transgender-Kind. Die Reise in eine neue Identität: Mia wird Jacob. In: stern.de. Retrieved from: www.stern.de/familie/kinder/transgender-kind-mit-fuenf-jahren--eltern-unterstuetzen-ihren-kleinen-jacob-6209988.html

Brill, S., & Pepper, R. (2011). *Wenn Kinder anders fühlen, Identität im anderen Geschlecht. Ein Ratgeber für Eltern*. Munich: Reinhard. Originally published with the title: *The Transgender Child – A Handbook for Families and Professionals*. Cleis Press, 2008.

Brocéliande, de, L. (2015). Fleur. In *Ma fille est un homme*. Suresnes: Les Editions du Net.

Drescher, J., Cohen-Kettenis, P., & Winter, S. (2012). Minding the body: Situating gender identity diagnoses in the ICD-11. *International Review of Psychiatry*, 24(6), 568–577.

Ehrensaft, D. (2011). *Gender born, gender made*. New York: The Experiment.

Ehrensaft, D. (2012). From gender identity disorder to gender identity creativity: True gender self child therapy. *Journal of Homosexuality*, 59(3), 337–356.

Ehrensaft, D. (2013). Look, mom, I'm a boy – Don't tell anyone I was a girl. *Journal of LGBT Youth*, 10(1–2), 9–28.

Ehrensaft, D. (2014). Found in transition: Our littlest transgender people. *Contemporary Psychoanalysis*, 50(4), 571–592.

Giordano, S. (2008). Ethics of management of gender atypical organisation in children and adolescents. *International public health policy and ethics*, M. Boylan (ed.). Berlin: Springer, 249–272.

Grossman, A. H., & D'Augelli, A. R. (2007). Transgender youth and life-threatening behaviours. *Suicide and Life-Threatening Behaviour*, 37(5), 527–537.

Hidalgo, M. A. e.a. (2013). The gender affirmative model: What we know and what we aim to learn. *Human Development*, 56, 285–290.

Hill, D. B. e.a. (2010). An affirmative intervention for families with gender variant children: Parental ratings of child mental health and gender. *Journal of Sex & Marital Therapy*, 36, 6–23. Retrieved from: http://transformingfamily.org/pdfs/Parents%20and%20Gender%20Variance.pdf

Hill, D. B., & Menvielle, E. (2009). You have to give them a place where they feel protected and safe and loved: The views of parents who have gender-variant children and adolescents. *Journal of LGBT Youth*, 6, 243–271.

Keins, P. (2015). Trans*Kinder. Eine kleine Fibel. Charleston, SC: CreateSpace Independent Publishing Platform.

Kennedy, N. (2013). Cisgenrisme et enfants trans: La perspective de l'activité sociale. Communication au colloque "Le droit de l'enfant et de l'adolescent à son orientation sexuelle et à son identité de genre," 02.05.2013, Sion, Suisse, organisé par l'Institut universitaire Kurt Bösch (IUKB), en collaboration avec le Conseil de l'Europe. Retrieved from www.iukb.ch/fileadmin/iukb/confl3/prog_e.pdf

Kennedy, N., & Hellen, M. (2010). Transgender children: More than a theoretical challenge. *Graduate Journal of Social Science*, Dec., 7(2). Retrieved from www.gjss.org/sites/default/files/issues/chapters/papers/Journal-07-02--02-Kennedy-Hellen.pdf

Kleeman, J. (2015). Transgender children: 'This is who he is – I have to respect that'. *Guardian*. Retrieved from: www.theguardian.com/society/2015/sep/12/transgender-children-have-to-respect-who-he-is

Langer, S. J., & Martin, J. J. (2004). How dresses can make you mentally ill: Examining gender identity disorder in children. *Child and Adolescent Social Work Journal*, 21(1), 5–23.

Lev, A. I. (2004). *Transgender emergence: Therapeutic guidelines for working with gender-variant people and their families*. New York: Routledge.

Li, G., Flores, C., Grossman, A. H., & Russell, S. T. (2013). Preferred name use and suicide and mental health risks among transgender youth. Conference: 2013 Society for Research in Child Development. Retrieved from: https://mcclellandinstitute.arizona.edu/sites/mcclellandinstitute.arizona.edu/files/Preferred%20Names%20USe%20and%20Suicide%20and%20Mental%20Health%20Risks%20among%20Transgender%20YouthLi_0.pdf

Lorriaux, A. (2015). La souffrance des enfants trans'. *Slate*. Retrieved from: www.slate.fr/story/95615/les-enfants-trans

Lüthi, A., & Fuchs, O. (2013). Transgenre, de plus en plus de consultations. In 20 minutes. Retrieved from: www.20min.ch/ro/news/suisse/story/Transgenre-deplus-en-plus-de-consultations-27482941

McBride, R. S. (2013). *Grasping the nettle: The experiences of gender variant children and transgender youth living in Northern Ireland*. Belfast: Institute for Conflict Research. Retrieved from www.teni.ie/attachments/b8e87333-747b-412b-98de-5973a5229f07.PDF

Menvielle, E. (2012). A comprehensive program for children with gender variant behaviors and gender identity disorders. *Journal of Homosexuality*, 59, 3, 357–368.

Olson, K. R., Key, A. C., & Eaton, N. R. (2015). Gender cognition in transgender children. *Psychological Science*, 26(4), 467–474.

Padawer, R. (2013). Mädchen? Junge? Ich bin ich! In *GEO. Die Welt mit andren Augen sehen*, 12/13, 98–114.

Pascual, J. (2015). Le sexe "neutre" reconnu pour la première fois en France. In *Le Monde*. Retrieved from: www.lemonde.fr/societe/article/2015/10/14/le-sexe-neutre-reconnu-pour-la-premiere-fois-en-france_4789226_3224.html

Pullen Sansfaçon, A. (2012). *Princess boys, trans girls, queer youth. Social action research project: Parenting a "gender creative" child in today's society*. Research Report, University of Montreal.

Pullen Sansfaçon, A., Robichaud, M. J., & Dumais-Michaud, A. A. (2015). The experience of parents who support their children's gender variance. *Journal of LGBT Youth*, 12(1), 39-63. Retrieved from: www.tandfonline.com/doi/pdf/10.1080/19361653.2014.935555

RADELUX II (2012). Retrieved from: www.ances.lu/attachments/155_RADELUX_transgender%2006-02-2013%20DINA4%20layout.pdf

Raj, R. (2002). Towards a transpositive therapeutic model: Developing clinical sensitivity and cultural competence in the effective support of transsexual and transgendered clients. In *The International Journal of Transgenderism*, 6(2). Retrieved from: www.iiav.nl/ezines/web/ijt/97-03/numbers/symposion/ijtvo06no02_04.htm

Riley, A. e.a. (2013). Recognising the needs of gender-variant children and their parents. *Sex Education*, 13(6), 644–659.

Schneider, E. (2012). Peur des psychiatres de prendre la mauvaise décision et influence des normes de genre. Talk on 5th of December at the conference "Le genre: quel défi pour la psychiatrie? Biologie et société dans les classifications et la clinique." Paris: Université de Paris Descartes.

Schneider, E. (2013). An insight into respect for the rights of trans and intersex children in Europe. (Original in French: Les droits des enfants intersexes et trans' sont-ils respectés en Europe? Une perspective.) Conseil de l'Europe (ed.). Retrieved from: https://rm.coe.int/CoERMPublicCommonSearchServices/DisplayDCTMContent?documentId=090000168047f2a7

Schneider, E. (in press). Trans'-children: Between normative power and self-determination. In *Normed children*. German title: Trans'-Kinder zwischen Definitionsmacht und Selbstbestimmung. In *Normierte Kinder* (E. Schneider, & C. Baltes-Löhr, ed.) (2014). Bielefeld: transcript.

- Schneider, E., & Keins, P. (2013). Périodes méconnues de la transidentité: De la petite enfance au début de la puberté. In *Le droit de l'enfant et de l'adolescent à son orientation sexuelle et à son identité de genre*. P. D. Jaffé, B. Lévy, Z. Moody, & J. Zermatten (ed.). Institut Universitaire Kurt Bösch.

United Nations (1989). *Convention on the rights of the child*. Retrieved from: www.ohchr.org/Documents/ProfessionalInterest/crc.pdf

Voß HJ (in press). Determining sex/gender: Genes and DNA precisely do not predict the development of a genital tract . . . *Normed children*. E. Schneider, & C. Baltes-Löhr (ed.). Bielefeld: transcript.

Wallace, R., & Russell, H. (2013). Attachment and shame. In Gender-nonconforming children and their families: Toward a theoretical framework for evaluating clinical interventions, *International Journal of Transgenderism*, 14(3), 113–126. Retrieved from: www.tandfonline.com/doi/pdf/10.1080/15532739.2013.824845

World Health Organization (1990). *International statistical classification of diseases and related health problems 10th revision* (ICD-10)-WHO Version for 2016. Chapter V. Mental and behavioural disorders (F00-F99), F.64.0-2. http://apps.who.int/classifications/icd10/browse/2016/en#/F60-F69

Yogyakarta Principles (2007). The application of international human rights law in relation to sexual orientation and gender identity. Retrieved from: www.yogyakartaprinciples.org/principles_en.pdf

Zinck, S., Pignatiello, A. (2015). External review of the gender identity clinic of the child, youth and family services in the underserved population program at the Centre for Addiction and Mental Health. CAMH CYF GIC Review. Retrieved from: www.camh.ca/en/hospital/about_camh/newsroom/news_releases_media_advisories_and_backgrounders/current_year/Documents/GIC-Review-26Nov2015.pdf

Zucker, K. J. (2008). Children with gender identity disorder: Is there a best practice? *Neuropsychiatrie de l'enfance et de l'adolescence* 56, 350–357.

Zucker, K. J. e.a. (2012). A developmental, biopsychosocial model for the treatment of children with Gender Identity Disorder. *Journal of Homosexuality*, 59(3), 369–397.

9
GOLDEN TICKET THERAPY

Stigma management among trans men

Elroi J. Windsor

The act of changing sex carries tremendous stigma. Restrictive gender norms pervade Western cultures, positioning transsexual[1] people as deviants. Consequently, transgender people may encounter problems during social interactions, including those with healthcare providers (Safer et al., 2016). Due to transgender people's report negative encounters in healthcare systems, advocates have stressed the importance of studying these settings (Bockting et al., 2004). In the last two decades, social research with transgender people has increased, including within healthcare. Transgender people typically must get approval from therapists before starting medical transition because psychomedical institutions pathologize transsexuality (Green, 2000). These interactions can be tense. They offer an important opportunity to understand how a stigmatized population uses mental health services.

This chapter examines how trans men negotiate stigmas of mental illness while pursuing medical transition. It explores how trans men navigated therapy to get the letter that would authorize medical transition—the "golden ticket"—or bypassed that process in accessing hormones and surgeries. Through interviews with trans men, the findings suggest that they used three strategies to minimize the stigma of mental illness: submission, manipulation, and resistance.

The historical construction of disorder

Getting approval from mental health professionals before accessing medical transition stems from a history of pathologization. Although gender diversity preceded clinical classification for centuries (Lev, 2004), the medicalization of transsexuality began around 1910 when science directed its authoritative lens to individuals with cross-gender identifications. By 1950, psychomedical communities began constructing the boundaries of the category of "transsexual," theorizing about its foundations and recommending treatment (King, 1993). As psychomedical professionals aspired to align the body with the mind, psychotherapy became important to sort candidates for medical intervention (King, 1993). This evolution of the role of therapy in treating transsexuals secured mental health providers' roles in authorizing medical transition.

As decades passed, clinicians refined diagnostic criteria to justify surgical procedures, and the first edition of *The Standards of Care for Gender Identity Disorders* was published in 1979 (Meyer et al., 2001). These standards became the official guidelines used by providers treating transsexuals. The most recent edition of the Standards of Care (SOC) was published by the World Professional Association for Transgender Health (WPATH) (Coleman et al.) in 2012. The WPATH SOC is a 112-page booklet that outlines ways for healthcare providers to assess clients' readiness and eligibility for medical transition (Coleman et al., 2012).

Although the WPATH SOC question the pathologization of transsexuality, they implicitly rely on classifications of psychological disorders. In 1994, the American Psychiatric Association (APA) replaced "Transsexualism" with "Gender Identity Disorder" (GID) in the fourth edition of the *Diagnostic and Statistical Manual of Mental Disorders* (Meyer et al., 2001). In 2013, the APA published the *DSM-5*, which renamed the diagnosis "gender dysphoria" (APA, 2013). These diagnoses have been used to signify eligibility for medical transition (Lev, 2004). The WPATH SOC further confirmed therapists' roles as gatekeepers of transsexuals' medical transitions through different specifications, such as recommending one authorizing referral letter for hormone therapy and chest surgery and two letters for genital surgery. They recommend that therapists' letters describe the individual's eligibility for procedures, including "a brief description of the clinical rationale for supporting the client's request" (Coleman et al., 2012, p. 26, 28). In writing referral letters, therapists authorize medical transition for transsexuals and may invoke the gender dysphoria diagnosis. The therapist letter is the "golden ticket" transsexuals present to physicians as proof they have been evaluated by a mental health professional. This letter is a crucial commodity for trans people.

Historically, transsexuals learned to adapt to psychomedical protocols. They learned that they could assert having a true self that needed to be freed to gain services (Meyerowitz, 2002). Clinicians soon realized their clients had read diagnostic literature and mimicked behaviors and narratives to expedite services (Meyerowitz, 2002). In this way, transsexuals asserted agency within the larger pathologizing structures, and some still use these strategies (Spade, 2006).

Despite increasing visibility of trans people, problems in therapy persist (Benson, 2013). Transgender people have reported feeling dissatisfied with therapy restrictions (Bockting et al., 2004), unhindered by them (Rachlin, 2002), or mixed (Denny & Roberts, 1997). Overall, trans people report positive outcomes through counseling, where negative encounters often result from therapists lacking experience with transgender clients (Bockting et al., 2004; Rachlin, 2002). Undoubtedly, therapy can be beneficial. But the WPATH SOC present an additional barrier for transsexuals who are certain about their decisions and do not want counseling. Thus, interactions between transsexuals and their therapists can become strained (Meyerowitz, 2002). To foster more productive therapy, some therapists proposed new models for working with transgender clients that are less pathologizing (e.g., see Lev, 2004; Raj, 2002). But adherence to the WPATH SOC limits therapists' abilities to apply more affirming models.

Managing stigma within the confines of pathology

Determining what behaviors and practices qualify as mental disorders is a socially constructed reality differing across cultures and throughout history. Between the third and fourth editions of the DSM, classifications of disorders rose from 180 to 297 (Shorter, 1997). The original 1952 *DSM* was 132 pages (Lev, 2004); the current version is nearly 1,000 pages long (APA, 2013). This upsurge begs the question of whether people in Western cultures truly are increasingly mentally ill. Even demonstrating reliability of diagnosing remains challenging for therapists who use the same criteria set forth in the *DSM*. The power to classify certain human conditions as mental disorders is a subjective social process often fraught with political tension (Spiegel, 2005). The labeling of "mental illness" creates "aristocracies of illness" where persons applying the label may denigrate some deviant behaviors over others (Szasz, 1961, p. 61). For example, clinicians may stigmatize the desire to change one's assigned sex, but may treat tomboys as acceptable.

Goffman (1963) described stigma as any "attribute that is deeply discrediting," such that stigmatized people are viewed as somehow socially different or devalued and then invoke purposeful strategies to conceal the negative label (p. 3). While healthcare professionals are expected to be more sympathetic to stigmatized groups due to having experience working with them (Goffman, 1963), interactions between providers and their clients can reflect dominant sociocultural values of stigmatization (Green & Platt, 1997). Although research on stigma management has been criticized for situating responses as primarily passive, defensive, or reactionary, studies have demonstrated ways stigmatized persons may challenge the stigmatized status and sway those with whom they deal (Siegel et al., 1998). Trans people's stigma management stems from being labeled with a psychological disorder while enduring counseling to procure their desired bodies. Their mental health experiences involve managing the stigma of gender dysphoria while affirming their identities as healthy. Advocates for transsexual self-determination resist the classification of gender diversity as mental illness. They argue for ending the pathologization of gender nonconformity in the *DSM* and oppose gatekeeping practices (e.g., Spade, 2006). In Western societies, cisgender people may obtain hormones and surgeries without authorization from mental health professionals. This disparity in treatment happens even though research has demonstrated similarities between transgender and cisgender people in terms of how they felt about their bodies before and after surgery (Windsor, 2011). Thus, the pathologization of trans body modifications represents a contested decision.

Methodology

This chapter examines how trans men negotiate the stigmatizing effects of pathologization. In interactions with therapists, how do trans men handle the stigma of mental illness? How do they respond to therapy expectations that rely on psychological labeling when accessing medical transition? These questions were examined in a larger study of trans men's healthcare experiences (Windsor, 2006). My IRB-approved research relied on in-depth interviews with 20 participants. Conventional grounded theory methods informed data collection and analysis (Strauss & Corbin 1998), leading to a core conceptual category of "psychomedical gatekeeping."

Accessing some aspect of medical transition was a criterion for selection in the study, but trans men's body modifications varied. Trans men in this sample had been accessing medical transition from 1 to 20 years, with an average of 4.3 years. Every trans man in this sample used testosterone, and chest surgery was the most common surgery ($n = 16$). Sixteen respondents saw a therapist to gain approval for medical transition.

Nine trans men lived in greater New York City, which had a large network of transgender-specific resources, including a community healthcare center. Eleven trans men lived in the Southeast United States in areas with fewer resources and no central transgender-specific clinic. Respondents ranged from 20 to 57 years old. Sixteen respondents were white; four were trans men of color.

Strategies for managing stigma: submission, manipulation, and resistance

Most trans men in this sample sought counseling to gain authorization for medical transition. In pursuit of the golden ticket, trans men saw therapists who held varying attitudes. Throughout these situations, trans men engaged in stigma management strategies to navigate the experience of psychomedical labeling. They developed three main strategies to manage the stigma of the therapy authorization process and stigmatizing interactions with therapists (see Table 9.1). Some trans men strategically *submitted* to stigma to expedite the authorizing process. Others *manipulated* stigma during therapy interactions. Lastly, many trans men in this study *resisted* stigma by actively critiquing it or avoiding therapy altogether. Trans men sometimes used more than one strategy in their interactions. These strategies present an opportunity to explore how transsexuals negotiate medical transition in a context that pathologizes their desires and compromises their bodily autonomy.

Submission: doing what needed to be done

When accessing therapy to gain authorization letters, some trans men submitted to the ways the WPATH SOC recommend therapy and may include a psychiatric diagnosis. Yet, most of the men who did so had no other choice. The WPATH SOC regulate medical transition, and trans men usually had to submit to them to

TABLE 9.1 Trans men's stigma management strategies

Submission	Manipulation	Resistance
• Passively accepting therapy (with or without critique) • Regarding therapy as a temporary means to an end • Constructing strategic narratives (confidence, typical transsexual trajectory)	• Openly addressing power imbalances with therapists • Strategically choosing transgender-friendly therapists (those who supported transition decisions, used flexible timelines, empathized with trans men)	• Ending relationships with disapproving therapists • Criticizing diagnosis • Emphasizing transgender diversity • Supporting elective therapy • Evading therapy

access hormones and surgeries. Trans men in this sample used submission as a strategy by regarding therapy as a means to an end.

A few trans men accepted the therapy expectation without critique. They did not complain much, and acquiesced to counseling as part of what they believed was required. These men tended to live in more isolated, rural areas and appreciated how therapy connected them with transgender communities and resources. For example, after meeting with several unhelpful therapists who tried to persuade him he was gay, Zack[2] expressed relief when he found a therapist who understood him:

> I went to [this therapist] and he just blew me away. He knew everything I felt. He knew *everything*. And then I started working with him and . . . he helped me start the letters for testosterone, and then from that moment, from that time on, he told me every doctor I need to go to . . ., he told me the different doctors for chest surgery, the different doctors for the hysterectomy. . . . And he just kinda pulled me into the community and gave me all the resources that I needed.

Complacency with undergoing counseling, however, did not mean trans men accepted the presumption that they were psychologically disordered. None of these men stated that they had a mental illness or wholeheartedly accepted a gender diagnosis.

Other men who passively submitted to therapy expectations experienced a loss of agency and critiqued the process. Nate stated: "It's this feeling of not being in control of your own future when you have to rely on other people to write all these letters to attest to your validity as far as being trans." Similarly, Jack felt like medical transition was out of his hands: "I'm gonna have to wait for everything. And other people are gonna have to sign off on everything. It's gonna be like I'm in this for the ride, and that I'm not driving this." These men understood therapy as a disempowering process. They managed the stigma of being expected to defend their decisions by reluctantly submitting to the therapy process. Voicing disapproval to me, a researcher, offered them an opportunity to air their frustrations. They expressed a critique of the way the process discredited and devalued their autonomy. These critiques further managed the lingering stigma of having to endure therapy.

More commonly, trans men who submitted to therapy regarded it as a temporary means to an end. Andrew saw a counselor so he could "do that three months and get my letter—like a means to an end." Zed described his therapy experience similarly: "It felt like I was doing what I needed to do to get what I wanted." In these cases, trans men managed stigma by going through the steps recommended by the WPATH SOC. Their reports demonstrate submission as an active process, performed consciously and purposefully. They managed the stigma of therapy by rationalizing it as fleeting.

Submission to therapy also included constructions of strategic narratives. During interactions with therapists, some trans men presented themselves as more confident about their decisions. They concealed fears about transition, worrying such disclosures would prevent them from receiving letters. John explained:

> I felt my therapist was really cool and I could have talked to him about whatever. He was trans, he wasn't wanting me to fit some mold, he didn't diagnose me with GID. He wasn't into wanting me to be like a real transsexual or something. But I was having a lot of doubts in starting hormones. But I didn't feel comfortable bringing them up, because I wanted to just get my letter.

Zed also relayed, "I felt like I should appear more sure about what I wanted than I really was. So I did. I just said, 'This is what I wanna do and I know it.' [laughs] Whereas, I probably had a lot more internal dialogue than that, but I didn't talk so much about that . . . I presented myself as being way more confident in my decision and what I wanted than I actually was." Rather than expressing their doubts and jeopardizing authorization, these men purposefully elected to reveal only the most certain attitudes in transitioning. They surrendered to the stigmatizing therapy process knowing that not doing so could compromise access to hormones or surgery. They managed the stigma of therapy expectations by avoiding risky disclosures. This strategy gave trans men some agency within the process.

A similar strategy of submission included trans men who relayed selective biographical information. Although the WPATH SOC do not currently endorse any mythical "true transsexual" narrative, historically psychomedical professionals expected one, which led transsexuals to relay narratives they believed therapists needed to hear (Mason-Schrock, 1996). In this study, some trans men believed invoking more conventional narratives would garner medical transition more efficiently. By invoking trajectories of the "true transsexual," these men submitted to ideologies that pathologize transsexuality. Their submission to such stigma, however, was part of a purposeful maneuver through the mental healthcare system, as M&M described:

> I don't think you could typecast it [being transsexual]. But back then you were probably trying to look for a particular person, had to say particular

things. So that's always in the back of your mind. So, I'm not sure what they're lookin' for, but I hope I say whatever it is. It's like you have to authenticate that I am what I already am. That's just like to say, if we went into another world and I already know I'm Black, but they have a list that says this is what Black people do and say and be. And so, if I don't do that, I don't get my Black card. [laughs] You know? That's the way I felt! Like, oh my God! I'm not gonna get my card.

Relaying a conventional narrative meant trans men accepted the stigmatizing therapy process in order to expedite services and get their golden ticket. Adam constructed a similar story in order to get authorized for chest surgery:

That was really ... the visit to a healthcare provider where I most felt like I had to tell the right story in order to get what I needed. Because I had a very set goal in mind. I just wanted this one piece of paper. And I didn't want to do anything to raise his suspicions about me. And nothing that I told him was *false*, but I told my story in such a way that it highlighted my discomfort in my body when I was a teenager, which wasn't clear to me at that time that it was a gender-related thing. But I told the story in the way that made it sound like the signs were pointing to gender as the source of my problems.

Adam also intentionally presented a carefully crafted narrative that resembled a more typical transsexual trajectory than what he actually experienced. He elaborated on this decision:

It was pretty much my strategy going in. I was sort of annoyed that I had to jump through that hoop anyway ... because it didn't feel necessary for me. ... I wanted to make it as quick and painless a hoop as I possibly could. So, I consciously, [laughs] I tried hard to seem very well adjusted and did not dwell on uncertainties that I had. Or didn't really talk about the long period of time that I identified pretty exclusively as genderqueer, and really just focused on more traditional transition kinds of details. ... This was not a therapeutic relationship. It was definitely a means to an end.

For trans men, submission to therapy expectations occurred out of necessity, but it also involved calculated decisions. Trans men knew they could present stories that were misleading or that supported stigmatizing protocol, but they used these preconceptions advantageously. Their submission to the protocol effectively reproduced the authority of the guidelines. But submission included purposeful and clever strategies that reflected their agency in using the system.

Manipulation: it was on *my* timeline

Submission to therapy sometimes included a critique of the WPATH SOC, but it left therapy requirements fairly unchallenged. A second strategy from this study shows how trans men manipulated the stigma of the SOC. For these trans men, negotiating stigma in therapy interactions differed from submission because trans men openly expressed their discomfort with therapy expectations directly to their therapists. They also strategically sought authorization letters from therapists who had reputations for being "transgender-friendly." In these cases, manipulation did not involve persuading therapists that they were good candidates for medical transition. Rather, trans men critiqued therapy expectations directly to their providers and sought letters from therapists who seemed sympathetic to disempowering gatekeeping practices.

Most men in this sample viewed therapy as a barrier. They lamented lacking control over their lives, and a few men, like Trevor, chose to address power imbalances with their counselors:

> I went into my story, and she asked me a couple questions. And then I talked about how there is this power dynamic between her and me. We both knew that I wanted a letter at the end of three months. And I was really worried about being gay-identified, because I heard a lot of horror stories about people not getting letters because they weren't gonna make a happy straight person. And still feeling a little genderqueer too, not fitting the mold of masculine man. And after 30 minutes of our session, she told me that she was gonna give me a letter.

By openly questioning the inherent power imbalances in the therapy relationship, trans men risked being denied authorization letters. That only a few men chose this overt strategy illustrates the limitations of agency within the confines of pathology. Challenging the authority of therapists was too risky for most trans men.

The most common way trans men manipulated the stigma of therapy expectations was by choosing therapists who had reputations for being flexible with the WPATH SOC. Trans men chose therapists who seemed to understand that the SOC were recommendations that could be adapted. These therapists supported trans men's decisions, used flexible timelines, and expressed empathy with the validation process. Drew explained:

> My therapist never had any doubt in her mind that [transitioning] was exactly where I needed to go. She didn't encourage it, but she never even asked me. She didn't ask me to validate my identity. She didn't ask how long I had known. It just never was a question. It was kinda like this is who I am, that's part of who I am and it was good. And so to have that, almost *more* confidence from *her* than me at some times, was really helpful. . . . She was just a good support network. She never had any expectation as far as a time limit.

Trans men reported that these therapists did not interrogate them about their life histories, or make them justify their identities before providing letters authorizing hormones and surgery. Trans men's decisions to see supportive therapists enabled them to manipulate the stigma of therapy expectations by seeing therapists who used the WPATH SOC more loosely.

Trans-friendly therapists also seemed less committed to upholding a fixed timeline for trans men to follow, as was also the case for Drew's therapist: "Fortunately for me, [she] was ready as soon as I was ready. 'Cause when I directly asked her if she'd done that before and written letters, she had. So it was on *my* timeline. It was on *my* watch. And that was exactly what I needed." Many trans men in this sample started medical transition when the WPATH SOC recommended at least three months of counseling prior to issuing an authorizing letter. But these trans men were able to manipulate this protocol through choosing experienced therapists they expected would be flexible. Kevin explained:

> When I walked in there, the whole gatekeeper stuff was in the back of my mind. And I'm like, "Look, this is what I wanna do." And he's like, "Well let me see you for a month, and I'll write your letter in a month." I know it's usually a three-month period where they make you wait before they write you a letter. But for one thing, he was just really easygoing about that part of it. Because I'm like, "Look I've been thinking about this for 14 years, so." He was really willing to work with me. Also, he's an FTM as well, so he'd been there before.

> This flexibility regarding timelines alleviated Kevin's stress about spending more time in an authorizing process after he had already spent years thinking through the decision.

In addition, by choosing transgender therapists, trans men believed their providers could empathize with the authorizing process. Trevor explained how his therapist, a trans woman, joked about having to use the language of disorder: "While she was writing [my letter], she was laughing about it. I think her being trans was really cool; we both could appreciate how ridiculous it sounded. She was just apologizing, like 'I'm really sorry I have to include all that stuff.' And was kind of making fun of it." This therapist also invited Trevor to collaborate in the letter-writing process, making the authorization process more transparent. This cooperative act deconstructed the power dynamics of the relationship. By helping his transgender therapist author the letter, Trevor was able to manage the stigma that made the letter necessary.

Cisgender therapists who candidly expressed their discomfort with the protocol also aided trans men in negotiating the stigma of therapy expectations. Drew explained:

> I asked her, "So what goes in this letter?" She told me about how she usually writes them. And she told me that she understands the importance of the letter, but she also feels frustrated in having to write one for the same reasons that I feel frustrated in having to get one. She said, "I'll include a few things in it about how long we've been working together." But she was like, "To be honest, when I write these letters I almost feel ridiculous. You wanna just

say, 'He's a big boy. He's made a grown-up decision.'" [laughs] And she's like, "But you can't, so I sorta say that in my own way." And so she wrote it and then she said, "When I'm done writing it, you can come in and read it. And if there's anything that you're uncomfortable with or want me to change, then I will." And so, that's what we did.

By empathizing with trans men, trans-friendly therapists moderated the stigmatizing effects of the pathologizing process.

These experiences illustrate the important ways therapists worked as allies to trans men. However, these therapists did not disavow the system of writing authorizing letters; they still chose to see transsexuals for this reason. Their participation in the WPATH SOC seemed influenced by the reality that trans men would likely encounter surgeons and hormone-prescribing doctors who required letters.

Resistance: we're not crazy

Many men in this study disapproved of how psychomedical systems pathologized them. This section highlights the strategy of resistance, where trans men actively opposed the stigmatizing protocol. They resisted the stigma of the pathologizing process by ending relationships with disapproving therapists, criticizing psychological diagnoses, emphasizing transgender diversity, supporting elective therapy, and evading therapy.

Some trans men encountered insensitive therapists who would not even consider authorizing medical transition. Drew explained how his therapist discounted his desire for chest surgery: "She couldn't understand the trans thing at all. And at one point, my third visit, she made a comment, 'I just don't understand why anyone would want to do that to their body.' And I was like, [laughing] 'Okay bye!'" When trans men in this study encountered therapists with these attitudes, they managed stigma by refusing to continue services with unsupportive therapists.

A point many trans men made during this study was to emphasize they were not crazy. These trans men felt insulted by the stigma of mental illness that informed the authorizing process for transsexuals. Dave emphasized:

> They don't seem to realize nobody *chooses* this. This is not something you go, "Oh well, hoo! I'm gonna be trans today!" We didn't ask for it, and they need to realize that. . . . They say we have *gender* disorder. Now they say that's mental disease, right? Now we're all crazy. But we're not crazy. And there's a lot more of us than they think there are.

Similarly, Zed stated, "I don't agree with the diagnosis [laughs]. I think that diagnosing people for who they are is sort of ridiculous." Trans men managed stigma by expressing discontent with the pathologization of transsexuality. They criticized the mental illness diagnosis, and asserted their right to self-determination.

Many trans men in this sample opposed a psychological diagnosis as a prerequisite for hormones and surgery. But a few men hesitated to totally discount it because they believed an official diagnosis might facilitate insurance coverage for transition services even though most insurance companies in the United States exclude transition-related care (Stroumsa, 2014). These men, however, believed their healthcare should be covered without accompanying psychopathology. Joey clarified:

> I don't think anybody should *have* to be diagnosed with gender identity disorder. For me, this is a situation that needed to be handled with *my body*. I just can't understand the corruption of not having it covered by medical insurance. I just can't get past that. It's just very difficult to deal with, because it really feels like something that would greatly improve the quality of my life in a lot of different ways.

Other trans men in this sample resisted the WPATH SOC by pointing out that not everyone's transitions follow the same path. These trans men complained about how psychomedical institutions viewed transsexuals' transitions as identical and linear. John expressed disappointment with the SOC because he felt they were "really focused on treating trans people like they have a psych disorder, diagnosing them with a psychiatric label. Everyone's expected to want to have bottom surgery, and all this stuff." As Sam explained, "You don't have to be transitioning from A to B or B to A. We're just people. . . . The bottom line is that all people should have access to *quality* healthcare." Trans men resisted the stigma of official diagnostic protocol by highlighting their heterogeneity. Emphasizing diverse experiences helped trans men minimize the stigma of a classification system that assumed transsexuals represent a homogeneous group.

Although some trans men reported benefiting from therapy, they expressed dissatisfaction with being expected to have their mental health evaluated during the authorizing process. Their resistance to therapy expectations did not mean they entirely objected to counseling. Indeed, many trans men in this study valued their relationships with competent therapists. They stressed that they believed in the general benefits of counseling, but they felt therapy should not be required to access medical transition. As Dave explained:

> It was an odd feeling to have to go see a psychiatrist, because I was, well there's nothing wrong with *me*. . . . But that was the first process, is going and getting *evaluated*—I guess would be a good term—to see if you *qualify*. . . . But I think it's a good process because not only do the doctors get to know you, but they start pulling out stuff that might have been sunk for years.

Kevin could not offer total support for therapy as a prerequisite to medical transition:

> I kind of understand why people might want you to go through therapy just because it changes *everything*. I don't know that it should be mandatory, but I would probably be in favor of it personally and if I were to talk to other

people, I would recommend it. I don't know if I could say you *have* to do this.

By acknowledging benefits of counseling but rejecting the expectation, trans men resisted the stigma of therapy expectations.

Finally, several trans men in this study resisted the stigma of therapy by evading therapy requirements. Three men in this sample were able to obtain hormones and another got chest surgery without having to produce authorizing therapist letters to these doctors. Two of these men saw providers who did not seem to follow the WPATH SOC, but one of these trans men noted that his surgeon had since started requiring letters. The other two trans men were able to get hormones in unconventional ways. Solomon got hormones through a retired doctor who did not require authorizing letters. Another respondent was able to get hormones without a letter because he had started masculinizing his body through a testosterone-boosting, over-the-counter product. He found that sufficiently passing as male eased his access to prescribed treatment.

Although these trans men were able to bypass therapy prerequisites at times, lifelong avoidance of the WPATH SOC was uncommon. When Solomon moved to another state and tried to renew his hormones, he found only one place that would do it: "They wanted me to jump through all the hoops again. I was like, 'I'm not doin' that.'" Solomon then found a way to get "private testosterone" and purchased testosterone through underground economies. Men who did not access therapy typically struggled to find medical providers, and sometimes compromised safe care in the process. Still, these trans men resisted therapy prerequisites and appreciated being able to alter their bodies without enduring psychological evaluation and authorization.

Trans men's negotiations of the therapy process reveal the ways they managed the stigma of pathologization. The WPATH SOC establish guidelines for providers, and transsexuals typically negotiate medical transition within these confines. But trans men in this study offered new perspectives on their experiences and reframed their decisions as non-pathological.

In response to the ways the SOC rely on pathological models, trans men asserted agency and managed stigma in therapy contexts. Trans men minimized the stigma of being treating as having a mental disorder. Therapy expectations exist only because gender nonconformity is pathologized in psychomedical institutions.

The findings in this study illustrate problems with therapy expectations, which some surgeons and hormone-prescribing doctors treat as fixed requirements. Although some therapists alleviated trans men's anxiety, tensions around the WPATH SOC compromised productive therapy for trans men. Trans men worried about saying the right thing in order to get authorizing letters. In pursuit of the golden ticket, they were more likely to present sanitized versions of their life experiences that reflected antiquated narratives about "true" transsexuals. Many felt burdened by therapy expectations. Consequently, therapy interactions for them were sometimes superficial or stressful. Under the WPATH SOC, therapists offered counseling to clients who guarded their true feelings for fear of not receiving authorizing letters. What resulted was a system based on fraudulent assertions. Getting therapy to procure letters of authorization limited both trans men and their therapists in achieving the most beneficial relationships. A model based on elective therapy and informed consent to medical transition might foster more sincere interactions between transsexuals and their providers. This model would also eradicate much of the stigma that informs these interactions.

Critiques and alternatives to the SOC exist, yet they remain popular. Whether or not therapist letters will continue to function as a golden ticket is best determined by psychomedical professionals' willingness to re-evaluate a trans person's right to bodily autonomy. Doing so requires an examination of sociocultural classifications of transsexual embodiment as disordered and in need of psychomedical management. When gender diversity and differently gendered and sexed bodies are no longer pathologized, then counseling can serve a more supportive and authentic role in helping people navigate these transitions.

Notes

1 In this chapter, I use "transgender" and "trans" as broad terms referring to having gender identities and/or expressions differing from those typically associated with assigned sex. I use "transsexual" to describe individuals that alter their bodies through hormones and/or surgeries to reflect a body that differs from their assigned sex, and "trans man" to describe an individual with a female-to-male transgender experience. These terms are not universally experienced by the respondents in this sample, but are used here uniformly for brevity's sake.
2 All names are pseudonyms chosen by respondents.

References

American Psychiatric Association. (2013). DSM-5. Retrieved from: www.psychiatry.org/dsm5.

Benson, K. E. (2013). Seeking support: Transgender client experiences with mental health services. *Journal of Feminist Family Therapy*, 25(1), 17–40.

Bockting, W., B. Robinson, A. Benner, & K. Scheltema. (2004). Patient satisfaction with transgender health services. *Journal of Sex and Marital Therapy*, 30, 277–294.

Coleman, E., Bockting, W., Botzer, M., Cohen-Kettenis, P., DeCuypere, G., Feldman, J., & Zucker, K. (2012). *Standards of care for the health of transsexual, transgender, and gender-nonconforming people*. World Professional Association for Transgender Health Inc. Retrieved from: www.wpath.org/uploaded_files/140/files/ Standards%20of%20 Care,%20V7%20Full%20Book.pdf

Denny, D., & Roberts, J. (1997). Results of a questionnaire on the Standards of Care of the Harry Benjamin International Gender Dysphoria Association. In B. Bullough, V. Bullough, & J. Elias (Eds.), *Gender blending* (320–336). Amherst, NY: Prometheus Books.

Goffman, E. (1963). *Stigma: Notes on the management of spoiled identity*. Englewood Cliffs, NJ: Prentice Hall.

Green, G., & Platt, S. (1997). Fear and loathing in health care settings reported by people with HIV. *Sociology of Health and Illness*, 19(1), 70–92.

Green, J. (2000) [2006]. Look! No, don't! The visibility dilemma for transsexual men. In S. Stryker & S. Whittle (Eds.), *The transgender studies reader* (499–508). New York: Routledge.

King, D. (1993) [1996]. Gender blending: Medical perspectives and technology. In R. Ekins & D. King (Eds.), *Blending genders: Social aspects of cross-dressing and sex-changing* (79–98). London & New York: Routledge.

Lev, A. I. (2004). *Transgender emergence: Therapeutic guidelines for working with gender-variant people and their families*. Binghamton, NY: The Haworth Clinical Practice Press.

Mason-Schrock, D. (1996). Transsexuals' narrative construction of the 'true self'. *Social Psychology Quarterly*, 59, 176–192.

Meyer III, W., Bockting, W. O., Cohen-Kettenis, P., Coleman, E., DiCeglie, D., Devor, H., & Wheeler, C. (2001). *The Harry Benjamin international gender dysphoria association's standards of care for gender identity disorders, sixth version*. World Professional Association for Transgender Health, Inc. Retrieved from: www.wpath.org/documents2/socv6.pdf

Meyerowitz, J. (2002). *How sex changed: A history of transsexuality in the United States*. Cambridge, MA: Harvard University Press.

Rachlin, K. (2002). Transgender individuals' experiences of psychotherapy. *International Journal of Transgenderism*, 6(1). Retrieved from: www.symposion.com/ijt/ijtvo06no01_03.htm

Raj, R. (2002). Towards a transpositive therapeutic model: Developing clinical sensitivity and cultural competence in the effective support of transsexual and transgendered clients. *International Journal of Transgenderism*, 6(2). Retrieved from: www.symposion.com/ijt/ijtvo06no02_04.htm

Safer, J. D., Coleman, E., Feldman, J., Garofalo, R., Hembree, W., Radix, A., & Sevelius, J. (2016). Barriers to healthcare for transgender individuals: Current opinion in endocrinology, *Diabetes & Obesity*, 23(2), 168–171.

Shorter, E. (1997). *A history of psychiatry: From the era of the asylum to the age of Prozac*. New York: John Wiley & Sons.

Siegel, K., Lune, H., & Meyer, I. H. (1998). Stigma management among gay/bisexual men with HIV/AIDS. *Qualitative Sociology*, 21(1), 3–24.

Spade, D. (2006). Mutilating gender. In S. Stryker & S. Whittle (Eds.), *The transgender studies reader* (315–332). New York & London: Routledge.

Spiegel, A. (2005, January 3). The dictionary of disorder: How one man revolutionized psychiatry. *The New Yorker*, 56–63.

Strauss, A., & Corbin, J. (1998). *Basics of qualitative research: Techniques and procedures for developing grounded theory*, second edition. Thousand Oaks, CA: Sage.

Stroumsa, D. (2014). The state of transgender health care: Policy, law, and medical frameworks. *American Journal of Public Health*, 104(3), 31–38. Retrieved from: http://search.proquest.com/docview/1508767081?pq-origsite=gscholar

Szasz, T. (1961). The uses of naming and the origin of the myth of mental illness. *American Psychologist*, 16(2), 59–65.

Windsor (née Waszkiewicz), E. (2006). *Getting by gatekeepers: Transmen's dialectical negotiations within psychomedical institutions*. Thesis, Georgia State University. Retrieved from: http://scholarworks.gsu.edu/sociology_theses/13

Windsor, E. J. (2011). *Regulating healthy gender: Surgical body modification among transgender and cisgender consumers*. Dissertation, Georgia State University. Retrieved from: http://scholarworks.gsu.edu/cgi/viewcontent.cgi?article=1055&context=sociology_diss

10
BORDERS OF BELONGING

Challenges in access to anti-oppressive mental healthcare for Indigenous Latino gender-fluid youth

Silvia Tenenbaum

Much has been written about decolonizing psychology as a profession, and even more about the necessity of incorporating a gender-fluid framework mindful of the intersectional positionality that implicates subjectivities in complex vectors of oppression, invisibility, and marginalization. Feminist and multicultural models have guided therapists in adapting therapeutic practices to reflect social justice perspectives, thereby improving their ability to offer psychotherapeutic treatment that is not compromised by sexist, racist, heterosexist, or classist bias (Smith, Chambers, & Bratini, 2009). Authors employing these models have invited socially aware therapists to analyze the pathogenic influence of structural oppression on the emotional well-being of individuals and communities, in order to increase the development of socially mindful interventions (Smith et al., 2009). Moreover, further consideration of the dynamics of oppression invites practitioners to transform their interventions to achieve an emancipatory psychology geared at "breaking the chains of personal oppression as much as the chains of social oppression" (Smith et al., 2009. p. 159), which include the patriarchal underpinnings of the American Psychiatric Association's Diagnostic and Statistical Manual of Mental Disorders (DSM V) (Smith et al., 2013). In the absence of conceptual tools to understand the pathogenic nature of structural oppression, mainstream psychology exhibits a tendency to cast oppression's damage as an individual disorder and thereby risks perpetuating an unequal status quo (Smith et al., 2009).

Critical psychology, on the other hand, offers an overarching framework of values, assumptions, and practices seeking to reduce or eliminate oppression in society (Hernandez, 2008). Social justice, feminist, and other critical analyses of mental health theory and practice have illuminated the sociopolitical origins of these epistemologies, as well as the embedded risk found in conventional psychotherapeutic interventions of maintaining and even reproducing the belief systems and power relations from which they emerged (Smith et al., 2009). "Therapists who wish to break from this position of complacency and allow their relatively privileged social positions to become the platform by which silenced members of society can begin to be heard ... becom[e] part of the solution" (Smith et al., 2009. p. 167). The research conducted since 2010 by Dr. Suzanne Stewart and her team at OISE leans on the paradigm of decolonizing psychology in order to problematize the epistemological foundations of mainstream clinical psychology, grounded in unexamined patriarchal values, Eurocentric approaches, and systemic oppressive practices. The consideration of mainstream psychology as another oppressive tactic is one of the premises of the decolonizing approach this essay follows. Such consideration would "open the Pandora's box of gender, race, privilege, and privileged roles in supervision" (Smith et al., 2009. p. 84) which are deeply embedded in educational programs and practices geared at incoming clinicians and psychology students at large. Dr. Stewart's pivotal work at the University of Victoria and the University of Toronto, and my own at OISE from 2009 to 2014, form the epistemological bases of a critical view of "traditional" psychology that historically has not taken into consideration geographic dislocation in border identities. The status quo of graduate psychological training still assumes a Eurocentric, heteronormative, and cisgendered viewpoint or, at most, a viewpoint that incorporates sexual difference as an "addendum" rather than as a core value that should inform a rigorous critique of the very ideologies that determine which sexual identities are hegemonic and which marginal. Likewise, this hegemonic model of psychological training has yet to incorporate a postcolonial and diasporic perspective to questions of geographical displacement and acculturation. As my decade-long clinical experience working with border-youth has taught me, gender-fluidity in Indigenous Latino populations must be approached intersectionally in order to understand how gender identities are shaped by migrant trajectories, and in turn, how one's border-gender comes to bear on the processes of migrancy and acculturation. To the extent that these questions and issues continue to be marginal to the main concerns of mainstream psychology as a discipline, border-youth will continue to face access barriers to culturally aware healthcare services. For instance, when gender-fluidity is framed solely in terms of granting of denying access to hormonal treatment or sex-reassignment surgery, there is no space to explore the process and meanings of gender-becoming amidst complex processes of cultural adaptation that engage the DNA of one's transgenerational history. Up-to-date training models for mental healthcare providers must address issues of center and periphery in clinical psychology by incorporating a critical analysis of the ways in which patriarchal and heteronormative values shape understandings of mental health and recovery, as well as the imbrication between individual suffering and systemic oppression. In addition, a decolonizing approach to mental healthcare must implement a contextualized approach that considers the intersectional nature of oppression and privilege that differentially positions individuals and groups in terms of their social equity needs and claims. Accordingly, the central claim of this essay is that extending mental health services to border-gender youth requires an extended consciousness about societal-embedded oppressive practices. This is of particular relevance in addressing the power differential between 'clients' and 'service providers' when defining mental health and illness, formulating a diagnosis, and planning intervention strategies to alleviate suffering.

It is within this theoretical and clinical orientation that I have approached the issue of access to mental healthcare services for Indigenous Latino gender-fluid youth, understood as a transitional and multiple subject position which I term "border-youth." Border-youth refers to an intersectional, in-process, and context-dependent subject position articulated through the negotiation of socially imposed categorizations around race, ethnicity, gender, migration status, linguistic identity, sexual orientation, and so on. Here, "border" signifies both the ways in which structural forms of oppression and marginalization strategically make identities visible or invisible, as well as the contestations that emerge from the capacity to recuperate, translate, and make one's cultural knowledge relevant in a diasporic context. In critically examining the counseling experiences of border-youth through the participants' own narratives[1] regarding mental healthcare access, I follow the cultural context model to address the following questions: How do border-youth's experiences of oppression undergone before immigration become augmented by cultural and institutional practices of invisibility actualized by mental healthcare services in Toronto? And how does the specific positionality of indigenous Latino border-gender youth vis-à-vis Canadian indigenous peoples, non-Latino gender-fluid youth, and Hispanic Latino immigrants further contribute to their invisibilization and lack of access to culturally relevant mental healthcare services?

Some key barriers to access identified in this study are:

1. There is an underuse of mental healthcare services by immigrant Latino gender-fluid youth because they need to consult and/or receive culturally competent counseling services, which are not presently provided in Spanish (Ivette Jaque, personal communication, August 13, 2010; Jose [Pepe] Mellado [counselor, Centre for Spanish Speaking Peoples], personal communication, November 15, 2010).
2. Precarious legal status creates complexity for this already vulnerable population. There is a lack of empirical data in counseling psychology related to immigrant border-youth in general and, in particular, to those who are Spanish-speaking (Marlinda Freire, personal communication, August 2, 2013).
3. There is a lack of understanding of specific cultural patterns of gender development for border-youth because clinical intervention has been predominantly implemented through a family approach, even though they might not share the same language and cultural practices with the rest of their family of origin, other counselors, and/or other members of the community using the services.

Indigenous Latino gender-fluid youth formed the fastest growing asylum seeker population in Canada before December, 2015, when 31,000 Syrian refugees began arriving (Statistics Canada, July 2016). Immigrant Indigenous Latino gender-fluid residents in Canada between the ages of 16 and 29 have a higher prevalence of mental health problems than their non-Indigenous gender-fluid youth counterparts, as reflected in depression and suicide rates, and education dropout statistics (Statistics Canada, 2009). Many Indigenous Latino youths' parents arrived in Canada as asylum seekers after being tortured, arrested, and forcefully displaced in their countries of origin, experiences that generate and continue the cycle of intergenerational trauma (Dr. Freire, personal communication, September 20, 2012). There is, however, a documented gap in culturally specific mental healthcare services for this population who typically does not have access to or remains in mainstream counseling services. Very little is currently known about their experiences of access to mental healthcare services, and even less is known about how their hybrid identities shape these experiences.

Indigenous[2] Latino gender-fluid youth are multifaceted and multilayered groups of individuals and are distinct from traditionally understood mestizo, Latin American, or Spanish-speaking LGBTQ youth. Despite sharing similar challenges with other Latino immigrants—such as precarious legal status, job insecurity, racialization, and language barriers—they often identify with their Indigenous roots, an identification that carries a complex history of Latin American racial relations.

Latin American Indigenous communities have faced a long history of discrimination and violence in their countries of origin. Immigrant seekers of Indigenous origin typically do not disclose their ancestry because it proliferates their sources of oppression. For instance, a massive Guatemalan exile occurred as a result of the Guatemalan genocide, but the crux of the reported reasons was political rather than ethnic (Marlinda Freire, personal communication, May 12, 2013). Indigenous families decided to keep their ancestry hidden as a strategy to secure refugee status, resulting in authorities undercounting and underserving these acutely oppressed minorities. Because these new immigrants do not disclose their Aboriginal status upon entering Canada, authorities assume that their first language is Spanish, their religion is Catholicism, and so forth. Two set of problems arise: first, a lack of proper disclosure and further invisibility of their specific social equity needs and challenges once they have landed in Canada; and second, immigrant organizations cannot apply for funding from institutions that will not acknowledge the existence of such an isolated community within the larger Latino community. This has perpetuated historical cycles of oppression, which only now are beginning to be recognized and addressed by the more politically aware members of the psychology community; however, an understanding of intergenerational trauma has yet to enter mainstream psychological training programs at the graduate level.

In discussing nonconforming gender identities among Indigenous Latino youth, I have chosen the term "gender-fluid" over transsexual or transgender, in order to better articulate these youth's lived experience of gender and sexuality. I ascribe to Prosser's understanding of gender-fluidity, as referring to a gender identity that changes over time through "a substantive transition: a correlated set of corporeal, psychic, and social changes" (Shelley pp. 4, 22). Gender-fluid has a psychological beginning and end, in terms of insight, awareness, accommodation, and acknowledgment of a paradoxical ongoing processing. Gender-fluid is a productive term as it allows us to pay attention to the flow of becoming, in all its intricacies, from a respectful stance that honors its timing. As a clinical social psychologist, my approach is framed mainly by therapeutic concerns, and therefore, I concur with Prosser that fluidity as a concept changes over time: both internal and historical time, although its manifestations vary. Gender-fluidity is the parameter that encompasses changes. This understanding of gender-fluidity assumes that gender shifts and transitions are always intersubjective. Therefore, they involve gender-fluid children, their non-traditional parents, their teachers, as well as activists and counselors—among other allies—who intervene in school programs and other institutional settings to problematize and challenge ideologies and practices that exert gender-based oppression by upholding hegemonic understandings of gender as dichotomous, self-evident, stable, and continuous with birth-assigned sex.

Identities in formation are transient by nature and need to be understood not as an incomplete process but as a process per se, that is, as defined by the praxis and movement of becoming. The term gender-fluid responds to this aim and suggests that identities in formation don't need to go anywhere, but rather just be, where Prosser's "substantive transition" navigates one's own intersubjective tempo. The concept of gender-fluidity also surpasses the gender binary paradigm which sustains patriarchal and heteronormative ideological frameworks and institutions. From a psychological perspective, the term gender-fluid connotes greater degrees of freedom in navigating one's gender experiences, identifications, and presentation, including the choice to remain illegible according to traditional gender markers.

Indigenous Latino gender-fluid youth often feel a closer affinity with their Canadian Indigenous counterparts than with other Latino immigrants, given important similarities in their collective histories of oppression. Despite these cultural similarities, Canadian First Nations and other marginalized groups from postcolonial nations also differ fundamentally in their share of wealth, education, resources, and access to public health services (Sherbourne Health Centre, 2009). Indigenous Latino youth, for instance, cannot make use of Indigenous supports because they do not yet have the language skills necessary to access English-language services directed specifically at Indigenous peoples, nor can they access resources allocated to Canadian First Nations in Indigenous native languages. Spanish-language supports exist in the city of Toronto. However, these services do not differentiate among the specific needs of various Latin Americans populations and, as a consequence, specific Latino Indigenous needs remain invisible.

Psychology research with border-youth

Gender research in the Latin American population residing in Toronto was initiated in 2012 (Ivette Jaque [counselor, Centre for Spanish Speaking Peoples], personal communication, March 20, 2012), but the specific variable of gender-fluidity has not yet been addressed even in sexual minority research, partly because the ever-changing aspect of gender-fluidity cannot be easily grasped in quantitative epidemiological research.

In the present research, Indigenous Latino gender-fluid youth were invited to examine their experiences with mental healthcare access in Toronto. An important aspect in researching border-youths' access to mental healthcare services from a social justice perspective is the need to understand the barriers to access as political in nature; that is, as systematic exclusions of experiences and social locations that do not fit hegemonic representations of Latino, mestizo, heterosexual, able-bodied immigrants who speak the Spanish language. When it comes to the immigrant population, for instance, access to mental healthcare services is framed as facilitating the process of incorporation understood as a linear and assimilationist process of securing legal status, finding employment, learning English, and so on. To the extent that Indigenous, Latino, border-fluid youth fail to conform to heteronormative, neoliberal, and assimilationist ideals of cultural adaptation, their mental healthcare needs remain invisible to mainstream services.

When participants were prompted to expand on their own understanding of the barriers, they provided ample examples: "Access is not about putting your name down for a wait list. Access is about getting an actually useful, pertinent group that is going to make me feel better, not worse" (Mona, p. 20). From a similar context, Pat stated:

> I don't need to have access to a token after a slice of pepperoni pizza and a talk about sexual health, as if my gender orientation puts me at risk, risk of what! I am gender-fluid or gender-independent, not a freak of nature! When I tried to speak to a counselor about spirituality, she sent me to a Catholic church! The doctor who made the referral thought that because we are both from Chile, we share a similar cultural background. What a farce! (Pat, p. 18)

Access may be compromised when issues of confidentiality and information sharing are not clear. As one participant stated: "Sometimes, I'm not sure about what can happen if I fill out an "intake" form. Who has access to this information? Where is it going?"

Another participant expressed her discomfort about being asked to participate in an exclusive gender-fluid group as it created a ghetto-like mentality. Indeed, this participant has accurately identified the problematic underlying assumption that border-youth struggle more with their gender-fluidity than with negotiating their difference in mainstream settings.

The implied uniformity assumed of all peoples based on place of origin—in this case, Latino—carries with it other generalizations about these individuals' class, sexual orientation, immigration trajectory, and status. This becomes problematic as it often takes precedence over an acknowledgment of the lack of resources, which the participant might have felt as more honest and real: "I know that there is no place for people like me, but I would have preferred to deal with the truth rather than a polite lie" (Pat, pp. 18–19). In general, participants' comments about barriers to access considered how immigration intersects with their social location; for example, not having services in languages other than Spanish (for Indigenous newcomers' youth), having predominantly white, upper-class, long-term residents in ethnic-based community centers (so participants could not easily relate to their societal standards and privileges), and a lack of training in gender-fluidity by frontline workers. Indeed, one should wonder why ethno-specific community centers do not reach out, hire, and assign professionals with lived experience in gender navigation or diverse cultural and ethnic backgrounds. Psychological research has consistently shown that a combination of clinical expertise and lived experience creates rapport, which is the basis of good outcome in the therapeutic alliance. Not surprisingly, peer-support groups coupled with self- and other-selected leaders from their own communities were a recognized need by all participants, across countries and situations. The present clinical support is insufficient, fragmentary, and not up-to-date in terms of gender.

Therapeutic guidelines: models of identification and grassroots mental healthcare initiatives

Generally speaking, the gender-fluid community struggles with finding role models. For such a small community as the gender-fluid Latino youth living in Toronto, the chances of encountering an all-encompassing leader are even more rare. However, communities tend to have natural leaders who, if given training and opportunity, may produce significant social change, strengthen social networks, and channel community resources to better serve underprivileged individuals and groups. As the participants in this study disclosed, many youth mentors have assumed leadership roles in important social initiatives; for instance, there is a group in formation applying for a small grant to participate in a trans march as a unique and distinct minority within youth groups.

The idea of leaders as being both innate and formed is one that resonates with Latin American political struggles all over the continent. Many youth can relate to this from their ancestral fights for land and social freedom through family stories, community circles, and from Indigenous notions of leadership which are grounded on principles of solidarity and collaboration. For this youth, taking the torch is, so to speak, part of a cultural desideratum, especially when forming certain aspects of the self such as body image, gender presentation, and representation, second-language acquisition, and re-defining a way of being in a new land. The words of Tabare form an apt summary to this aspect: "Leaders should come bottom up, and as part of our community movements" (Pat, p. 11). The identification, selection, and acceptance of grassroots leaders is a difficult process, particularly for recently formed diasporas, as is the case for the Latin American community in Toronto which began to form in the 1960s. Moreover, the incorporation of an LGTBQ agenda within Latin American and Latino activist movements is even more recent (since 1980), and gender-fluid identities have only become visible in the past decade at the most. Furthermore, partly because of the process of acculturation, some community leaders would incite gender-fluid youth to assimilate in order to access mainstream society and its perceived privileges. On the other hand, mental healthcare practitioners' perception of this population as homogeneous and stable—e.g. traditional heteronormative—limits their capacity to see gender-fluidity and to approach it in non-essentialist terms.

The idea that desired models of identification should emerge organically from within their own communities is coherent with the participants' own understanding of what a culturally sensitive mental healthcare model would look like: a long-term supported grassroots process, where initiatives are driven by the identified needs of the population and not by insurance company guidelines or budget restrictions. They would be interested in receiving support, including clinical direction, in configuring autonomous grassroots self-help groups that could facilitate mental healthcare services, such as securing safe and affordable housing for people struggling with mental illness, support in the process of requesting sex-reassignment surgery —with cultural interpreters if requested—and therapeutic support for transitioning individuals. Art-therapy based group and community counseling groups were also suggested, as a means to securing a healthy attachment to their newly formed communities of care. Needless to say, none of these services are currently available as they would require a paradigm shift in mainstream mental healthcare services. As Tabare articulates:

> For me, seeing any link between me as a person, my mental health needs, and community connections through any existing leader in the [. . .] community center is as foreign as going to a Dyke March. Trans Pride is the best community connection I have felt in years, but there is nothing yet for Indigenous Latino youth (that meant, in psychological terms, and in Spanish language as a clinical intervention), not a support or self-help group. The existing gay Latino group [. . .] is all about drugs, cross-dressing for fun, and excess not to feel their pain while keeping them marginalized from other opportunities. I don't want to be part of that. I have other dreams to dream.
>
> Tabare, pp. 7–8

Understanding themselves as diasporic selves—that is, as individuals made foreign through geographic, cultural, and linguistic displacement—Indigenous Latino gender-fluid youth do not see themselves fully reflected in a Queer community such as Toronto's, which still struggles to diversify and decolonize their political movement. While acknowledging the choice they themselves—or their parents or other family members—have made to migrate, they still harbor mixed emotions and ambiguity towards having roots in a foreign land as their diasporic condition imposes the challenge of having to negotiate between different and often contradictory value systems and worldviews.

An intersectional approach to gender-fluidity

Understanding gender-fluidity within an immigration process is no doubt challenging but absolutely necessary if we are to reduce barriers to mental healthcare access.

Border identities are, by definition, produced in sites of "occult instability" (Fanon, 1952), that require complex, contextually situated, and contingent negotiations of sociocultural meanings and identity/legibility markers. We live in a world where identity and critical subjectivity depend upon the process of translating a profusion of intersecting cultural meanings, and gender-fluid immigrant youth face the challenge of crafting a diasporic voice that integrates their multiple knowledges, temporalities, and geographical belongings through a reflexive and relational understanding of numerous, and often conflicting, cultural codes. The results of this study provided the researcher with a vivid reminder that we live in an oppressive regime in which identities are "teleologically" inscribed toward a standard end: the employable citizen (McLaren, 1995, p. 65). Most gender-fluid youth and many of their allies do not want to inscribe in this type of socially insular and politically marginal existence, as all the participants in this study expressed difficulty in conforming to what is expected of them in the deregulated, precarious, and labor-flexible economy. Border-youth have the possibility of living multidimensional lives through actively contesting oppression and marginalization through their ability to recuperate, translate, and make one's cultural knowledge relevant in a diasporic context. As participants explained, living a multidimensional life often means choosing to obscure or underplay certain aspects of their life; for instance, their preferred gender presentation in the workplace, or gender aspects or Indigenous background in processing refugee claims or in dealing with immigration authorities. These strategic negotiations constitute a form of translative knowledge through which border-youth navigate, resist, and actively transform their living conditions and integrate themselves into the larger community. Untrained clinical staff might pathologize these strategic identity negotiations when they, in fact, constitute productive and resourceful coping mechanisms that help these individuals navigate mainstream institutions.

One unexpected finding from this research was the fact that gender presentation resolution took precedence over immigrant trajectory and foreign origin, as all participants named the gender-fluidity aspect as more crucial than the geographical one. To clarify: while participants expressed that their gender-fluidity is not in itself a problem to resolve or a pathology to cure and displayed unusual insight for their chronological age regarding their gender choices, they were puzzled about the mental healthcare system's approach to their gender non-conformance and felt uncertain about its implications for accessing services. This added a new layer of complexity to experiences of discrimination and oppression previously undergone in their countries of origin. They expected that migration to Canada would ease gender oppression rather than impose on them the need for new translative learning in navigating mainstream institutions and settings. Most of the original literature on counseling the "different one" (Sue & Sue, 2008) presents a romanticized version of cultural adaptation that assumes that most people settle and assimilate into the receiving culture after a decade. Later research has shown (Tenenbaum, 2014) that this is clearly not the case since settlement is rarely a linear and unidirectional process and the migration itself poses adds challenges, drawbacks, and loss of status—social, cultural, and economic. Despite the fact that participants felt that Toronto has provided them with more opportunities for self-expression than their countries of origin, their institutional experiences did not mirror such openness or tolerance, which resulted in the participants' choice to discontinue their use of counseling resources.

Participants who are ambiguous in their gender presentation feel that they cannot access mental health programs. Pat, for instance, stated that "counsellors feel uncomfortable with me, always calling me by the wrong pronoun" (Pat, p. 2). The issue of how to call a border-gender youth is an important aspect of access and equity; it is important to ask rather than trying to guess. "I understand people might be confused by my appearance, and I don't mind to state my choice of pronoun, but most people are afraid to even approach me" (Rodrigo, p. 5). This could indicate the need to have a simple and honest communication with a teenager whose gender presentation is unconventional. Overall, a significant shift in perspective in what concerns therapeutic means and ends, the role of the clinician, and the purpose of mental healthcare services is paramount to the ability of counselors to be able to function in the real Toronto of today.

The results of the present study suggest that border-youth may engage in strategies of racial or gender passing as a protective mechanism when navigating the intersectional sources of oppression they face. For instance, they may conceal their indigenous identifications or gender-fluidity when needing to pass as Latino immigrants in accessing current programs. A culturally sensitive researcher thus needs to consider how the domains of sexuality, gender, cultural/linguistic, and political identity coexist in complex and often conflictual ways. Present frustrations with program guidelines and counselors/facilitators appear to arise from discrepancies among these domains and their rigid categorizations that usually focus on gender-fluidity as the most problematic aspect of border-youth identity.

These individuals are insightful pioneers, the makers of a newly emerging sub-community that is part of a larger sexually diverse community. They are also aware of the fact that they share common needs with other first-generation immigrants: securing permanent residence status, acquiring an acceptable level of proficiency in the English language, and obtaining safe housing (getting out of the shelter system and no longer being under-housed or at risk of homelessness, as declared by Rodrigo). These are their priorities, not their gender expression. As these participants expressed, they are new to the city and its institutional systems, not to their bodies:

> I know that I am living at the margins of society, but at least I am not at the margins of my most authentic identity: a gender-fluid teen that feels closer to Indian roots than to the white middle class, whether Canadian or Latino, and I get support and strength from the two people I know similar to me in my circumstances. Lonely? No, I rather have a community of three, than an alienation of millions out there. It would be nice if I can get counselling too, like anybody else, I have emotional needs to resolve.
>
> *Tabare, p. 16*

In these participants' experience, gender is an agentic project, an aspect of a self-affirming developmental process, and what they require from counselors and other mental healthcare providers is respect for their choices—including the right to determine and prioritize what is experienced as problematic in their lives—and genuine openness for exploration that is not driven by implicit agendas that pathologize or fail to recognize the social origins of individual suffering. "I have bigger fish to fry" was Rodrigo's response when asked whether he experienced his gender-fluidity as problematic. His comment resonates with most participants' experience that gender is not a problem to solve and that other needs, material and symbolic, take precedence as they struggle to make themselves at home in their new country while trying to heal the sedimented wounds of history and generating a connection to nature, spirit, and self.

In summary, solidarity—understood as the provision of care and safety for one another—and the possibility to freely and safely express their gender non-conformance were identified as key aspects of experiencing gender-fluidity as less problematic than their intersectional social location as racialized Indigenous Latino immigrant youth. One implication of these findings is the need to critically address the ways in which community counseling and clinical practices may be embedded in, complicit with, and at risk of replicating colonially oppressive practices that further marginalize, make invisible, and oppress these communities. Both Mona and Rodrigo expressed concerns over the generalized denial of the existence of Indigenous populations—both Canadian and South American—and over gender-oppressive practices that are common among mainstream clinicians, even guidance counselors in schools. For instance, Mona explained that "they [school guidance counselors] are always asking me the reason I want to dress like this and stated that I have a choice to dress differently to reduce the bullying I am regularly subjected to in high school" (Mona, p. 3). Mona further stated that we live in a "rape culture, as everybody knows" (Mona, p. 5) and she did not feel that the school counselors were willing to acknowledge or address systemic gender barriers, thus making gender harassment 'her' problem and failing to provide a safe space.

Lack of trust appears to be at the crux of the inability of existing programs to provide culturally-sensitive services. Trust was a concept defined by these participants as the fit between the client's expectations of therapeutic work and the counselor's ability to prioritize the client's needs and frame of reference. For instance, when assessing and treating culturally diverse clients, it is recommended that counselors ask clients for their expectations of therapy (Paniagua, 2005) instead of imposing their own perceptions and goals on them (Tenenbaum, 2008). Furthermore, Paniagua (2005) has recommended that "mental health professionals should be familiar with the meaning attached to the term 'therapist' across different cultural groups. American Indians often see therapists as medicine men or medicine woman and many Hispanics view therapists as 'folk healers'" (p. 22). This is consistent with the views expressed by these participants as they search for credibility less in the counselor's credentials than in their shared agreement around the therapeutic process and its aims, rapport-ability, and from appraisals of the therapist's healing power from other respected members of the community.

This essay has addressed key access-barriers to mental health services encountered throughout a decade of clinical work with border-youth at various university, hospital, and community settings in Toronto. My work's goal has been to support each and every participant in the process of becoming an integrated being, and from a psychological and culturally-sensitive compass, to accompany their flourishing and their search for harmony, self-fulfilment, and creative self-expression. My research findings advocate for a social justice approach that offers an alternative to individualistic therapeutic practice and proposes a shift towards a community-based model by linking interpersonal processes and larger social systems (Hernandez, 2008). Such an approach implies a contextual understanding of the other within the self, a basic tenet of the newcomer who brings their ancestors' history on their shoulders, a transgenerational inheritance that adds complexity and texture to the 'adaptation' process. Providing access to meaningful, culturally-aware, and socially just mental health programs and services requires making institutionally visible the needs of the Latin-American community in all their multiplicity, including the situated needs of a gender-fluid youth who do not accept working within the hegemonic parameters of the medical approach, border-youth individuals who do not live their gender-fluidity as disempowering pathology, and Spanish-speaking newcomers who are proud to claim their Indigenous ancestry.

Notes

1 Through the implementation of a narrative methodology that included two questionnaires, two interviews, and some quantitative data, my project was geared at identifying the historical and current impact of oppressive social forces, including "sexism, racism, homophobia, and classism in the practice of counseling psychology and family therapy" (Hernandez, 2008. p.10).
2 In this research, the term "Indigenous" refers to the collective name for the original peoples of what is the whole American territory today and their descendants, who before settlement by Europeans, thrived and met all their material and spiritual needs through the resources that the natural land had to offer (Waldram, 2004) The Canadian Constitution (1982) recognizes three distinct groups of Indigenous peoples: "Indians, Inuit and Metis" (Aboriginal Affairs and Northern Development Canada [AANDC], 2011; Assembly of First Nations [AFN], 2002). The Canadian government, through the *Indian Act* in all its subsequent amendments until the present iterations and after its major overhaul in 1985, legally defines what it is to be "Indian," but not "Indigenous." However, Indigenous is defined in the Constitution, the highest law of Canada. Thus, "First Nations" is not a legally recognized term for an individual by the Canadian government. Most countries in Latin America follow similar silencing tactics. The Indian Act's terminology is often used by Canadian Indigenous people themselves, while their Latin American counterparts living in Toronto tend to self-identify as Indigenous. Because the term indigenous has no legal standing, individuals seeking landing status in Canada, such as Latin Americans with international Indigenous ancestry, cannot use their origin as grounds for a claim as part of the refugee seeking process, limiting the reasons claimants can cite for fleeing oppressive existing realities in Latin American countries.

References

American Psychiatric Association (2013). *Diagnostic of Statistical Manual of Mental Disorders*, 5th Edition.

Cohen-Kettenis, P. T., & Wallien, M. S. (2008). Psychosexual outcome of gender-dysphoric children. *Journal of the American Academy of Child & Adolescent Psychiatry, 47*(12), 1413–1423. doi: 10.1097/CHI.0b013e31818956b9

Cohen-Kettenis, P. T., & Friedemann, P. (2003). Transgenderism and intersexuality in childhood and adolescence: Making choices. *Developmental Clinical Psychology and Psychiatry*, Vol. 46. Thousand Oaks, CA: Sage.

Dolski, M. (2013, December 30). The two solitudes of two-spirit. *DailyXtra*. Retrieved from: http://dailyxtra.com/canada/news/the-two-solitudes-two-spirit

Fanon, F. (1952). *Black Skin, White Masks*. New York, NY: Grove Press.

McLaren, P. (1995). White terror and oppositional agency: Towards a critical multiculturalism. In C. E. Sleeter & P. McLaren (Eds.), *Multicultural education, critical pedagogy, and the politics of difference* (pp. 33–63). New York, NY: SUNY Press.

Paniagua, F. (2005). *Assessing and Treating Culturally Diverse Clients: A Practical Guide*. Thousand Oaks, CA: Sage.

Shelley, C. A. (2008). *Transpeople: Repudiation, Trauma, Healing*. U of T Press.

Smith, L., Chambers, D., & Bratini, L. (2009). When oppression is the pathogen: The participatory development of socially just mental health practice. *American Journal of Orthopsychiatry, 79*(2), 159–168.

Statistics Canada. (2009). *Aboriginal peoples in Canada in 2006: Inuit, Métis and First Nations, 2006 Census*. Ottawa, ON: Statistics Canada. Statistics Canada. (2010). Ottawa, ON: Statistics Canada. http://www12.statcan.ca/english/census06/analysis/labour/pdf/97-559-XIE2006001.pdf

Sue & Sue (2008). *Counselling the Culturally Diverse*, New York.

Tenenbaum, S. (2012, May). *Process of schooling an Aboriginal Mexican refugee in a punitive educational system: A Canadian case study*. Paper session presented at Trans-Rights as Human Rights: The Implications for Trans-Healthcare, Linköping, Sweden.

Tenenbaum, S. (2011, August). *Trans-sensuality in a rigid society: A comparison Uruguay-Canada*. Paper presented at the Gender Odyssey Family Conference, Seattle, USA.

Tenenbaum, S. (2010a, February). *Identity, otherness, and attachment struggles in a gender-affirming child and his family of origin: A Canadian ethnographic account through the evolution of his drawings*. Paper session presented at the third Bi-annual Gay & Lesbian Affirmative Psychotherapy Transgender Symposium, New York, USA.

Tenenbaum, S. (2010b, November). *Application of the "Ulysses Syndrome" in Toronto*. Paper session presented at the World Conference on Ethno-Psychiatry, Barcelona, Spain.

Tenenbaum, S. (2008). The concept of the "other" in counselling: Diversity and clinical implications for a better practice. In: *Honouring the Past, Shaping the Future: 25 Years of Progress in Mental Health Advocacy and Rights Protection* (pp. 170–172). Toronto, ON: Psychiatric Patient Advocate Office.

Valentine, D. (2007). *Imagining transgender: An ethnography of a category*. London, UK: Duke. University Press.

11
TRANSGENDERISM IN IRAN

Mehrdad Eftekhar Ardebili

In this narrative review, the concept of transgenderism will be discussed in Iranian culture, and its distinctive features will be highlighted. Considering the differences between Iran and Western countries in terms of religion and its role in ordinary life, religious authorities' hegemony, and the attitude towards gender and human rights, transgenderism is conceptualized in a completely different framework in Iran. This study aims to answer these questions: How does the social context, including patriarchal, ideological, heterosexist attitudes, and the traditional binary gender model, affect the presentations of transgenderism in Iran? In what ways is the present medicolegal approach shaping the phenomenon of transgenderism and how is it perceived by the society and transgender individuals? What are the effects of this approach on the other sexual minorities? What is the outcome of sex reassignment surgery (SRS) in this community?

Transgenderism in this study is used as a term broadly encompassing all expressions of gender variance characteristics (Buck, 2016). Transsexuality is a medical term and is used for strong and persistent cross-gender identification and seeking for sex-reassignment surgery.

Overview of the current situation

Undoubtedly, the history of contemporary situation of transgender phenomenon in Iran goes back to Imam Khomeini's Fatwa in 1967 (Ayatollah Khomeini, 1967). He considered SRS permissible in response to Ms. Molkara, one of the first transwomen who underwent this surgery in Iran. His influence, charisma, and position after the Islamic revolution in Iran in 1979 led other *faghihs* to accept this; sex change became an acceptable medical, legitimate, and legal process after the revolution.

The applicants for gender reassignment, either independently or through a referral made by the judiciary system, can go to certain "diagnosis and evaluation centers" (for a period of time, the only reliable center in Iran had been a center in a university, Tehran Psychiatric Institute). The psychiatrists, clinical psychologists, and social workers of the centers are expected to be in contact with the patient for at least a period of six months. The main task of the centers is to approve the proper diagnosis, rule out differential diagnosis such as psychosis and homosexuality, and help the patient in his/her decision by delivering individual and family counseling. Psychiatrists and clinical psychologists in these centers use their clinical judgment to identify "true transsexuals," who will receive the certificate of having the disorder. The patients and the records are then referred to the Forensic Medicine Organization (FMO) at the end of this period. Judges arrive at the verdict of "permission to sex change" after the approval of the FMO committee—which is situated between the medical and judiciary systems. Afterwards, the patient may seek hormonal treatments and surgical reconstructions. They can obtain their personal ID only after the FMO approves the main surgical procedures that have been performed.

The prevailing attitude toward transsexuality among psychiatrists, psychologists, religious authorities, and judges is based on the medical model; transsexuality is regarded as a biological error, with transsexuals born into the wrong body, needing surgical intervention to reform their bodies. The medical model serves to support and reproduce the binary gender model (Rosqvist et al., 2014). Therefore, we can say that the gender variances are acceptable only when there is a need for SRS; other gender variances are not recognizable. The prevailing medical model rejects transsexuality as a natural form of human variability (Dallas Denny, n.d.); so, there is no such thing as transgender identity in Iran. This medical view is condemned and criticized by many influential psychiatrists and psychologists who believe sex change could not essentially be regarded as a therapeutic intervention.

Clinicians are not obliged to back their ideas by scientific research evidence. Rather, they defend their views based on presuppositions, their own clinical experience, and a few published case reports (Khodayarifard & Abedini, n.d.). A number of psychiatrists that were asked to lead a panel in the Annual Conference of Psychiatric Association 2015 emphasized psychotherapeutic drug treatment and psychotherapy as the only acceptable therapy. These psychiatrists oppose reassignment surgery altogether and recommend a combination of medications (mainly anti-psychotics) along with a form of religious inspired psychotherapy, aimed at "converting" the trans person ideas about their desire to transition. Although many of these psychiatrists are influential in universities, they have not been able to change the ongoing process yet.

The possibility of performing sex change in Iran is a significant event and has attracted a lot of attention worldwide, though it could not be regarded as a sign of sexual freedom or human rights. The legitimate solution for transgender individuals is be labeled with a disorder, transsexuality or gender dysphoria, and undergo SRS. Therefore, if a trans person decides not to undergo SRS, it will be illegitimate to present as his/her current gender. Cross-dressing is illegal and illegitimate too, and a transgender has to perform all religious practices according to the anatomical sex before the main surgeries. The determined fate of sex change may be aligned with normative social desire to protect the current discourse and acceptable formal existing conceptions of masculinity and femininity, and to prevent blurring the boundary between them. The permission to undergo sex change, therefore, is regarded as an attempt to eliminate a group of sexual minorities, and the concept of gender variance, and an avoidance of the traditional society to encounter sexual otherness.

In this inflexible perspective on gender and sexuality, changing the discourse of conceptualization of transgenderism from medical to human right will probably abort the possibility of sex-reassignment surgery in Iran and, at the same time, will pin transsexuality to other sexual and gender variances into the domain of perversion and immorality. It seems that since human rights discourses are understood and treated differently in different parts of the world, the excision of the category from the classification system in the next version of the International Classification of Diseases (ICD) might eliminate any conceptualization or acceptance of the term in Iran or some other countries.

The effects of legal favoritism toward transsexuality

The double standard approach to transsexuality and homosexuality—placing one in the medical/legal/legitimate framework and subsuming the other under the category of sins deserving to be punished severely—has some consequences. Here are some articles pertaining to same-sex behaviors illustrating the harsh approach to same-sex behavior (Islamic Penalty Codes, 2013):

Article 110: The prescribed punishment for homosexual relations in case of intercourse is execution and the mode of the execution is at the discretion of the religious judge.
Article 111: Homosexual intercourse leads to execution provided that both the active and the passive party are of age, sane, and consenting.
Article 112: Where a person of age commits homosexual intercourse with an adolescent, the active party shall be executed and the passive party, if he has not been reluctant, shall receive a flogging of up to seventy-four lashes.
Article 113: Where an adolescent commits homosexual intercourse with another adolescent, they shall receive a flogging of up to seventy-four strokes of the whip unless one of them has been reluctant;
Article 127: Lesbianism is [defined as] homosexuality of women with their sexual organs.
Article 129: The penance of lesbianism is one hundred lashes for each party.
Article 131: If lesbianism is repeated three times and after each time the penance is executed, the penance on the fourth time is execution.

Nevertheless, the presence of these articles does not mean homosexuals are executed in Iran, as some may imagine. It has been said that homosexuals are persuaded to undergo sex change in Iran, facing the options of either sex change or death (Carter, 2011). This hypothesis is portraying a cruel and revengeful situation in Iran similar to what is depicted in the Almodovar film *The Skin I Live In*. This however, is not supported by evidence. To the best of my knowledge, there is no known report of individuals who have been forced to undergo SRS. That said, there is some truth in this hypothesis, which relates to the overlap between transgenderism and homosexuality. In fact, the more plausible hypothesis is that persons who have questioned their gender identify themselves as transsexuals in order to conform to social norms. In order to handle guilt feelings about their homosexuality, some indeed select to undergo SRS.

We should be reminded that the criminalizing attitude toward homosexuality is internalized in Iranian culture, and thus there is an internal pressure and guilt in addition to external demands. According to this hypothesis, SRS, as the only exit door available to sexual minorities to feel accepted and not persecuted socially, may attract Iranians who are in lesser conflict with their gender and who may not identify as transsexuals, as compared with Western countries. However, this hypothesis is in contradiction with three known fact. First, the reported epidemiologic findings about the lower rate of sex change in Iran than Western countries do not support this hypothesis. Second, in a patriarchal society that idealizes masculinity, men who become woman are stigmatized and rejected at the same rate as homosexuals. Thirdly, homosexuals and transsexuals have their own distinct groups and communities in Iran; illustrating two highly stigmatized communities (Khoshnnod et al., 2013) which also tend to stigmatize each other in the attempt to demarcate and differentiate themselves. This reaction may be considered as a coping response to identity threats that target their core existence, which leads persons in each group to react by approaching and identifying more closely with their group (Major & O'Brien, 2005).

Epidemiology of transsexuality and sex-reassignment outcomes in Iran

In one descriptive cross-sectional study, all psychiatric records of transsexuals referred between April 2002 and March 2009 to the Tehran Psychiatric Institute (TPI) were reviewed. In this time frame, 281 subjects with the official diagnosis of Gender Identity Disorder were seen. Male-to-female and female-to-male GIDs made up 49.1% and 50.9% of cases, respectively. Therefore, the sex ratio of MTF: FTM transsexuality was 0.96:1. Given the assumption that the majority of GID subjects in Iran were referred to TPI in that period of time, the authors concluded that the prevalence of GID (with similar rates in two types) in Iran during 2002–2008 would be at least 1/141,000 population. The authors warn that the calculated prevalence is possibly an underestimated prevalence because factors such as low public awareness, legal and religious limitations, family rejection due to traditional values, social stigmatization, and limited social services also affect help-seeking behavior in subjects with gender dysphoria.

One of the interesting findings of this recent study was the equal presentation of transsexuality among both sexes. A prior research in 1996 reported the male-to-female to female-to-male ratio among transsexuals as 1.85/1 (Mehrabi, 1996). The implied conclusion is that the sex ratio of transsexuality has been changing during the past 20 years: more biological females ask for sex change. In a study (Saeedloo et al., 2013) 32 female-to-male and 15 male-to-female transsexuals who had been admitted between 2005 and 2010 to the TPI were interviewed. According to this study, surgical process was considered as the most problematic part of their sex reassignment journey. Going through the process of transitioning in an organization associated with forensic medicine, obtaining psychotherapy treatment, and meeting a psychiatrist were ranked next. Meanwhile, 23.4 percent of patients did not recognize any difficulty in the process of their treatment. None of the patients had regrets about undergoing surgical reassignment, though two of them were not satisfied with the quality of their surgeries. In addition, none of the patients had ever thought of going back or regretting their transition. The religious attitude and practice of trans persons changed during the experience of gender transformation; a moving from religiosity to spirituality (Safavifar et al., 2016).

Stigma

Iranian society is a traditional society with two officially recognized genders, each having its own separate and different attires, roles, rights, and so on. In preschool years, the difference is not prominent and children of both genders can freely play together. The sharp demarcation between the two gender starts on the first day of school, when boys go to boys' school and girls go to girls' school. Many trans persons recount how they faced the conflict between their anatomy and gender for the first time in their life on the first day at school. The age at whicht religious practice is mandatory comes sooner for girls at 9 and, from then on, they have to wear hijab which gives them a completely different look from boys. In Iranian two-gendered society, persons who blur the demarcation between genders are labeled with a disorder. In a qualitative study conducted in Iran (Eghbalian et al., 2012) trans persons expressed the social challenges in their everyday life: their appearance attracts others' attentions in various social situations, they were labeled with a disorder, satirized, mistreated, and at times prosecuted. Many trans persons are not able to withstand the difficulties in workplaces and schools and other educational centers, and are forced to leave or hide. They may struggle to tolerate their discomfort, and behave in accordance to the expectations. High school and university dropout rates as well as unemployment are a common experiences in trans persons narratives. In some cases, this social pressure leads to self-imposed complete isolation. The situation inside the home is not better than the external environment. When a trans person shares his/her feeling with relatives, others often react as if this was the first time they have noticed their child's conflicts with his/her gender.

Iranian families commonly believe that trans persons' identity is caused by media and social network influence. In the mentioned study, the trans persons recounted stories of being insulted, intimidated, forced to wear hijab and do military service, and even imprisoned. Some have been forced to get married due to their family's belief that there is not a serious problem in their child's core identity, and suppose these feelings will fade with marriage. Since families in Iran have more authority over their female child and have the right to decide about their child's marriage, the pressure to get married is more prominent in female-to-male trans persons.

Ahmadzad et al. have shown that 7.4 percent of their study female-to-male transsexuals had a history of prior marriage (2011), which is higher than the rate in some other countries. For example, in a study in Japan, the frequency of marriage as a female in female-to-male transsexuals has been reported to be very low (Okabe et al., 2007). At the same line to illustrate more limitation in female-to-male transpersons, one study shows that the first psychiatric visit and first SRS are respectively 4.4 and 2.5 years later in female-to-male that male-to-female trans persons (Saeedloo et al., 2013), which may mean that they are more likely to disclose their own identity and begin to live according to their own wish later than male-to-female transsexuals.

Families of trans persons themselves are mocked in society; they feel they have lost their face, have to hide their child's problem, or force him to change his idea. In fact, it may be supposed that the families are transferring the pressure that the society is exerting upon them onto their child. One study conducted on the family environment of transsexuals and homosexuals in Iran found that most families are disorganized and conflict-oriented, which the authors interpreted as an expression of the effect of stigmatization on the family (Shayestehkhou et al., 2008). Given the patriarchal culture of Iran, there is less tolerance for the transitioning of a boy to a girl and in such cases the family of the trans person typically experiences significant shame (Eftekhar & Moshtagh, 2007).

There is a very interesting finding in another qualitative study (Bidaki et al., 2010) in Iran. The participants of this study, who were all female-to-male transsexuals in the process of screening for being medically eligible for sex change, expressed discomfort over the generally pathologizing attitudes of Iranians toward transsexuality, who are being morally categorized as perverts: "they see us as problematic individuals like homosexuals". The negative social attitude is so disturbing, however, that trans persons prefer to be categorized as having a medical disorder (gender dysphoria), accepting the pathologizing view, to get rid of social pressures. Trans persons often feel that the public is largely ignorant about transgender/transsexuality, and call upon social groups and medical authorities to provide education about this disorder, believing that once they are recognized as having a diagnosable disorder, they will obtain greater financial access and emotional support from organizations.

In the past 15 years trans persons have formed some nongovernmental organizations (NGOs) and support groups. One of the recent organizations is Mahta (n.d.), the center for supporting Iranian trans persons. The organization provides information and skills that will help trans persons challenges they may encounter socially, at work and at home. Joining such groups, often assists trans persons in reframing the stigma of mental deviancy. The current reframing, however, often involves relying on a medical model that considers the root cause of their identity to be linked with childhood trauma or mental illness, rather than moral deviancy. In such groups, individuals are often encouraged to "be brave" and accept that they are suffering from a disorder similar to other medical diseases like diabetes. In this meaning-making process (Frost, 2011), trans persons may realize that they do not deserve to be blamed for their condition, and attribute the cause of the stigma to social factors. This, in turn, may contribute to dramatic positive effects on their wellbeing, mood, and sociability.

In this chapter, the distinctive features of transgenderism in Iran were reviewed. Although it appears that there is a legal favoritism towards transsexuality in Iran, as compared with homosexuals, the attitudes toward transgenderism and homosexuality are, in essence, similar. Trans identity has no place in a dichotomous two-gendered society, and, like homosexuality, is disavowed. The discourse currently used is predominantly a medical one, where language around trans identity is framed using vocabulary associated with mental illness (e.g. usage of terms such as transsexuality or gender identity disorder rather than transgenderism). It is also framed around a medicolegal discourse. It could be assumed that if there was surgical treatment of homosexuality, it would be a legal and acceptable intervention. To accommodate to this situation, trans persons in Iran are defining themselves within this recognizable framework. Changing the discourse from a disease (medical) to that based on human rights (similar to the approach taken in many Western countries, where transsexuality is no longer conceptualized as a mental disorder and will be taken out of the next edition of the ICD) may have some deleterious effects on their condition in Iran and perhaps other similar cultures. In the current medico-legal framework, trans persons are attempting to improve their condition through founding NGOs, enabling groups, presence in media, and enhancement of general population knowledge about transgenderism. The effects of these activities on their condition, health indicators, and stigma have yet to be explored.

References

Ahmadzad-Asl, M., Jalali, A., Alavi, K., Naserbakht, M., Taban, M., Mohsennia, K., & Eftekhar, M. (2011). The epidemiology of transsexuality in Iran. *Gay and Lesbian Mental Health*, 15, 83–93.

Ayatollah Khomeini, R. (1967). Commentaries on the liberation of the intercession. In R. Ayatollah Khomeini, *Tahrir al-w'asila* (pp. 753–755). Najaf: Matba'at al-Adab.

Bidaki, R., Ahmadzad-Asl, M., & Taban, M. (2010). *The experiences of female to male transsexuals in Tehran*. Tehran: Iran University of Medical Sciences.

Buck, D. M. (2016). Defining transgender: What do lay definitions say about prejudice? *Psychology of Sexual Orientation and Gender Diversity*, 3(4), 465–472.

Carter, B. (2011). Sex-change or die option as the alternative to the death sentencing of homosexuals. *The Journal of Gender, Race & Justice*, 14, 797–832.

Dallas Denny, M. (n.d.). Changing models of transsexualism. *Journal of Gay & Lesbian Psychotherapy*, 8(1–2), 25–40.

Eftekhar, M., & Moshtagh, N. (2007). Transsexualism, Iran. In S. Josef (Ed.), *Encyclopedia of women & Islamic cultures*, Vol. IV (pp. 145–146). Leiden, Boston: Brill.

Eghbalian, M., Eftekhar, M., & Negarandeh, R. (2012). *Experiences of stigma in trans persons referred to sex-clinic of Tehran Institute of Psychiatry.* Tehran: Iran University of Medical Sciences.

Frost, D. M. (2011). Social stigma and its consequences for the socially stigmatized. *Social and Personality Psychology Compass,* 5(11), 824–839.

Islamic Penalty Codes. (2013). Tehran: Supreme Court.

Khodayarifard, M., & Abedini, Y. (n.d.). *Treatment of gender identity disorder based on cognitive behavioral family Therapy: A case report.* Retrieved from: psyedu.ut.ac.ir/acstaff/khodayarifard/. . ./APF-22.pdf

Khoshnnod, K., Hashemian, F., Moshtagh, N., & Eftekhari, M. (2013). Social stigma, homosexuality and transsexuality in Iran. *sexologies,* 17(null), S69.

Mahta (n.d.). Retrieved 05 17, 2016, from: www.mahta.com.

Major, B., & O'Brien, O. T. (2005). The social psychology of stigma. *Annual Review of Psychology,* 56, 393-421.

Mehrabi, F. (1996). Some characteristics of Iranian transsexuals. *Iranian Journal of Psychiatry and Clinical Psychology,* 2(3), 6–12.

Okabe, N., Sato, T., Matsumoto, Y., Ido, Y., Terada, S., & Kuroda, S. (2007). Clinical characteristics of patients with gender identity disorder at a Japanese gender identity disorder clinic. *Psychiatry Research,* 15(157), 315–318.

Rosqvist, H. B., Nordlund, L., & Kaiser, N. (2014). Developing an authentic sex: Deconstructing developmental-psychological discourses of transgenderism in a clinical setting. *Feminism & Psychology,* 24(1), 20–36.

Saeedloo, M., Jalali, A., & Eftekhar, M. (2013). *Evaluation of the outcome of genital reconstruction surgery in gender identity disorder Patients in Iran.* Tehran: Iran University of Medical Sciences.

Safavifar, F., Eftekhar,, M., Alavi, K., Negarandeh, R., Jalali, A., & Eftekhar, M. (2016). Religious experiences of Iranian trans persons: A qualitative study. *Medical Journal of the Islamic Republic of Iran,* 30, 385–392.

Shayestehkhou, S., Moshtah, N., Eftekhar, M., & Mehrabi, F. (2008). T01-O-17 Family environment of homosexual and transsexuals in Iran. *Sexologies,* 17(Supplement 1), S55–S56.

PART III
Cultural montage

12
TO RETURN TO SCHREBER
Trans literatures as psychoanalysis[1]

Trish Salah

What might it mean, to call for "a return to Schreber"? And why might one want to? The former Saxon judge and subject of Sigmund Freud's *Psycho-Analytic Notes on an Autobiographical Account of a Case of Paranoia* has long been known as "by far the most famous mental patient ever" (Allison et al., 1988, p. 2), and is prominently positioned within the canons of psychoanalytic and psychiatric and, for that matter, anti-psychiatric and anti-psychoanalytic thought. Further, given Schreber's associations with psychoses, abuse, homophobia, misogyny, racism and fascism, why turn to Schreber as a resource for thinking a trans-positive psychoanalysis?

In this chapter I contend that psychoanalytic reading of (trans) sexuation may be substantially enriched by turning to the creative writing of transgender authors,[2] whose texts offer rich if ambivalent representations of sexuality's relationship to identity, desire, and knowledge. Transgender literature is currently enjoying something of a renaissance, and throws into critical relief not only analytic discourses but the phantasmatic uses made of trans figures in the writing of cis authors, and elsewhere I explore this work under the rubrics of trans genre and Tiresian poetics (Salah, 2017). Much of what is exciting about the new transgender writing is that it imagines and speaks to trans audiences first,[3] contra a tradition of memoir writing, which as Jay Prosser has shown, originates in the clinician's office in conditions that require the author warrant her (or his) self intelligible, diagnosable, and palatable to the non-trans expert (Prosser, 1998, 140–152).

In this chapter, however, I want to make the perhaps paradoxical argument that a text elaborated as memoir before it became case study—Daniel Paul Schreber's writing of subjective dissolution and feminine rebirth—provides analytic and imaginative resources for thinking about not only sexuation, but dialectics of desire and abjection in the formation of cultural, racial, and gender identifications, as well as occasions reflection on the relationship of transsexuality, transgender, psychoanalysis, and the clinic. I propose that Schreber's *Memoir* might allow us to do so for three reasons: first, because as a reading, Freud's interpretation of Schreber's "cross sexed wish" has been historically influential in constituting contemporary discourses of sexual orientation, gender identity, and mental health; second, because Schreber's text grapples with many of the philosophical and sexological concerns animating the Freudian project, from an incipiently transgender sexed position; and third because Schreber's text offers a poetics of identity that complicates and perhaps decenters psychoanalytic and social constructivist accounts that too readily equate narrative and subjective formation. In this chapter, then, I want to consider both how Schreber has been written and how Schreber might write us otherwise.

Cultural and psychoanalytic commenters often underline that Schreber "was not a transsexual" even while deploying Lacan's reading of Schreber to diagnose transsexuality as, or as overly proximate to, psychosis. This is the trajectory at least since Catherine Millot's account of transsexuals in terms of Lacan's later formulation of "horsexe," the outside of sex, in a position at one remove from psychosis, structurally speaking. According to Millot, transsexual women identify with *The Woman*, attempting to embody the phallus in a near psychotic state, while trans men might either identify with ordinary men, simply evidencing an atypical assumption of sexed position, and phallic lack, or with a third gender category, beyond male and female—a position Millot references as the sex of Angels, and clinically designates as another form of phallic identification, a refusal of any lack in being. While Millot acknowledges the possibility of ordinary transsexuals, the gesture seems disingenuous given the ways her text spectacularly thematizes trans femininity as psychotic, most emblematically via Daniel Paul Schreber. And under the name of Schreber much clinical literature has proceeded as if transsexual psychoses were the rule.[4]

Against thematic, decontextual and overly interpretive deployments of Freudian concepts, Lacan staged his return to Freud as one of close reading, a tarrying with the difficulties Freud's text poses, a polemic against its premature closure in the service of peace of mind and profession. So, then, too, to return to Schreber, we must ask what's difficult, what interrupts the sense, the use we've made of hir[5] name or text. In a word, then, to return to Schreber is to return the repressed. But whose? And to whom?

Daniel Paul Schreber's *Denkwürdigkeiten eines Nervenkranken* or *Great Thoughts of a Nerve Patient* was published in 1903 and it was some years later, through Jung, that Freud came to be its most famous reader, one who declared "the wonderful Schreber . . . ought to have been made a professor of psychiatry and director of a mental hospital" (Woods, 2011, p. 245).[6] The book details Schreber's second period of illness, one preceded by dreams that a previous illness had returned, and the liminal yet prefigurative daydream or thought that it might "be very nice to be a woman submitting to the act of copulation" (Freud, 1911/1963, p. 108).

Schreber's book chronicles a metaphysically forced feminization in which his body was changed from male to female through the medium of "nerves of voluptuousness," and the agency of Schreber's doctors, and later in accord with the will of a God (or Gods) whose motives change over time but ultimately require Schreber's unmanning to preserve or restore the Order of World. Freud's reading of the case discovered a version of the Oedipus complex run amuck: on this account Schreber assumed "a feminine position" in relation to the father, which later became the object of Schreber's persecutory transference toward his physician, Dr. Flechsig, and onto God himself. Schreber's fantasies of persecution, which took the form of a question about the Other's destructive desire, were over time rearticulated as a savior fantasy, one in which Schreber acceded to the necessity or desirability of becoming a woman for the sake of the order of the world.

A feature of Schreber's narrative that is much remarked upon is the way in which the "delusion" uncannily encodes Freud's libido theory and his theory that psychoses in paranoia arise from repressed homosexuality. "Schreber's delusional formation sounds almost like endosomatic perceptions of the processes whose existence I have assumed . . . as the basis for paranoia" (1911/1963, pp. 181–182).

More than well known, as a signifier the name of Schreber has become both overwrought and overdetermined. It would take more space than I have here to do more than sketch a partial and thematic history of the reception, interpretation, and reiteration of Schreber's text and thought.[7]

- Freud and Lacan read an *Oedipal Schreber* arising from family complexes and linking paranoia and delusions of grandeur (apocalypse and salvation), psychoses, repressed homosexuality, and forced feminization (to salve the desire of the Other). Ida Macalpine and Richard Hunter quarrel with Freud's equation of feminization and repressed homosexuality, arguing the latter is less significant than Schreber's pregnancy wish, and articulate a counternarrative to this framework.
- *Abused Schreber* is read by psychiatrists Niederland and Schatzman as suffering delusions directly recapitulating the various "torturous" techniques and regimes to which he was subjected as a child by his father Moritz Schreber, a theorist of medicalized pedagogies for rescuing the German volk from fin de siècle decadence.
- *Fascist Schreber* is understood by Elias Canetti, in *Crowds and Power*, to have unwittingly transcribed, in his symptomatology, aggressively xenophobic and nationalist social fantasies and an annihilating and submissive desire for an absolute leader that anticipated the rise of National Socialism.
- Deleuze and Guattari's *Anti-Oedipal Schreber* combines elements of the previous versions and signifies the reductiveness of an instrumental contraction of life-story to case history, person to analytic example; though *the person* is a fiction no less subject to critique. This Schreber serves as metonym for the antipsychiatry strand within the larger liberationist movement of their text, but as one ambivalently weighted as they accept, by and large, Canetti's diagnosis of Schreber as proto-fascist. Anti-Oedipal Schreber ghosts Foucault's accounts of institutional and discursive power which, as Santner demonstrates, closely replicate the rhetoric and the (metaphysical) analytic of Schreber's Order of the World.
- *Anti-Semitic Schreber* is a further specification of *Fascist Schreber* that is also a reading of Freud (what we might call the Schreber-in-Freud), by Sander

Gilman, Jay Geller, and Daniel Boyerin, in which Schreber's identifications with Jewishness, feminization, rot, etc. take on particular force in light of Freud's reduction of them to suppressed homosexuality. Read through nineteenth-century discourses of racial degeneracy that concatenate effeminacy, homosexuality, Jewish manhood, sexual diseases, and madness, and through Freud's own complex and repressed identifications with homosexuality, femininity, and Jewishness, this Schreber emerges in the intersections of anti-racist and new historicist projects as a sign for psychoanalysis's foundational blind spots and self-inflicted wounds.

- As mentioned above, Catherine Millot's *Horsexe* is one of a number of Lacanian accounts that inscribe transsexuality as or through psychoses. Another name for this iteration might be the *Push-towards-Woman*. MacAlpine and Hunter render a more sympathetic iteration of *Transsexual Schreber*, one invested with the possibility of non-psychotic transsexualities. *Schreber-as-Transsexual* functions to highlight the (historical) valences and violent productivity of institutional discourses that take up the gender-crossing subject without regard for how s/he might live in the world, and deepens our consideration of how the over-determination of sexual identity engages similarly overdetermined affective, narrative, generic, and cognitive identifications of and with otherness.
- *Abject Schreber*, variously given shape by Lyotard, de Certeau, and most fully by Santner, is read for a more ambiguous, ambivalent, and potentially ethical movement of disidentifications with God, Phallicism, Race-purity and identifications with luder, rot, women, prostitutes, non-Europeans, and Jews. This *Schreber* correlates to growing interest in the ambivalences and violence determining individual and collective identities.

In *Please Select Your Gender* Patricia Gherovici proposes that Schreber's *Memoirs of My Nervous Illness* be read as a prototype of the genre of transsexual autobiography. She notes that "Schreber was to Freud what Joyce is to Lacan," a name under which was written jouissance as sinthome, one holding text and body together (2010, p. 232). Developing Lacan's view that sexuation turns finally upon the subject's relation to the figure of loss and the discernment of death, Gherovici distances herself from clinical narratives that seem to render transsexuals psychically rigid, or entrapped. After all, there is no subject without a sinthome.

Conversely, Oren Gozlan's *Transsexuality and the Art of Transition* thematizes transsexuality as both a mode of sexuation among others, and an aesthetic and analytic repertoire which enables us to think the sexed body as mysterious, and unsettled in its meanings. Reading for the novelty of sexes' emplotment in the memoir of the famous "nineteenth-century hermaphrodite" Herculine Barbin,[8] and Jeffrey Eugenides' bestselling "gender novel" *Middlesex*, a picaresque fictional memoir of a late twentieth-century hermaphrodite, Gozlan approaches these intersex narratives for the trans genre fantasies they both encode and invite (2015, pp. 30–31).

I take the term "gender novel" from Casey Plett's definition: "books . . . penned by cisgender—that is, non-transgender—authors . . . a very twenty-first-century sub-genre: sympathetic novels about transition by people who haven't transitioned" (2015). Importantly, for Plett, these novels "fail to communicate what it's actually like to transition" relying instead upon a series of clichéd and often transphobic tropes and sentimental, unidimensional depictions of heroic outsiders struggling against adversity (2015). Underlying much of Plett's criticism of such texts is the argument that such "gender novels" are not only not written by transsexuals, they are neither for transsexuals nor actually about us. My own argument exploits the hopefully productive tensions between this important identity political argument and Gozlan's appeal to trans aesthetics as a way of reconceiving our approach to sexuality and the human. Of course as Gozlan notes, neither Herculine Barbin nor Cal, the protagonist of *Middlesex*, are transsexual. Both texts are perhaps trans genre, however, in as much as that genre marks an assymetrically inhabited

It is in this spirit that I take up Gherovici's proposal, to rethink accounts of transsexuality and psychoses, and their clinical and social conditions of possibility, through a reading Schreber's text as a source of theoretical insight, as well as a persistent enigma, one that can be productively put into dialogue with both the history of its reception and contemporary trans genre writing.

To do so I suggest we read Daniel Paul Schreber's textualization of jouissance and phantasy of involuntary feminization less as the memoir of a psychotic and more as a biomythography[9] contoured by racial and sexual anxieties and psychic suffering. Schreber's text is not only richly generative for psychoanalysis's theorizing of sexuality, the ego and the unconscious, the psychotic, but also displaces psychoanalytic certainties as to what is a sex, sexual difference, the difference between theory and fantasy or transference and influence, neurosis or psychosis. If the unconscious knows no contradiction, we might say Schreber knows them all.

I should say that if this approach is novel, the idea that Schreber might offer a critique of the clinic is not. In the first instance it is Schreber's, with Freud coming in a close second.[10] The relevance of this idea for thinking about transsexuality turns up in the translator's introduction to the English-language edition of Schreber's memoirs, that of the Ms. MacAlpine (and the unnamed Mr. Hunter) so scathingly dismissed by Lacan. And in an early corrective to a queer feminism that seemed to be taking its cues from Millot's version of Lacan, Diane Morgan underscores the radicality of the non-pathologizing construction of transsexuality produced in MacAlpine and Hunter's introduction to their translation of Schreber's book (Morgan, 1999, p. 226–227). At a time marked by the appearance of "cases of change of sex reported in the newspapers" (MacAlpine and Hunter, 1955, p. 405), rather than cast Schreber as suffering from repressed homosexuality, they describe hir as a "transvestite," a term then used interchangeably with transsexual. Schreber is described as having a "fantasy of being transformed gradually 'over decades if not centuries' into a reproductive woman, carrying neither a castration threat, nor passive homosexual wishes" (1955, p. 7, p. 24). Morgan, and indeed MacAlpine and Hunter, lay the ground for this chapter's attempt to unsettle psychoanalysis's certainties with regards to the cross-sexed wish, as well as how it (and the broader culture) reads psychosis through the transsexual figure.

Laplanche's revision of Freud's seduction theory provides a way to think about Schreber's delusional structure as actually being encountered as an "endo-somatic perception" of libidinal processes, working on an enigma introduced by the desire of another. Laplanche's formulation is of seduction as a general condition, one in which the signifier of the other's desire is implanted in the infant, prior to the formation of the ego, and inaugurates its own unconscious process as it attempts to translate this enigmatic extimité (1999/2015, pp. 8–12). Laplanche rethinks the temporality of trauma through a process of deferred translation: "This message is then retranslated following a temporal direction which is sometimes progressive and sometimes retrogressive (in agreement with my model translation—detranslation—retranslation)" (1999/2015, p. 56).

I've elsewhere argued that Schreber's importance for Freud has to do with the entwining of a reading of the fantasy of changing sex as symptomatic of a repressed, pathological homosexuality with Freud's own feelings admiration and anxiety of influence (2009, pp. 68–72). But Schreber's fantastic transformation is not limited to sex change. Santner observes Schreber's passional identifications with the abjected terms of German Romantic and racial nationalism (Women, Jews, prostitutes, effeminacy, filth) traumatically encodes the symbolic refusal and refuse of their constellation under National Socialism (1996, p. xi). This certainly seems to be true at times, but in other moments, Schreber's cross-sexed and non-European dis/identifications seem less abject than aspirational:

> in a future transmigration of souls. I was cast in several roles consecutively ... becoming a 'Hyperborian woman' seemed a sign that the earth had lost so much of its heat that general glaciation had either occurred already or was imminent ... my becoming a 'Mongolian Prince' appeared to me as a sign that all Aryan peoples had proved themselves unsuitable to defend the realms of God, and that a last refuge would now have to be taken with non-Aryan peoples.
>
> *Schreber, 1903/1955, p. 93*

This situation, contrary to, as Schreber calls it, the Order of the World, is one in which an external agency, or agencies, affect the flesh with speech. Elsewhere Schreber characterizes these voices in a mode that hovers between metaphor and its literalization:

> the miraculously created birds do not understand the meaning of the words they speak; but apparently they have a natural sensitivity for the similarity of sounds. Therefore if, while reeling off the automatic phrases, they perceive either in the vibrations of my own nerves (my thoughts) or in the speech of people around me, words which sound the same or similar to their own phrases, they apparently experience surprise and in a way fall for the similarity in sound; in other words the surprise makes them forget the

rest of their mechanical phrases and they suddenly pass over into genuine feeling.

1903/1955, pp. 167–169

Freud's reading of this passage is justifiably infamous, for what Santner characterizes as its "patriarchal complacency and rhetorical virtuosity" (1996, p. 35): "As we read this passage we cannot avoid the idea that what it really refers to must be young girls" (1996, p. 36). And as Santner notes here, "Freud's deduction repeats the crucial structural features of the object under investigation: the experience is one of an irresistible linguistic or ideational 'implantation'" (1996, p. 35). Freud, in other words, seems to contend here with his own experience of the imposition of a coercive and compelling language, and given his own reading of Schreber's birds, he too seems to be subject to a kind of feminization by linguistic association. As Santner suggests, it is as if by reading Schreber Freud was subjected to, or abjected by, a "*drive dimension of signification* . . . that is purely 'dictatorial' in that it positions its bearer as a kind of bird-brained stenographer taking dictation" (1996, p. 35).

Patricia Gherovici notes that both in Schreber's memoir and Freud's reading of it, the cure proceeds by way of writing "the delusion" (2010, p. 232). The process of writing is impelled by a rent in the subject, and does the work of repair. Schreber does narrate and comment upon compulsive thinking, though the narration also seems unable to formally contain its compulsion. Suffusing the wish for, and fantasy about feminization, Schreber's narrative invests both specific words and language in general with a particular quality of thingness; that is, it performs (or in-voices) libidinal cathexis as an objectification of words as things.

Working on and through the gendered (and sexist) limits on this conception of the (masculine) subject's capacity for voluptuousness, can we say that Schreber enacts a version of the death of the subject and simultaneously elaborates an exorbitant locution of the subject which *in-voices* the possibility of feminine pleasure, an Other jouissance? In other words, if the speaking subject is symbolically masculine, must Schreber *cease to be* (a speaking subject), in order to speak, or be spoken, in the feminine?

To in-voice, with its root meaning of "envoy," usually means to send a bill, but here I want to draw upon George Otte's plotting of the work of desire and fantasy in our commonplace hearing of voice as expressive of authenticity and identity (1995, p. 150–153). For trans subjects this commonplace often articulates a cisnormative imperative to pass. But how does anyone learn to speak, after all, if not by taking in and emulating the speech of others and their adult, as yet enigmatic, sexes? Where and when to do we introject our racial locution? Doesn't that inevitably precede our encounter with its signification? What imperatives are contracted between desiring (and) identification and knowing the difference? In Otte's usage, which is pedagogical, I understand "in-voicing" as working to highlight a tension between the demand for authenticity and the inevitability, even desire-ability of ventriloquism. This double usage asks us to think about the costs incurred (debt's representative, delivered) for thinking about the locution of Schreber's gender- and race-crossing voices of jouissance as belonging with desire.

If we concur with Gherovici's generic description of Schreber's *Memoir* as prototypical transsexual autobiography, how does its signifying bear upon the process of narrative self-authorship that trans theorist Jay Prosser highlights as both constitutive and as the function of subsequent transsexual memoir? For Prosser, transsexual subjects contend with the trauma of bodily agnosia within our sex of assignment, and constitute ourselves as sexed subjects through the narrative inscription of the bodily imago or an "alternatively gendered imaginary" (1998, p. 77). As he says, "Autobiography is very determinedly an act of remembering... Autobiography's conventions are both the means to passing through transsexuality and to passing back into it" (1998, p. 131). In turn Patricia Elliot asks us to query where Prosser's theorizing elides the difference of language from the body, which is to say where the sensuous body is invoked as the ground of a bodily imago prior to processes, and cuts, of symbolization (2010, pp.100–102).

Elliot's objection is Lacanian, anti-foundationalist, to the extent that it refuses the self-evidence and priority of the body as object of perception. Might it be that for Prosser, then, as opposed to Schreber (or Lacan), it is narrative rather than affectively cathected disjunctive and intensively figural language that has the capacity to organize a libidinal body? What might be the stakes of this difference, between a narratively organized or organize-able body, a perceptually knowable body as it were, and a body of specifically concretized and metonymically associative signifying language, we might even say poetic language—a body one might cobble together or work at in spite of a recalcitrant flesh and/or an cissexist socius in which the trans subject is unthinkable?

Perhaps the answer has something to do with how we might read repetition, remembering and working through across the fragmentation within Schreber's narrative, which does emerge even as its disjunctive signifying resists narrative and indeed temporal coherence. Does Schreber effect a cure by getting lost in language? What losses might appear in language, if not castration as such? Or rather do we have in the *Memoirs* an inscribed surface or body of language Schreber made to dwell in and against experiences of language's thingness, her Real?

In-voicing significations' seriality, fragmentation, destruction, and permutation, might it be that Schreber plays with and upon "cuts in the real," draining from signification its impossible grounds—the recurrence of a cryptic if alluring insistence—and her own? If so, perhaps it is in her text's "literal profusion," its relentlessly baroque, one might even say ornamental inscription of the excess of excess that this siphoning is made.

Martin notes of all the neologisms performed in the memoir, Schreber's "bellowing miracle" (*das Brüllwunder*) appears most often, and suggests this might indicate the presence of some variety of adult tic disorder (2007). However, we might also ask if it is not also legible as a repeated bodily eruption of a gap between the signifier and meaning, or better, perhaps as a voice's repetitive (and repeatedly failing) attempt to reach for, or touch upon, speech that is barred?

Most obviously, Schreber's crisis of symbolic investiture, inaugurated by the unthinkable thought of "succumbing to pleasure as a woman," points to the extent to which becoming feminine is so hegemonically abjected that a subject supposing himself to be a man might collapse under that identification. In relation to Schreber's suit to secure her freedom, how might we think this affectively hypercathected and concretized language of enjoyment and suffering as an uncanny remainder of and precursor to cross-sexed subjects' attempts to write ourselves into the social, out from under the (paternal) law? It is worth noting that in 1902 Schreber's petition to have civil rights restored was successful, and Schreber was released. Schreber was among the first "mental patients" to successfully sue for her freedom (MacAlpine and Hunter, 1955, p. 5). Subsequent to her release and until death Schreber continued to maintain the truth of her great thoughts, and it was largely when alone that Schreber would incorporate signifying elements of feminine presentation into her appearance (make-up, earrings, other jewelry, feminine hairstyles) (Freud, 1911/1963, p. 20).

MacAlpine and Hunter suggest Freud's defensive inscription of the feminine as repressed homosexuality had consequences beyond that particular case study; the psychoanalytic equation of repressed homosexuality as expressed by the fantasy of changing sex, paranoia, and psychosis entered the canon of psychiatric thought as the diagnosis of pathological homosexuality in the first edition of the Diagnostic and Statistical Manual of Mental Disorders (DSM) (1955, pp. 8–11). It also articulated the psychoanalytic distinction between neurosis and psychosis, and translated into an Anglo-American psychiatric discourse, significantly set the terms for the basic classificatory distinction organizing the DSM (1955, pp. 15–18).

While Freud challenged the criminalization of conscious homosexuality, Freud's reading of Schreber's feminine reverie as symptomatic of repressed homosexuality crystallizes a clinical logic of narcissistic differentiation from feminine (and trans) identifications that are understood to be psychotic. To the extent that the Freudian text exerted a force on the popular imagining of sexuality as well as playing a key role in determining the psychiatric clinical framework, it installed transgender and femininity as spectral threats to "healthy" homosexuality and non-pathological womanhood. In this context, it should perhaps come as no surprise that queer theory's uptake of Schreber has largely recapitulated the most conservative moments in Freud's and Millot's reading of the case.[11]

Returning to Schreber as literature, as trans genre or even, perhaps, transgender literature allows us to look at this history of cisnormative reception anew, even as it offers analytic and imaginative resources for rethinking sexuality's relation to linguistic, cultural, racial, and gender formations.

Notes

1 Early versions of this chapter were delivered at Psychoanalysis and Freedom/LACK Conference, Colorado College, April 22–23, 2016 and at *The Freudian Legacy*, Canadian Network for Psychoanalysis and Culture, University of Toronto, Sept. 22–24, 2013. My thanks to Pat Elliot, Dina Georgis, Oren Gozlan, Larry Lyons, and Beau Molnar for their insightful feedback.

2 A note on nomenclature. In this essay I use the term transsexual to refer to persons who have or who are in the process of changing sex, surgically, hormonally, or socially, and/or who self-describe as transsexual. I use the terms trans and transgender more or less interchangeably to refer to persons who claim those as identities to mark their gender variance or cross sexed identification, or adjectivally to describe gender variant phenomenon or cultural productions. This usage may include transsexuals who signify in this register, though many do not. Additionally, the terms trans, trans*, transgender, transsexual are used by different authors as heuristics or analytics. (See, for examples, Stryker et al. 2008 and Gozlan 2014.) Where I am using these terms to activate such analytics that is explicitly articulated in the text.
 3 This movement in turn depends upon a distinction made by trans historian Susan Stryker. Drawing upon Foucault's *Society Must Be Defended*, she notes that moving from discourses that take transgender phenomenon as their object to discursive fields constituted by embodied transsexual and transgender subjects, entails both the unearthing of "historical contents that have been buried in functional coherences or formal systematizations" and the upsurge from below of "knowledges that have been disqualified as nonconceptual knowledges, as insufficiently elaborated knowledges, naïve knowledges, hierarchically inferior knowledges, knowledges that are below the required level of erudition or scientificity" (in Stryker, 2006, pp. 12–13). Such a movement excavates the obscured, instrumentalized, naturalized deployments of such contents in psychiatric, anthropological, and other discourses concerned with gender, sex, and their variance, as well as excavating and activating the delegitimated knowledges of those who trans sex.
 4 Fortunately, this position has not gone unchallenged. Again, the early example is that of MacAlpine and Hunter. More recently, in her *Lacanian Analysis and Transsexuality: Take 2*, Patricia Elliot surveys new interventions in discussions of transsexuality and psychoanalysis, including work by Shanna Carlson, Oren Gozlan, and Patricia Gherovici, to delineate a new relation between trans subjects and the clinic, "a path that mandates respect for the desire to change sex as a sinthome, which signifies a positive form of self-transformation."
 5 I use here the ungendered and transgendering pronoun hir, a neologism but not one of Schreber's.
 6 Portions of this section of the chapter have appeared in somewhat different form in Salah (2017). Both that article and this chapter draw upon and develop arguments made in the first chapter of my doctoral dissertation, *Writing Trans Genres* (2009).
 7 This taxonomy of readings is adapted from *Writing Trans Genres* (Salah 2009, pp. 66–68), and is indebted to Eric Santner's extensive discussion of Schreber's significance in *My Own Private Germany: Daniel Paul Schreber's Secret History of Modernity*.
 8 Introducing the Dossier of public accounts and anatomies of Herculine Barbin, Foucault justifies his scanty commentary on the texts thusly: "I have been content to bring together some of the principal documents that concern Adélaïde Herculine Barbin. The question of strange destinies like her own, which have raised so many problems for medicine and law, especially since the sixteenth century, will be dealt with in the volume of the *History of Sexuality*, that will be devoted to Hermaphrodites" (Foucault in Barbin, 1980, p. 119).
 9 African-American lesbian poet, theorist, and activist Audre Lorde coined the term biomythography to name her memoir *Zami: A new spelling of my name*. Biomythography moves beyond autobiography by entexturing the telling of an individual life in that of the family, community, ancestors, struggle. Composing story as history, as mythic in scope, and as partial and partially fictive record of collective life, biomythography is also an insurgent prayer and documentary form.
10 See, for instance, Schreber's "Open Letter to Professor Flechsig" (1903/1955, pp. 33–36).
11 There are two determinations involved, which may be easily confounded: one is structurally cisnormative in its foundational approach to the sexes, and the other historically embedded in and reiterative of cisnormative psychoanalytic knowledges. Consider Butler's early queering of Freudian and Lacanian accounts of sexuation and kinship in order to trouble the "heterosexual matrix." Freud's account of Oedipalization is predicated upon the necessary separation of ego libido and object libido. Lacan draws upon woman's place in Lévi-Strauss's elementary structures of kinship, as an element of exchange, the mobile

signifier passed between men, to elaborate the symbolic constitution of the phallus (and sexual difference). The prohibition of the paternal metaphor simultaneously articulates the prohibition on incest, and following Butler the prohibition of same-sex desire, which on her account installs gendered identity as a melancholy afterthought (Butler, 1995, pp. 134–135). But this ban is itself only intelligible through its own founding naturalization of a sex prior to cross-sex identification; i.e. if "before" the incest taboo there is a ban on same-sex desire, then logically "before" if temporally coincidental there is a foreclosure of cross-sex *identification* prior to the organization of sexuality.

References

Allison, D., de Oliveira, P., Roberts, M., & Weiss A. (Eds.). (1988). *Psychosis and sexual identity: Toward a post-analytic view of the Schreber case*. Albany, NY: SUNY Press.

American Psychiatric Association. (2000). *Diagnostic and Statistical Manual of Mental Disorders* (4th ed., Text Revised), Washington, DC: American Psychiatric Association.

Barbin, H. (1980). In M. Foucault (Ed.), *Herculine Barbin: Being the recently discovered memoirs of a nineteenth-century French hermaphrodite*. (R. McDougall, Trans.) New York: Pantheon Books. (Original work published in 1978.)

Butler, J. (1995). *The psychic life of power*. Redwood City, CA: Stanford University Press.

Canetti, E. (1984). *Crowds and power*. (C. Stewart, Trans.) London: Farrar, Straus and Giroux. (Original work published in 1960.)

De Certeau, M. (1986). *Heterologies: Discourse on the other*. (B. Massumi, Trans.) Minneapolis, MN: University of Minnesota Press.

Elliot, P. (2011). *Debates in transgender, queer, and feminist theory: Contested sites*. Farnham: Ashgate.

Elliot, P. (2013, Sept. 22–24). Lacanian analysis and transsexuality: Take 2, the Freudian legacy, *Canadian Network for Psychoanalysis and Culture*, University of Toronto. Retrieved from: https://cnpcrcpccom.files.wordpress.com/2015/12/7-elliot-lacanian-analysis-and-transsexuality-take-2.pdf

Eugenides, J. (2003). *Middlesex*. Toronto: Vintage Canada.

Fanon, F. (2008). *Black skin, white masks*. New York: Grove Press. (Original work published in 1952.)

Foucault, M. (2003). *Society must be defended: Lectures at the College de France 1975–1976*. New York: Picador. (Original work published in 1997).

Freud, S. (1963). *Psycho-analytic notes on an autobiographical account of a case of paranoia* (Dementia paranoides). SE 12: 3–82. (Original work published in 1911.)

Freud, S. (1949). *The ego and the id*. London: The Hogarth Press. (Original work published in 1923.)

Gellar, J. (1992, Summer). The unmanning of the Wandering Jew. *American imago* 49, 227–262.

Georgis, D. (2013). *The better story: Queer affects from the Middle East*. Albany, NY: SUNY Press.

Gherovici, P. (2010). *Please select your gender*. New York: Routledge.

Gilman, S. (1993). *Freud, race and gender*. Princeton, NJ: Princeton University Press.

Gozlan, O. (2015). *Transsexuality and the art of transitioning: A Lacanian approach*. London; New York: Routledge.

Lacan, J. (1977). *Écrits: A selection*. (A. Sheridan, Trans.) New York: Norton Books. (Original work published in 1970.)

Lacan, J. (1978). In J.-A. Miller (Ed.), *The four fundamental concepts of psychoanalysis*. (A. Sheridan, Trans.) New York: Norton. (Original work published in 1973.)

Lacan, J. (1993). In J.-A. Miller (Ed.), *The seminar of Jacques Lacan, book III: The psychoses*. (A. Sheridan, Trans.) New York: Norton. (Original work published in 1981.)

Laplanche, J. (1999). Time and the Other. In J. Fletcher (Ed.), *Essays on otherness* (pp. 234–259). London: Routledge. (Original work published in 1992.)

Laplanche, J. (2015). Notes on après-coup. *Between seduction and inspiration: Man*. (J. Mehlman, Trans.) (pp. 46–56). New York: The Unconscious in Translation. (Original work published in 1999.)

Laplanche, J. (2015). *Seduction, persecution, revelation: Between seduction and inspiration: Man*. (J. Mehlman, Trans.) New York: The Unconscious in Translation. (Original work published in 1999.)

Lorde, A. (1982). *Zami: A new spelling of my name: A biomythography*. Watertown, MA: Persephone Press.

Lothane, Z. (1992). *In defense of Schreber: Soul murder and psychiatry*. London: The Analytic Press.

MacAlpine, I., & Hunter, R. (1955). Translator's introduction. In D. P. Schreber. *Memoirs of My Nervous Illness*. (I. MacAlpine and R. Hunter, Eds. & Trans.) (pp. 1–28). Cambridge, MA and London: Harvard University Press.

Martin, G. (2007, September). Schreber's "bellowing miracle": A new content analysis of Daniel Paul Schreber's *Memoirs of My Nervous Illness*. *Journal of Nervous & Mental Disease*, 195(8), 640–646. DOI: 10.1097/NMD.0b013e31811f404c

Millot, C. (1990). *Horsexe: essay on transsexuality*. (K. Hylton, Trans.) New York: Autonomedia. (Original work published 1983.)

Morgan, D. (1999). What does a transsexual want? The encounter between psychoanalysis and transsexualism. In K. More & S. Whittle (Eds.), *Reclaiming genders: Transsexual grammars at the fin de siècle* (pp. 219–239). London, New York: Cassell.

Niederland, W. (1974). *The Schreber case: Psychoanalytic profile of a paranoid personality*. New York: Quadrangle.

Otte, G. (1995). In-voicing: Beyond the voice debate. In J. Gallop (Ed.), *Pedagogy: The question of impersonation* (pp. 147–154). Bloomington, IN: Indiana University Press.

Plett, C. (2015, March 18). The rise of the gender novel. *The Walrus*. Retrieved from: https://thewalrus.ca/rise-of-the-gender-novel/

Prosser, J. (1998). *Second skins: The body narratives of transsexuality*. New York: Columbia University Press.

Salah, T. (2009). *Writing trans genre: an inquiry into transsexual and transgender rhetorics, affects and politics* (unpublished doctoral dissertation). Department of English, York University, Toronto Ontario.

Salah, T. (2014). *Lyric sexology*, Vol. 1. New York: Roof Books.

Salah, T. (2017). 'Time isn't after us': Some Tiresian durations. *Somatechnics* 7(1), 16–33.

Santner, E. (1996). *My own private Germany: Daniel Paul Schreber's secret history of modernity*. Princeton, NJ: University of Princeton Press.

Sass, L. (1995). *The paradoxes of delusion: Wittgenstein, Schreber, and the schizophrenic mind*. Ithaca, NY: Cornell University Press.

Schreber, D. P. (1955). *Memoirs of my nervous illness*. (I. MacAlpine & R. Hunter, Trans.) Cambridge, MA and London: Harvard University Press. (Original work published 1903.)

Stryker, S. (2006). (De)subjugated knowledges: An introduction to transgender studies. In S. Stryker & S. Whittle (Eds.), *The transgender studies reader* (pp. 1–17). New York: Routledge.

Stryker, S., Currah, P., & Moore, L. J. (2008, Fall–Winter). Introduction: Trans-, trans, or transgender? *WSQ: Women's Studies Quarterly*, 36 (3–4), 11–22.

Woods, A. (2011, Fall). 'I suffer in an unknown manner that is hieroglyphical': Jung and Babette en route to Freud and Schreber. *History of the Present*, 1(2), 244–258.

13
WRONGING THE RIGHT-BODY NARRATIVE

On the universality of gender uncertainty

Laine Hughes

The discourses that comprise the field of transgender studies—from early medical texts to contemporary gender theory—demonstrate great diversity amongst those who identify with the term "trans."[1] However, trans people seeking medical intervention have repeatedly been asked to tell a particular life story in order to acquire transition-related care: that story is commonly referred to as the "wrong-body narrative" (WBN). The project of recognizing difference across trans narratives is relatively recent. Historically this perspective was obscured by the limits of a diagnostic criteria that constructed gender dysphoria as a measurable condition, and the WBN as the marker of trans against which all transitional aspirations could be evaluated. In order to resist a taxonomy that would re-inscribe this divide and risk hierarchizing trans people, this chapter uses the term "trans" as a broad modifier to describe and include anybody with a desire, realized or not, for surgico-hormonal intervention into their gender presentation.[2] As trans people have increasingly found themselves the subject of public interest,[3] the associated tales of moving from one gender category to another to solve the "problem" of being born in the wrong body have become entrenched in the cultural imaginary. What appears in some ways as the growing acceptance of trans is limited as it has occurred almost entirely along the lines of how closely one can conform their life story to that of to the WBN. Indeed, the WBN is regularly held up as a hallmark of trans, the barometer with which authentic claims of trans can be distinguished. While it may accord a diagnosis to those who can adhere themselves to it, the WBN serves as a border that contains how bodies and identities may be conceptualized and lived in. I am interested in examining the costs of such normalization, and in considering how the WBN has been used to construct a kind of trans-normativity that is predicated on assuring that the myth of cisgender certitude endures.

In Canada, access to transition is regulated on a provincial level and, while specifics vary, generally one must demonstrate enough gender distress to warrant an initial diagnosis after which medical services can be obtained.[4] This requirement is in part responsible for the development and proliferation of the WBN, as it is commonly relied upon to illustrate the feeling of a gender-based disjunction between body and mind. The underlying clinical principle is that access to a medically augmented transition should be granted when an individual believes that they were born with an incongruous psychological gender and physical sex; hence the colloquial designation of being "in the wrong body." As Ulrica Engdahl (2014) explains: "the notion of 'wrong body' consists of a dichotomous explanation of the transgender experience as a state of "being in the wrong body" . . . the wrong body is envisioned as a state in which gender body and gender identity do not match; hence a disparity between body (materiality) and self (subjectivity) embodied in the narrative" (pp. 267–268). However, because early trans diagnoses were granted primarily according to how closely one's story echoed the WBN, it must be understood as a compulsory act rather than an essentialized element of a trans identity. In this case, it may be argued that the WBN demonstrates trans people's recognition that certain stories (such as being born in a body that is incorrectly sexed) align more comfortably with sought after diagnoses (like that of gender identity disorder) and can thus be deployed in a scripted fashion to access transition related medical care. In a context where trans affirming intervention is carefully guarded and highly regulated, the price of admission is acquiescing to the notion one was born in the wrong body.

In this chapter I examine how the WBN has come to stand in as the dominant signifier of trans, and as the acceptable symptom for surgico-hormonal intervention, problematically posited as treatment and solution. Rather than recapitulate the WBN, I am interested in questions designed to investigate what is at stake in the concept. First I offer a consideration of what appeals about the WBN, paired with an examination of the effects that internalizing a feeling of "living in the wrong body" might have on a person, and of the ways that the WBN has been used to construct a normative trans narrative. I will elaborate on how the construction of a "normal trans person" relies on an ableist notion of a cure against which bodies that cannot be gender-rehabilitated are further marginalized; and for how such an idea is mobilized by neoliberal capitalism in that it offers this cure through the construction of trans subjects as economically productive citizens. In order to work toward a de-pathologized understanding of trans that does not foreclose access to life affirming surgico-hormonal interventions for trans people, a critique of the ways in which the discourses of trans have been complicit with ableism and neoliberalism is necessary. Psychoanalysis is particularly useful as a method of considering the WBN in that it encourages a close reading of all defenses against gender uncertainty, trans or otherwise. Indeed, there is something about the fantasy of total sexual reassignment often associated with trans—as the surgical correction of the wrong body—that forecloses the recognition that trans is not a radical formation, but rather reflects gender as a question that must be answered by all, and in so doing touches upon the uncertainty at the heart of *all* gendered subjectivity. It is my contention that through such an analysis it may be possible to recognize that there is no such thing as a right body: that *everybody* must mourn the imagined certainty contained by the body, and uncertainty does not compromise, but rather structures identity.

Producing a wrong-body

> I do not recognize as proper, as my property, this material surround; therefore I must be trapped in the wrong body.
>
> *Jay Prosser in* Second Skins: The Body Narratives of Transsexuality, *p. 77*

Although it has become highly significant to the ways in which trans is understood and explained, the WBN has its roots in the study of sexuality, more so than gender. Patricia Gherovici (2010) fleshes out the link between early studies of gender and sexuality, noting that it was in an attempt to challenge laws criminalizing homosexuality that Karl Heinrich Ulrichs: "gave the name of 'Urnings' or 'Uranians' to men who were sexually attracted to men. He wished to eradicate the association of homosexuality with pathology by arguing that these men had 'a woman's mind trapped in a man's body'" (p. 85). With this simple explanation of homosexual desire, palatable because it relied upon a heterosexual imaginary, and reduced the threat of queer desire to a problem it also made solvable through biomedicalization, Ulrichs planted the seeds that would germinate into the WBN of contemporary transgender formations. The irony is that while narratives asserting the wrongness of bodies represented attempts to legitimize homosexual or transsexual desires, they served precisely the opposite function by marking these ways of being as incorrect, and dangerously outside the norm. Rather than serve any project of de-pathologization, wrong-body narratives came to stand in as a diagnostic criteria, and thus as a primary marker of a pathologized condition. It is not surprising then that individuals seeking to affirm trans lives have often relied on the same language as Ulrichs, explaining surgeries as medical solutions to the medical problem of being born in the wrong body. However, when a subject position has been deemed radical to the point of wrongness in the way that trans has, it is important to be wary of any push towards normalization, and to be critical of instances where social acceptance is offered to subjects from whom it was once stripped away.

Regardless of its status in the Diagnostic and Statistical Manual of Mental Disorders (DSM), or its clinical appellation, be it transsexuality, transgenderism, gender identity disorder, or gender dysphoria,[5] the shifts in the institutional understanding of gender variance reflect that the desire to transition[6] has long been understood as problematic, evidence of a psychological abnormality in need of treatment, and, ideally, a cure. For this reason many of the initial critical interventions that consolidate as the early work of transgender studies revolve around challenging the pathologization of trans, and on advocating the notion that trans people are not the problem, rather that transphobic social structures are. Talia Mae Bettcher (2014) draws an analogy with a social understanding of disability that centralizes a critique of an ableist social environment to make the point: "there are some people who have congruence between identity and body (cissexuals) and others who do not or who did not (transsexuals), but the social world is constructed in such a way that it privileges the former" (p. 386). Bettcher is correct in her assertion, generated as a response to the lack of adequate housing, healthcare, and employment opportunities facing many trans people, often in part because they are trans. The logic of trans-normativity suggests that the only viable solution to a transphobic social world is to transition. The critique I am suggesting here is not of gender-affirming surgeries or individuals who opt for surgico-hormonal intervention, but rather of the trans-normative claim that the desire for transition can be read in any one specific way, particularly as a solution to being born in the "wrong" body. The risk of an uncritical acceptance of trans-normativity then, is that it offers the appearance of normalcy at a significant cost, that being the preservation of the concept of normalcy itself. Self-identified disabled genderqueer poet and author Eli Clare (2013) describes his observation that:

> I watch marginalized people in a variety of communities yearn towards – or make declarations of – normality. So many FTMs aspire to be normal men, MTFs to be normal women . . . personally I'd like to grind the idea of normality to dust. I don't mean that everyone in my worldview ought to be queer; it's just the very idea of normal means comparing ourselves to some external, and largely mythical standard. But being normal or being queer aren't the only choices.
>
> p. 6

Indeed, within a neoliberal[7] context like Canada wherein social value is promised to those who can best approximate the mythical ideals of settler-colonial whiteness,[8] normalcy will only ever be accessible to those for whom "trans" is the singular disruption to a white-settler, able-bodied, heterosexual, middle-class identity. For these reasons, and in order to avoid falling into a politics of neoliberalism, critiques of the pathologization of trans, the DSM, and challenges to the construction of trans as mental illness must resist securing arguments that rest on trans normalcy.

The desire for transition-related medical intervention has long been met with great scrutiny and doubt, and people seeking these services have been required to submit themselves to extensive observation of both mind and body. The gate-keeping role of clinicians involved in the diagnosis and treatment of trans patients has been well critiqued by Jay Prosser (1998), Joanne Meyerowitz (2002), Sandy Stone (2006), and James Green (2006) among others. One of the results of gate-keeping practices is the production of a "real" trans narrative that confers authenticity against which falsified tales can be rooted out. In the case of regulating trans, the gate-keeping function served to legitimize those who could best reproduce a WBN by granting access to surgico-hormonal transition, while refusing it to those deemed inauthentic, whose experiences were not painful enough, not "wrong" enough to justify intervention. The WBN, while describing a particular relationship to gender and embodiment, also emerged in part as a tool that could be employed by those seeking transition related healthcare when navigating the phobic, clinical distrust of trans people. The irony here being that the institutional concern with trans people's potential for what Bettcher (2014) calls: "outright lying in the therapeutic context through falsification of narrative" (p. 402) has in large part been responsible for the production of a highly specific, stylized narrative that has come to stand as the "authentic" version.

It seems that the WBN serves, among others, two key functions for trans people: first, it provides a certified foundation for securing access to medical intervention; and second, it offers a way of navigating the experience of feeling a disjunction between gender identity, and one's sex coercively assigned at birth. The importance and value of the latter should not be lost in a critique of the former. The WBN appears in the discourses of trans with great frequency because those who seek surgico-hormonal intervention are aware of its heft as a diagnostic criterion, and learn when and how to deploy it in the process of gaining a medically assisted transition. As Bettcher (2014) points out: "while the traditional wrong-body account makes a political gesture in helping to secure transsexual identities as belonging within a particular binary category, it does so in a way that feeds the very oppression it opposes" (p. 388). Trans people are required to articulate a life story that justifies surgical intervention, and the WBN has served that purpose. One of the reasons it has been accepted on such a large scale is that the WBN consolidates a binary that posits cisgender authenticity against trans artificiality. Exposing the WBN's role in the construction of trans as a fraudulent gender formation is important, because the act of self-explanation remains a central component of transition.

It has been argued that at some point in the process of transitioning, the practices of gender self-determination that make life livable become something like the process of writing an embodied autobiography. As Jay Prosser (1998) put it: "Transsexuality is always narrative work, a transformation of the body that requires the remolding of the life into a particular narrative shape" (p. 4). Trans autobiography is an extensive genre, a hearty discourse that works in part to bridge an imagined gap in understanding between people who seek transition and those who do not. It is important to note, however, that even as it opened space for some trans people to be heard, trans autobiographical practices were and are still limited to those with certain types of privilege (like class, ability, race, and settler status in Canada) who can, and often choose to access surgico-hormonal intervention, and who have the resources to disseminate their stories. It is also worth noting that many of the biographies produced conform to the WBN. While this may have happened in part to facilitate access to surgeries and to highlight the ordinariness of trans lives, it has also functioned to reify an authentic/inauthentic binary within the overarching trans umbrella, according to the WBN and how one relates to it. Indeed, the notion of authenticity as contained by the WBN can only grant authentic status to some by taking it away from many. Prosser is correct that some trans people use autobiography to construct a livable life narrative, but what he misses is that the strategy of writing a life story to underscore one's claims to gender integrity is not unique to trans people.

For each trans autobiography that uses the medium to mold a life into a particular shape that confirms gender certitude, there are many more autobiographies by non-trans people that attempt to do the very same. What this demonstrates is that while the WBN may be deeply entwined with trans identification, a lack of gender certitude and the need for a narrative that eschews it, is not uniquely trans. An illustrative example might be the biography of tennis player Renée Richards, which delves into her early life as a male athlete, and details her transition from male to female. While her book serves as an example of the kind of trans autobiographical work Prosser holds up, it is far from the only of its kind, and there are reams of pages written by male athletes designed to prove manliness and secure their connection to masculinity, and by female athletes who seek to feminize themselves, and shed the stereotype of a brutish woman enduring a man's game that is often associated with women who dare succeed in sport. We may find that in comparing Renée Richards' tale of transition and sport, with that of Andre Agassi who endured a violent and overbearing father in his quest for tennis greatness, or Amelie Mauresmo who was "criticized by fellow tennis players Hingis and Davenport who commented on her 'playing like a man' and suspected [her] of 'not being [a] real woman'" (La Croix, 2007, p. 19) that there are many more similarities between these narratives than radical differences. These biographies may be grouped in various ways: according to profession, in this case athletics, or for a shared focus, in that they grapple with notions about gender and the transgression of these ideals. Reading for these similarities may provide more insight and be more productive than would a practice of categorizing texts according to a trans/non-trans binary.

A critical feature of the WBN is that it comes to serve a trans/cis dichotomy, and functions as one of the ways in which the important similarities between trans and non-trans experiences of gender are obscured. The work of psychoanalyst Oren Gozlan (2008, 2011, 2015) is particularly useful when examining gender and its fantasies, as he has written extensively on his clinical work in the area. Gozlan's book *Transsexuality and the Art of Transitioning: A Lacanian Approach* is the culmination of years of research, and is part of a trans-affirmative shift occurring within psychoanalysis.[9] Particularly relevant here is Gozlan's observation in his essay "The Accident of Gender" that: "the phantasy of being a boy for the anatomical girl is not different from the phantasy of being a girl for the same anatomical girl" (p. 561). What Gozlan identifies, then, is that the act of taking on gender is something performed equally by everyone. It is the universal quality of selecting gender—of taking up an imagined, coherent gender identity—regardless of its specificities that is significant. That all subjects must respond to the question of whether or not to transition is avoided by the fantasy undergirding the WBN that some bodies are right and others are wrong. The WBN serves the project of confirming cisgender-certitude by constructing the notion that there could be a "right" body to be born into in the first place. What this model fails to account for is the fact that gender certitude is a myth for all subjects, cis, trans, or otherwise. As Gozlan rightly identifies: "gender itself is a compromise formation, a product of identifications and renunciations. Gender is born of the loss of a unity that could never have been and is a symbol of a fight for the preservation of unity" (p. 567). Gozlan makes apparent that trans is not an exceptional gender formation; rather it is but one of many possible responses to a question that we must all answer. This is not to discount the suffering that trans people may experience as a result of the disjunction between felt gender and how the body is perceived to be gendered, but rather to call attention to the ways in which this phenomena extends well beyond what we might refer to as trans. In other words, there is precious little difference between the cisgender refusal of surgico-hormonal intervention, and the trans appeal for surgico-hormonal intervention, in that both decisions equally reflect gender desire.

Although every subject must take up the question of gender in some way, it would be an exercise in reductionism to collapse all gender formations and disregard the ways in which approaches to the question may differ. Indeed, those who undertake gender-related transition, medically assisted or otherwise, make different decisions about how to live in their bodies than those who do not. Rather than focus on the specifics of the interventions one may undergo as a response to a trans identification, or examine how a surgically altered body may differ from a body that has yet avoided surgery, my interest is in the relationships between exteriors and interiors—bodies and psyches—that gender engages. I would argue that the primary difference between cis and trans narratives that articulate the fantasy of a concrete gender identity is whether or not they bother to answer the question of how one came to their (imagined) position of gender certitude. In other words, most autobiographies that identify themselves as specifically trans in nature contain within them an acknowledgment of the conundrum that emerges from the question: "how can I be X if my body tells me I'm Y?" A query conspicuously, yet necessarily absent from those autobiographies that are not trans, as it is its very absence that serves to naturalize certain fantasies of gender (particularly the fantasy of cisgenderness) whilst delegitimizing others (trans). In her award-winning essay "Mourning the body as bedrock: Developmental considerations in treating transsexual patients analytically" psychoanalyst Avgi Saketopoulou (2014) identifies a defense against the binary positing cisgender realness against trans artificiality:

> some transsexual patients resort to the unconscious fantasy that one's natal sex is not real and never has been. This permits them to hold onto their own sense of their gender without having to confront the material reality of their sex.
>
> *p. 781*

The WBN stands in as explanation and solution to the predicament of having been born in the wrong body, and surgico-hormonal intervention as a follow-up is intended to "correct" the problem and make it right. Notable here is that the solution offered by medical intervention does not, and indeed cannot address the internalized premium placed on natal sex as a determinant of gender, as outlined by Saketopoulou. In other words, regardless of what procedures one may undergo, flight from the body one was born with is never fully possible. Indeed, there is no surgico-hormonal intervention that can change the past, nor is there any kind of complete "sexual reassignment" procedure that can alter every characteristic associated with sex. In this context, the WBN risks prolonging suffering rather than assuaging it, in that it can function as a permanent condemnation of those who take it up. The WBN has gained currency as a model for understanding trans not because it is trans affirming, but because it works to concretize the wrongness of trans bodies, and exceptionalizes trans forms of gender against a naturalized cisgender.

It is worth noting that the language of wrongness and the stigmatization of mind and body are not exclusive to trans, and critical disability theorists and activists have generated an excellent critique of pathologization, the notion of "healthiness" and how it comes to be defined, as well as a commentary on some of the intersections of disability and trans. One common understanding of trans that is particularly ableist is that of trans as a birth defect. Clare (2013) has written about the ways in which able-bodied trans people often refer to being trans as having a birth defect, and the belief that with adequate medical care, a cure is possible. The two-fold issue he identifies with comparisons that equate trans and disability is that they are largely the product of an otherwise en-abled imaginary that relies on the assumption that those who live with disability have easy unencumbered access to healthcare, and that disability and trans are both individual problems that require a cure. Such a perspective on disability runs counter to the critiques of medical models that have been generated by critical disabilities theorists who argue that disability in and of itself is definitely not a guarantor of good enough medical care.

Although both may include some interaction with medical discourses, the experiences associated with being trans or living with a disability simultaneously differ and yet are not mutually exclusive: indeed, there are trans people living with various forms of disability who often go unrepresented. The lack of visibility facing trans people with disabilities is not accidental, and is due in part to the difference in how the categories—and the bodies that fit into them—are conceptualized. As Jasbir Puar (2014) points out: "while the exceptional disabled body can overcome its limits, the trans body can potentially rehabilitate itself" (p. 77). Puar maps out the ways in which trans has been constructed as a medical category and situated as a treatable health issue, manageable through a system of diagnosis and care. While the development of this system has been useful in that specific procedures and medications have become more widely available, the tradeoff is that it has been built on a foundation that assumes trans bodies are a problem that can be solved through medical rehabilitation. It is an internalization of the imagined wrongness of trans bodies and potential for rehabilitation that Eli Clare touches upon when he speaks of trans declarations of normality. It is important to resist normality, or attempts to distinguish trans from classifications of disability, in that it serves a neoliberal[10] effort to continue marginalizing people with disabilities. Even if trans were removed from the DSM entirely and depathologization was undertaken in earnest, those who are simultaneously alienated by the relations of production as they are structured by capitalism would still face far fewer life chances.[11] When it is determined that there is a singular, proper way of being, and that way of being is informed by neoliberalism, the productive potential of that body to accrue capital will inevitably become the crux of how that body is valued. Much of the social recognition that trans allies, activists, researchers, and doctors have fought for has been absorbed by capitalism, and trans people are often measured against their ability to participate in its framework. Often this comes to mean that one's worth is determined by how convincingly they can move from one clearly defined gender category to *the* other, from female to male, or male to female, no exceptions. Clearly such an equation excludes many trans, non-binary, and gender non-conforming people who either cannot or do not wish to fit into such a narrow version of gender. It is very important to avoid efforts to interpolate trans people into existing systems of social legibility—to pursue a notion of trans normalcy—because these attempts are inevitably structured by capitalism and fail to challenge the overarching frameworks of neoliberalism that administer and regulate gender.

The desire to make trans legible and coherent did not emerge in a vacuum, and is a result of the ways in which trans life chances have, and continue to be, deeply restricted in neoliberal political contexts. As cultural theorist Dan Irving (2008) points out, this has occurred in part due to: "the urgency to gain social legitimacy for transsexuality (that) often forecloses possibilities for critically theorizing the formation of transsexual subjectivities within a socioeconomic and political context" (p. 50). His critique of neoliberalism and the possibility it offers some trans people, that opportunity to accrue social currency, seeks to recognize and attend to this urgency—to the distress faced by trans people—while remaining critical of capitalist modes of production. If the medical treatment that is intended to alleviate the distress associated with being trans is to be viable, it cannot be restricted to one model with one goal: it cannot be exclusively attached to a notion of surgically repairing a wrong body, and in so doing, "curing" trans people.

However, it cannot be stressed enough that surgico-hormonal interventions are a valuable and important resource that trans people must have access to. Saketopoulou (2014) points out that through these procedures, "a new bodily materiality *can* be created that conforms better to the contours of psychological experience" (p. 793), and approaches that deny or downplay the importance of access to transition-related care, especially in order to advocate exclusively non-surgical approaches to trans, are at best grossly misinformed.[12] Medical care can be a significant component of affirming trans lives, and trans people should be able to acquire surgico-hormonal intervention with far less regulation of personal narratives than is currently in place. However, holding such procedures up as a cure for trans—a solution to the supposed anguish of dysphoria that results from the condition of wrong-bodiedness—is not only limiting for transgender expression, it is impossible, for as Saketopoulou notes: "Even after the most sophisticated and successful hormonal and surgical interventions, however, the difference is one of degree. The body does not come to fully align with gender experience; it only aligns much better than it had before" (p. 793). The key here is the notion of "better than it had before." In other words, the gendered appearance of a body can be improved upon, but the before always lingers, and the before is some of the important messiness that the WBN attempts to overwrite.

As seductive as the notion of gender certitude may be, such bodily cohesion is nothing more than a very popular fantasy, demonstrative of a universal longing for self-certainty that can never be realized.

The WBN offers structural support to the fantasy of bodily cohesion, and uses trans identifications to re-consolidate the (non-trans) "body as bedrock" through the prescription of corrective sexual reassignment surgeries for trans people. In this model, trans is situated as the radical other against which the fantasy of gender for those who are not trans is insulated and protected. It serves as an attempt to make non-transgender formations appear authentic, and to restrict trans people's psychic wellbeing in that it insists the past can and must be removed from the body, that the lacking, mismatched "before" can be disappeared. The body's history cannot be erased, however, nor should it be, as adequately accounting for the body's past is a necessary part of mourning the fantasy of gender. The WBN risks foreclosing one's capacity to accept the past—psychic, somatic, and experiential—which is a loss far greater than that of giving up the notion of gender certitude. Through her work with trans analysands Saketopoulou (2014) observes that: "even after medical interventions have been completed, it is the mourning of the unconscious fantasy that the past can be excised that best facilitates adaptation in one's identified gender" (p. 793). It is the incorporation rather than the denial of loss that is truly liberating. In the case of trans subjectivity it may be that by incorporating a working through of the gender one was coercively assigned at birth, rather than refusing that history as the WBN requires, one may begin to find relief from the push to gender certitude, and recognize that gender certitude is equally fantastical for trans and non-trans people alike.

Notes

1 Stryker and Whittle (2006) collected early writings on trans in the edited collection *The Transgender Studies Reader*, a seminal text in transgender studies. It contains formative work developed in the field of Sexology, including selections from psychiatrist Richard von Krafft-Ebing's *Psychopathia Sexualis*, physician Magnus Hirschfeld's *Transvestites: The Erotic Drive to Cross-Dress*, and endocrinologist Harry Benjamin's *Transsexualism and Transvestism as Psycho-Somatic and Somato-Psychic Syndromes* which served in the development of his "standards of care" for the treatment of what he termed "gender identity disorder" and are still often relied upon in delivering trans-specific healthcare. Transgender studies has since evolved as its own field of study, distinct from and often in contestation of the trans taxonomies developed by medicine and psychiatry.
2 This is one of many approaches to nomenclature when taking up questions about gender and transition. Indeed the use of language has been and continues to be extremely important to trans theorists, activists, and community members as it is central to self-determination. Such a broad application of the term trans has its hazards, but precision is risked in the interest of prioritizing inclusive language. There has been a shift towards gender neutral language more broadly, thanks in large part to the political interventions made by trans and gender variant people.
3 The life stories of (some) trans people have now made their way into the mainstream of popular culture. Particularly appealing to a cisgender imaginary are those biographies that focus on trans individuals who move from one clearly specified gender category to another. These include the early biographies of Christine Jorgensen and Billy Tipton,

to the stories of modern athletes like Michelle Dumaresq, Keelin Godsey, and Caitlyn Jenner that appear with increasing regularity in print and screen media. There are a growing number of trans actors including Laverne Cox and Tom Phelan who both play trans characters on popular television shows. There is still a dearth in representations of intersex individuals, genderqueer people, two-spirit, and disabled trans folks, however, and trans visibility in pop culture has largely been a project depicting those who appear to conform most closely to gender norms.
4 For the current diagnostic criteria used to determine access to transition-related medical services, please see "Gender Dysphoria" in Section 2 of the *Diagnostic and Statistical Manual of Mental Disorders, Fifth Edition* (DSM-5) (2013). For the standards of care guiding the medical treatment of trans people, see: "Standards of Care for the Health of Transsexual, Transgender, and Gender-Nonconforming People, Version 7" (2011) in the *International Journal of Transgenderism*, and for more on the medical approach see *Principles of Transgender Medicine and Surgery* (2007) edited by Randi Ettner, Stan Monstrey, and Evan Eyler.
5 For a thoughtful reflection on the shifts in the DSM, the clinical language used by healthcare professionals in delivering trans healthcare, and the conundrum of pathologization, see Heino F.L. Meyer-Bahlburg's (2010) article "From Mental Disorder to Iatrogenic Hypogonadism: Dilemmas in Conceptualizing Gender Identity Variants as Psychiatric Conditions" in the *Archives of Sexual Behaviour*.
6 Here "transition" refers to any self-defined exodus from the gender one was coercively assigned at birth. This notion of transition does not depend on one's personal experience of medical phenomena, including surgico-hormonal intervention.
7 The term neoliberalism refers to governance whereby a "free" economy based on competition and the open flow of goods and capital is believed to be achievable only through minimal governmental regulation, and the restriction of social welfare. A neoliberal agenda is one that promotes resource privatization, limited governmental oversight on trade, and the destruction of social support networks, but simultaneously demands enhanced border securities and tighter restrictions on immigration.
8 As the practices of colonial settlement in Canada are far-reaching and ongoing, the term "settler-colonial whiteness" is used to denote the contemporariness of colonial relations, and the racialized privilege that it affords its citizens. For more on settler colonialism see Scott Lauria Morgensen's (2011) *Spaces Between Us: Queer Settler Colonialism and Indigenous Decolonization*. A consideration of the links between settler colonialism and neoliberalism is offered by David Lloyd and Patrick Wolfe (2016) in their article "Settler colonial logics and the neoliberal regime."
9 The relationship trans individuals, communities, and theoretical approaches have shared with psychoanalysis is fraught, and the move towards a more trans-affirmative practice is relatively recent. Along with Gozlan, some key contributions to this shift have been made by Patricia Elliot (2009), Shanna Carlson (2010), Sheila Cavanagh (2010), and Avgi Saketopoulou (2014).
10 As Puar (2014) notes: "neoliberal mandates regarding productive, capacitated bodies entrain trans bodies to recreate an abled body not only in terms of gender and sexuality but also in terms of economic productivity and the development of national economy" (78). The problem being that even while seeking to achieve greater social justice for trans people, these efforts run the risk of normalizing exploitative social relations rather than challenging them. Critical disability theorists analyzed the ways in which capitalism placed a singular focus on individual impairments to make disability the property—and the problem—of those it identified as disabled, and critical trans analyses work best when they also address the forces of capitalism in similar ways: when they acknowledge that some trans people are offered the prospect of normalcy vis-à-vis transition (the cure) while restricting many more who do not, cannot, or would prefer not to transition.
11 The term "life chances" comes from trans lawyer professor and critical cultural worker Dean Spade to describe the neoliberal and capitalist conditions of unequal distribution, and how they disproportionately impact trans people. In a 2011 interview with *Guernica Magazine*, Spade states that: "'life chances' is a phrase that captures the many, many vectors

of harm and well-being that are being distributed in ways that I'm concerned about. For example, whether or not fresh groceries are available in your community, whether there's toxic waste and polluting industry nearby where you live, whether in your whole life you're likely to have a job that interests you, what level your local schools are funded at, whether someone in your family is dying or suffering from lack of healthcare and you're carrying around the stresses of that."

12 For more on psychoanalytical approaches to trans that advocate against surgery, see Catherine Millot (1990), Colette Chiland (1998), and Marie-Helene Brousse (2007).

References

Almassi, Ben. (2010). Disability, functional diversity, and trans/feminism. *International Journal of Feminist Approaches to Bioethics*, 3(2), 126–149.

Berlant, L., & Edleman, L. (2013). *Sex, or the unbearable.* Durham, NC: Duke University Press.

Bettcher, Talia Mae. (2014) Trapped in the wrong theory: Rethinking trans oppression and resistance. *Journal of Women in Culture and Society*, 39(2), 383–406.

Brousse, Marie-Helene. (2007). Sexual position and the end of analysis. In V. Voruz & B. Wolf (Eds.), *The later Lacan: An introduction* (pp. 251–260). Albany, NY: State University of NY Press.

Carlson, Shanna. (2010). Transgender subjectivity and the logic of sexual difference. *Differences: A Journal of Feminist Cultural Studies*, 21(2), 46–72.

Cavanagh, Sheila. (2010). *Queering Bathrooms.* Toronto: University of Toronto Press.

Chiland, Colette. (1998). Transvestism and transsexualism. *International Journal of Psychoanalysis*, 79(1), 156–159.

Clare, Eli. (2013). Body shame, body pride: Lessons from the disability rights movement. In S. Stryker & A. Z. Aizura (Eds.), *The transgender studies reader 2* (pp. 261–265). New York: Routledge.

Diagnostic and Statistical Manual of Mental Disorders, Fifth Edition (DSM-5). Retrieved from: www.dsm5.org/Pages/Default.aspx

Eigen, Michael. (1996). *Psychic deadness.* London: Karnac Books.

Elliot, Patricia. (2009). Engaging trans debates on gender variance: A feminist analysis. *Sexualities*, 12(1), 5–32.

Engdahl, Ulrica. (2014). Wrong body. *TSQ: Transgender Studies Quarterly*, 1(1–2), 267–269. doi:10.1215/23289252-2400226

Ettner, R., Monstrey, S., & Eyler, E. (2007). *Principles of transgender medicine and surgery.* New York and London: Routledge.

Gherovici, Patricia. (2010). *Please select your gender: From the invention of hysteria to the democratizing of transgenderism.* New York and London: Routledge.

Gozlen, O. (2008). The accident of gender. *Psychoanalytic Review*, 95(4), 541–570.

Gozlen, O. (2011). Transsexual surgery: A novel reminder and a navel remainder. *International Forum of Psychoanalysis*, 20(1), 45–52.

Gozlen, O. (2015). *Transsexuality and the art of transitioning: A Lacanian approach.* New York: Routledge.

Green, Jamieson. (2004). *Becoming a visible man.* Nashville, TN: Vanberbilt University Press.

Green, Jamieson. (2006). Look! No don't! The visibility dilemma for transsexual men. In S. Stryker & S. Whittle (Eds.), *The transgender studies reader* (pp. 299–508). New York: Routledge.

Irving, Dan. (2008). Normalized transgressions: Legitimizing the transsexual body as productive. *Radical History Review*, special issue "Queer Futures," 100, 38–59.

La Croix, Rachel. (2007). *'You've come part of the way, baby': The status of women and women's sports in intercollegiate athletics 28 years after title IX* (doctoral dissertation, The Florida State University).
Lloyd, David, & Patrick Wolfe. (2016) Settler colonial logics and the neoliberal regime. *Settler Colonial Studies*, 6(2), 109–118.
Mbembe, Achille. (2003). Necropolitics. *Public Culture*, 15, 11–40.
Mbembe, Achille. (2006). On politics as a form of expenditure. In J. Comaroff & J. Comaroff (Eds.), *Law and disorder in the postcolony* (pp. 299–336). Chicago: University of Chicago Press.
Meyer-Bahlburg, Heino F.L. (2010). From mental disorder to iatrogenic hypogonadism: Dilemmas in conceptualizing gender identity variants as psychiatric conditions. *Archives of Sexual Behavior*, 39(2), 461–476.
Meyerowitz, Joanne. (2002). *How sex changed: A history of transsexuality in the United States*. Cambridge, MA: Harvard University Press.
Millot, Catherine. (1990). *Horsexe: Essays on transsexuality*. New York: Autonomedia.
Morel, Genevieve. (2010). *Sexual ambiguity*. London: Karnac Books.
Morgensen, Scott Laura. (2011). *Spaces between us: Queer settler colonialism and indigenous decolonization*. St. Paul, MN: University of Minnesota Press.
Namaste, Viviane. (2005). *Sex change, social change*. Toronto: Women's Press.
Prosser, Jay. (1998). *Second skins: The body narratives of transsexuality*. New York: Columbia University Press.
Puar, Jasbir. (2014). Disability. *TSQ: Transgender Studies Quarterly*, 1(1–2), 77–81;
Saketopoulou, Avgi. (2014). Mourning the body as bedrock: Developmental considerations in treating transsexual patients analytically. *The Journal of the American Psychoanalytic Association*, 62(5), 773–806.
Spade, D. (2003). Resisting medicine, re/modeling gender. *Berkeley Women's Law Journal*, 15–37.
Spade, D. (2011). *Normal life: Administrative violence, critical trans politics and the limits of law*. Boston: South End Press.
Stone, Sandy. (2006). The 'empire' strikes back: A posttranssexual manifesto. In S. Stryker & S. Whittle (Eds.), *The transgender studies reader* (pp. 221–235). New York: Routledge.
Stryker, S and Whittle, S. (Eds.). (2006). *The transgender studies reader*. New York and London: Routledge.
Winter, Meaghan. (2011). Trans-formative change: Interview with Dean Spade. *Guernica: A magazine of art and politics*. www.guernicamag.com/interviews/spade_3_1_11/

14
BIOPOWER AND THE MEDICALIZATION OF GENDER VARIANCE

A Foucauldian analysis of trans subjectivity

Kinnon Ross MacKinnon

Foucault once said:

> By breaking down the door of the asylum, by ceasing to be mad so as to become patients, by finally getting through to a true doctor, that is to say the neurologist, and by providing him with genuine functional symptoms, the hysterics, to their great pleasure, but doubtless to our greater misfortune, gave rise to a medicine of sexuality.
>
> *2003, p. 323*

His theoretical framework of biopower is useful to contemplate the way in which transgender/transsexual bodies are constructed, subjected, subjugated, and controlled by medical institutions. For this reason, the primary goal here is to use biopower to trace the discursive production and disciplining of gender-variant bodies. Becoming knowable as an authentic transgender/transsexual subject is engineered through psychomedical discourses and institutions embedded in the authority of medicine to diagnose and treat individuals who present with gendered experiences that are at odds with their birth-assigned sex. For this reason, a medicalized definition of transgender/transsexual (trans) people is given primacy in this project. That is, a trans person is someone who accesses medical technologies for the purpose of living as another sex.

Medical research on gender-variant individuals in the mid-twentieth century was the first to differentiate psychological gender identity from anatomical sex. This research grounded in clinical work with intersex and trans patients gave rise to the belief that transition technologies, such as hormone replacement therapy (HRT) and/or sex reassignment surgery (SRS), could cure gender variance, including cross-sex identification. This is an important line of inquiry as much trans health scholarship today is buttressed by studying HRT, SRS, and other transition-related medical technologies (see Giami & Beaubatie, 2014; Monstrey et al., 2011). Rather than jettisoning advocacy for transition-related medicine, this chapter deconstructs the medicalization of gender variance for the purpose of demonstrating a critical position on trans subjectivity while highlighting certain paradoxes trans people encounter while resisting subjectification.

Trans subjectivity is hinged upon psychosexual discourses designed to integrate sexually deviant bodies into systems of control organized to cultivate life. This investigation is thus concerned with problematizing psychomedical powers that shape, act upon, discipline, and regulate gender non-normative bodies. To this end, the following questions are explored: What are the major historical processes and medical discourses that hail gender-variant subjects? How do mechanisms of biopower circulate within trans intelligibility? Can trans persons critique, or even resist, psychomedical discourses while simultaneously transitioning from one sex to another? To unravel these questions, Foucault's theory of biopower is discussed to outline its many notions of power and the production of knowledge about psychosexual patients. Next, specific events and processes that have contributed to the medicalization of gender variance are illustrated. Finally, the last section of this chapter will incorporate Foucault's ideas on the arts of existence and assujettissement: I argue that technologies of the self offer subjugated trans subjects instances to creatively practice resistance within normalizing medical discourses. For instance, I explore the many ways that trans subjects reproduce, repurpose, and subvert normative medical discourses within the use of transition technologies of the self.

In concert with poststructuralism, I acknowledge that much of this inquiry's use of language applies ideas and terms specific to gender-variant populations produced through scientific discourse. While these words represent points of reference to discuss the subjects at hand, here is a brief rationale for some of the concepts I employ: "gender variance" is used loosely to draw attention to the historical existence of sexes and genders outside of the binary order of male/female and their correlates—man/woman, penis/vagina, and heterosexual/homosexual. Interestingly, whereas gender variance seems to describe species variability, I use the term "gender nonconformity" to expose liberal discourses of autonomy, choice, and resistance. And the term "intersex" is employed to refer to individuals born with mixed sexual anatomy, rather than the literature's use of "hermaphrodite" which has been proclaimed as derogatory by intersex individuals.

Although it may be strategic to distinguish gender identity from sexuality within some areas of trans studies, this is a relatively new practice. While some authors (Fassinger & Arseneau, 2007; Tando, 2011) caution against collapsing "trans" into issues of sexuality, this may not be a useful distinction. In fact, their segregation may be a function of medical discourses designed to produce deviant subjectivities and taxonomies of psychopathological conditions. Thus, where it seems necessary, the topic of non-normative sexualities and sexed bodies are integrated to create a salient site for historicizing gender non-normativity and the construction of psychosexualized trans subjectivites. The purpose of this chapter is to employ the theory of biopower to delineate the inherent dangers of psychomedical discourses designed to subjugate and control sexually deviant bodies, and to highlight the contradictions of resisting subjectification through advocating for transition-related medicine.

Biopower: anatomopolitics, biopolitics, and the deployment of (hetero)sexuality

In *The History of Sexuality: An Introduction*, Foucault (1978) refers to two poles of biopower that operate in the seventeenth century for the purpose of dispersing power over life. These two forms of power over life are distinguished as disciplinary (anatomopolitics) and regulatory (biopolitics). The first form, described as "the disciplines," centers the body as a machine to optimize its effectiveness, while increasing its usefulness and submissiveness (Foucault, 1978, p. 139). Also named the anatomopolitics of the human body, the first pole of biopower assimilates bodies into systems of control, and treats the body as an entity to be worked upon. In *Psychiatric Power*, Foucault (2003) writes that "disciplinary power is a discreet, distributed power; it is a power which functions through networks and the visibility of which is only found in the obedience and submission of those on whom it is silently exercised" (p. 22). Rabinow and Rose (2006) explain that anatomopolitics can be conceptualized as an integration of the human body into efficient systems. Meanwhile, the second pole of biopower is known as biopolitics of the population, characterized by "regulatory controls" (Rabinow & Rose, 2006, p. 139). Biopolitics consists of developing knowledge about populations, statistical measures, and state policies on reproduction and healthcare. Foucault (1978) states that biopolitics is concerned with biological processes such as "propagation, births and mortality, the level of health, life expectancy and longevity," arguing that the ultimate goal of such technologies of power is to foster life "through and through" (p. 139). Walters (2012) suggests that biopower is an aggregate for the human population, encompassing life, death, and production. In summary, biopower is bifurcated as a biopolitical strategy to manage and regulate the life of the species, and the anatamopolitics of the body in which individual material bodies and their functions are disciplined.

Sexuality and categories of biological sex formulate the "great technologies of power" that were instrumental in joining disciplinary and regulatory power processes together in the nineteenth century (Foucault, 1978, p. 147). Through sexuality—the subject of much unspoken fascination—bodies were joined for the strategic management and continuation of life through birth regulation, continued labor capital, and social relations. In other words, biological sex was deployed within the conceptualization of sexuality. Foucault (1978) is skeptical of the naturalness of sex categories, asking "is 'sex' really the anchorage point that supports the manifestations of sexuality, or is not a rather complex idea that was formed inside the deployment of sexuality" (p. 152)? So while sexuality was the vehicle through which biopolitical techniques moved through the body in terms of sensations and pleasures, it was this construct of anatomical sex that ordered the population. Sex went beyond the bounds of human bodies and their organs, encompassing normative internally driven behaviors to differentiate between sexed roles, sexual functioning, and the pleasures of sexuality. Foucault uses the example of the reduction of women's bodies to their reproductive functions to illustrate the idea of sex operating tacitly, but distinctly within the deployment of sexuality. Thus, sex and sexuality exist discretely but are not to be taken for granted as natural categories. Rather, these ideas have been disseminated as powerful tools to bring about, and to order, the human population.

The production of knowledge is a major tenet of biopower, particularly with respect to the engineering of truths, the rendering of subjects as normal or abnormal, and how subjects constitute themselves through discourses. Importantly, Foucault (1978) identifies two modes of truth manufacturing: the confession and incitement to "scientific discursivity" (p. 65). By espousing transgressive experiences, physicians interpret and taxonomize subjected individuals' confessions through the lens of science. In fact, the primary ritual for establishing truth in the area of sexuality can be traced to Christian confessions, which transformed sexuality to discourse via language. In a lecture from *Abnormal*, seventeenth- and eighteenth-century sexuality is described as being not what one does with their body, but what one confesses to having done (Foucault, 1998). But a confession of the truth cannot be liberating for subjects, as confessors espousing the truth then contribute to their own subjugation (Foucault, 1978). Butler (2004) declares that discourse functions to pull the speaking subject into hegemonic systems of control in order to participate in the very system that seeks to subjectify and discipline. At the same time, a confession is contingent on an audience. The confessor's observer is the authority who demands a confession, "prescribes and appreciates it, and intervenes in order to judge, punish, forgive, console and reconcile" (Foucault, 1978, pp. 61–62). Confessions of sexuality were said in secret in the name of transgression, reducing sexual desires and behaviors to shame and deviancy. Later, nineteenth-century sexual practices were analyzed and archived by sexologists who also obtained their information by collecting confessions, and disseminated this knowledge as scientific discourse which instigated the rise of a medical authority on sexuality. Scientific medical disciplines such as medicine, psychiatry, and psychoanalysis began codifying sexual practices, desires, and behaviors into signs and symptoms, all collected through the confession and listening techniques.

Knowledge production and the subjectification of patients

Biopower circulates within medical institutions, creating subjugated patients within the doctor–patient relationship. In his *Psychiatric Power* lectures, Foucault (2003) asks "who are the agents of this disciplinary power? Curiously, the doctor, the person who organizes everything and really is in fact, up to a certain point, the focal element, the core of this disciplinary system" (p. 22). The doctor and the sick patient, together within the hospital walls, discursively produce knowledges about disease and the diseased. The hospital is the conduit that allows the doctor's gaze to bring illness to life, in that the truth and reality of malady comes to life within the clinical establishment designed to treat pathology. From this line of thinking a paradox emerges in which it becomes apparent that there are no a priori pathologies, and the sick become subjectified when seeking attention for their ailments. Illness, and subsequently, patients, are produced in the clinic by the physician who interprets, treats, and manages. To further depict this thesis, Foucault (2003) sheds light on Pasteur's biological research which charged that it was the hospital doctor, going from bedside to bedside, and the patients he examined in the crowded hospital, who were the major agents of the spread of disease. Pasteur's research illustrated that not only was the hospital doctor the purveyor of disease for many patients, but it was also through his ignorance of microorganisms which caused him to propagate illness (Foucault, 2003). In this case, it was the truth-producing function of the doctor and the patient's reproduction of the distinctive symptomatology of illness that engineered an intelligible sick patient. This literal depiction of molecular biology and disease works to underscore the role that the hospital, the doctor, and patients play in bringing pathology to life—physiologically and discursively.

Foucault's ideas on biopower, which outline microphysical processes determined to discipline and regulate bodies into life-optimizing systems of control, reveal many useful linkages to gender variance and trans subjectivity that will be taken up in the following sections. Next, the conversation explores, how exactly, anatomopolitics commands the development of non-normative psychosexual subjects who require biomedical treatments, fostered through the fantasy of a natural social order, and ultimately the propagation of humanity.

Psychiatric questioning, confessions, and psychosexual deviance

Parallels can be drawn between the production of madness in the nineteenth century through psychiatric questioning and confessions, and trans people who seek mental health treatment for clinical symptoms associated with gender dysphoria, such as having a strong cross-sex identity, or a desire to transition to another gender not assigned at birth. Both instances require the "patient" to make a declaration of mental illness which is then vetted through the doctor's etiologic theories of psychosexual deviance. Within the clinical apparatus of madness, nineteenth-century psychiatrists, psychoanalysts, and neurologists were highly concerned with symptomatology required to diagnose mental illnesses theorized to be caused by underlying sexual drives, especially hysteria and neuroses (Foucault, 2003). Within these psychiatric institutions doctors required that patients describe their symptoms. Doctors asked "Are you or are you not mad?" which was followed by (1) an affirmative response to secure the doctor's status; and (2) descriptions of the specific symptoms of madness to receive a diagnosis (Foucault, 2003, p. 311). Hence, psychosexualized mental patients were born in the clinic, and scientific discourses about madness caused by sexual deviance were introduced to the scientific lexicon. When persons present to mental health professionals today with symptoms of gender dysphoria, they are automatically imprinted with a psychosexualized body. Standardized criteria required to diagnose gender dysphoria include classificatory items on sexuality, organized as sexual fantasy and sexual behavior (Drummond et al., 2008). Like the clinical apparatus of psychosexual madness and psychiatric questioning, trans patients must confess their life stories of non-normative gender behaviors and sexual desires before medical professionals are able to provide a diagnosis based on symptomatology.

One of the most compelling events that provides evidence for the psychosexualization of gender variance and the porous distinctions between gender identity and sexuality occurred when homosexuality was removed from the Diagnostic and Statistical Manual of Mental Disorders (DSM) in 1973, only to be followed by the addition of gender identity disorder (GID) in 1980 (Reicherzer, 2008; Toscano & Maynard, 2014). This decision has been interpreted as an indication that homosexual behaviors and same-sex object choice continue to be considered deviant and subject to medical surveillance, concealed within GID (Toscano & Maynard, 2014). It could also be speculated that before the introduction of GID in the DSM, homosexuality acted as a proxy for pathologizing deviant genders, ensuring that individuals who displayed non-normative gender could be medically disciplined. While some political advocates for trans rights have distinguished gender identity from sexual identity, sexuality is in fact inextricable from trans subjectivity due to discourses of sexuality within the history of madness.

One of the dangers of knowledge production about madness is that it remains localized within professional bodies of expertise. Rose and Rabinow (2006) explain that biopower arranges medical authorities in such a way that they are constructed as competent to "speak the truth about the vital character of human beings" (p. 197). For Butler (2001) speaking the truth always involves an apparatus of knowledge applied to the intelligibility of a person and a body. She remarks that

> the act of self-reporting and the act of self-observation take place in relation to a certain audience, with a certain audience as the imagined recipient, before a certain audience for whom a verbal and visual picture of selfhood is produced.
>
> *Butler, 2001, p. 629*

At the same time, the vital character of contemporary gender nonconforming individuals is visibilized at clinics where they must confess a gender identity that is at odds with their anatomical sex (along with a plethora of gendered behaviors and sexual fantasies), which is then interpreted by the doctor in order to ensure diagnostic criteria are met to obtain access to transition technologies. As we have seen so far, confessions act as a technical strategy of biopower which forms the basis of the discursive production of intelligible psychosexualized trans subjects.

Sex reassignment techniques and the invention of gender identity

Sex reassignment technologies are highlighted below to further detail the function of biopower to discipline and normalize gender-variant bodies. Gender-variant individuals, who display incoherently ordered bodies and sexualities, disrupt the discursively produced natural sex/gender/sexuality system which is imagined necessary for birth and the continuation of the population. As Foucault (1978) argues that biopower optimizes life "through and through," it could be similarly observed that sex reassignment is designed to foster life "through and through" via surgical and hormonal interventions on non-normative bodies (p. 139).

The belief in gender identity, distinct from physiological sex, originated from the clinical treatment of transsexuals and intersex children in the 1950s. In 1955, sexologist John Money of Johns Hopkins University authored several articles in which he claimed that a person's psychological sex was learned, rather than simply determined by biological anatomy. Money declared that "gender role" was a new category of sex which could be learned irrespective of anatomy (Repo, 2013, p. 232). This theory of psychological gender identity was exemplified in his use of a combination of SRS, HRT, and behavioral interventions to socialize intersex children into their new sexed social roles. Repo (2013) describes this process as the *sexual apparatus*—a biopolitical tool of biopower that disciplined (anatomically and psychologically) children with mixed sex organs to maintain the social order necessary for the continuation of life. That is, children who were indistinguishable as either male or female represented a threat to the schema of reproduction in their inability to satisfy the anatomical requirements for heterosexual sex. Thus, Repo's (2013) concept of the sexual apparatus highlights a new order of knowledge about sex and gender whereby intersex children were subject to disciplinary power, worked upon and surgically aligned, to be assimilated into a normative gender system. These surgical technologies and gender therapies represented dominant sex and gender discourses which differentiated between psychological gender and biological sex. Doctors who aligned biological sex with psychological gender claimed that if genitalia looked "normal," a patient were more likely to fit into the corresponding gender role and practice heterosexuality, thus reproducing the social order of sex, gender, and heterosexuality (Repo, 2013, p. 234).

While the sexual apparatus underscores the authority of Money's case management of intersex bodies, the deployment of the truth of psychological gender identity, and the rise of clinical sex reassignment techniques in children, this biopolitical mechanism must be cautiously applied to trans subjectivity and the phenomenon of adults who transition sexes. Medical disciplinary powers may act upon gender-variant children and adults differently due to life stage and the presence or absence of family in the gender role socialization process. The following explains the importance and power of the family in the sexual apparatus in terms of strengthening the subject's new gender identity.

Family members take a commanding position in the microphysics of gender and the management of sex reassignments. Individuals closest to the subject are engaged in the supervision of gender role, which is taken up through family discourses of care and support. Foucault (1989) explains in *The Birth of the Clinic*, that the family is drawn into disciplinary apparatuses by stating that "the natural locus of disease is the natural focus of life—the family" (p. 19). Parents took the lead of the micro-clinic to reinforce the intersex subject's new gender role in order to facilitate their child's chance at a seemingly normal life. Conversely, many trans persons are estranged or maintain strained relationships to their birth families who fail to validate their felt gender identity (Levitt & Ippolito, 2014). However, due to much societal and biological family rejection, the discourse of "chosen family" is enacted within trans community (Majowski, 2014). Close friends become a trans person's chosen family. For Repo (2013), the family presented a parental panopticon in which, outside of the Money clinic, the child's non-natal gender was enforced within their family structure. In this way, a similar argument could be applied to adult trans persons for whom family often translates to a chosen family of friends and other trans individuals who affirm their gender identity. For adult trans persons, their chosen family, rather than family of origin, represents the micro-clinic that manages and confirms the subject's new gender, which in turn fosters life ordered by the normative gender system. Ultimately, familial relations and discourses of support and acceptance act as extensions of biopower techniques pulling gender-variant individuals into male or female sexed subjectivities designed to reflect the social order of reproduction

Similarly, there are interesting parallels within the language used to support the psychomedical treatment of intersex children and adult transsexuals of the mid-twentieth century, interlaced with the belief in "curing" gender variance. While the first documented SRSs in the United States were performed in the 1950s, Money's infamous research on the treatment of intersex children began circulating in 1955 (Meyerowitz, 2004). Money's aim in performing SRS and teaching children gender roles correlated to sex was done in the name of making "the best decision" for the child, and to prevent "psychological disturbances" (Repo, 2013, pp. 235–236). According to Harry Benjamin, the doctor whose early clinical work with transsexuals eventually created the Harry Benjamin Standards of Care, surgery was the only "successful cure" for authentic cases of gender disorder, and would "make life easier for such persons" (as cited in Meyerowitz, 2004, pp. 103–104). The production of new medical knowledge surrounding sex and psychological gender greatly influenced medical interventions for curing gender variance. In *Psychiatric Power*, Foucault historicizes psychiatry and the architected hospital, suggesting that this institution has been constructed to remedy mental health conditions. He states "it is the hospital itself that cures . . . the hospital is the curing machine" (2003, p. 101).

Medical discourses infiltrate the contemporary trans rights movement and have been repurposed to advocate for easier access to transition technologies. In fact, trans people ingest and regurgitate medicalized narratives for the purpose of navigating interactions with healthcare professionals (Johnson, 2015). Language used to justify sex reassignment surgeries today is permeated with biopolitical discourses aimed at fostering life and health. For example, trans health activists argue that improved access to publicly funded transition services will relieve high rates of depression, anxiety, and suicidality due to gender dysphoria (Hodge, 2010), while doctors surgically operate on intersex children in the name of doing the right thing (Creighton, 2000; Karkazis, 2008). SRS and transition technologies invest life-affirming strategies on the gender-variant body in order to improve the overall health of the individual, and maintain the social order necessary to facilitate population growth through reproducing normative male and female subjects. Allowing gender-variant individuals to exist outside of these categories presents a threat to the system of propagation and, as medical discourses hold, is unethical. But again, where sex reassignment technologies are presented as a therapeutic cure, trans subjects must first confess their illness within the clinic before being granted the "cure," thus participating in their own subjectification.

Resisting medical discourse: trans subjects and *assujettissement*

It is difficult to imagine resistance for gender nonconformists within these matrices of discursive power and repression, but the following section attempts to untangle this web of omnipresent biopower. Foucault (1982) states that subjects "are faced with a field of possibilities in which several kinds of conduct, several ways of reacting and modes of behavior are available" (p. 342). This topic has specifically been left for the final section of the investigation as trans resistance to biopower occurs within the deployment of transition technologies of the self and in normative medical discourses about individuals with gender dysphoria.

Foucault's (1984) "arts of existence" and "techniques of the self" are central tenets to the concept of biopower, describing the trickledown of power whereby subjugated individuals begin to constitute and work on themselves for the purpose of transformation and personal aesthetics (pp. 10-11). Harrer (2005) states that Foucault thinks about "self-constitution as a derivative of, or a complement to, the constitution of subjects through normalizing power and subjugation. The genesis of subjects essentially includes these two sides: subjugation and self-constitution" (p. 78). In the *Use of Pleasure*, Foucault employs the notion of *assujettissement* to describe power's inscription on individuals which is the key to creating subjugated subjects. Yet he claims that there are distinct practices of freedom within techniques of the self (Harrer, 2005, p. 79). *Assujettissement* refers to the paradoxical process of becoming a subject through the many different ways of conducting oneself (Harrer, 2005). Milchman and Rosenberg (2007) describe the arts of existence and the ethics of self-fashioning one's lifestyle or body as not unlike an artist carefully preparing a painting or sculpture. Foucault (1994) also notes that like creative objects, everyone's life could be seen as a work of art. As such, this chapter now explores how apparatuses of biopower groom trans subjects into partaking in their own subjugation, while offering opportunities to play with power through the arts of existence. Though it appears that subjects who internalize discourses present an example of self-governance, I instead suggest that *assujettissement* gives subjugated trans individuals a method for resistance within the grip of biopower. The many complex community and scholarly debates on non-normative sexes, genders, and sexualities (Elliot, 2010; Fassinger & Arseneau, 2007; Sullivan, 2007) present a salient site for the interplay of the arts of existence, revealing the layered ways that subjects affected by dominant medical discourses resist and reuse these hegemonic powers.

Assujettissement can be applied to understand trans persons who work to distinguish themselves as unique and apart from other groups within the lesbian, gay, bisexual, trans, and queer (LGBTQ) community. This self-constituting freedom of expression, however, has the unintended consequence of confirming the psychomedicalization of trans intelligibility. There is a body of literature within trans studies, and anecdotal evidence, that condemns the "queering" of trans subjects (Elliot, 2010; Sullivan, 2007). That is, some trans persons resent theorists who use the existence of gender variance to disrupt taken for granted dualistic notions of male/female, man/woman, and heterosexual/homosexual. Meanwhile, intersex activists have taken offence to being added to the larger LGBTQI acronym which connotes a community of sexual and gender outliers, reminding LGBTQ folks of the non-consensual medical violence done to intersex children through corrective surgeries, and that intersex is a congenital medical condition (Queers United, 2010).

Trans subjects who advocate against the conflation of non-normative sexuality and gender identity are paradoxically forced to forge their existence through medical discourses and taxonomies of deviance. As much of the gay and lesbian liberation movement entailed de-pathologization, a schism occurs within these sexual and gender minority groups. Much trans advocacy is centered around demanding improved access to state or health insurance-funded SRS and other services required to transition sexes, which are arguably not necessary for sexual minority groups. In order to politically organize for increased trans-related healthcare coverage, trans groups are forced to present themselves as pathological medical subjects. Advocates for trans healthcare find themselves caught repurposing psychopathologizing narratives of having an illness or being "trapped in the wrong body" because these are the stories that led to the proliferation of the idea that SRS and HRT cures gender variance.

As power increases, so does the impression of autonomy drawn from technologies of the self. Medical technologies constructed as techniques of self-improvement, such as SRS, HRT, Botox, silicone injections, hip reductions, and facial feminization/masculinization surgeries, to name a few, are used by trans people to transition from one sex to another in the name of freeing one's internal gender. The paradox, however, is that biopower is oriented around liberal notions of choice and a sense of freedom. Heyes (2006) explains that "a crucial part of freeing oneself consists in understanding an alternative picture in which increasing capabilities are closely tied to intensification of power relations" (p. 131). This reading of *assujettissement* may paint trans subjects as duped by biomedical powers, but it has also been argued that through the use of these techniques trans individuals also speak back to their medicalization through artistic mediums and their aesthetic bodies (Davy & Steinbock, 2012). Thus, it remains important to be open to the contradictions of constructing oneself using technologies of self-enhancement.

Biopower renders trans individuals as docile in their use of normalizing transition technologies and medical discourses for self-construction. But through *assujettissement*, gender nonconforming individuals subvert these discourses in order to gain access to medical transition technologies, regardless of the person's actual internal sense of gender. While it is well documented that many trans-identified persons do not internalize dualistic notions of gender (Bauer et al., 2013; Sanger, 2008), a patient who enters the clinic critiquing the practice of gender, or with a sense of multiple genders, will be significantly less likely to convince doctors for sex reassignment technologies (Butler, 2001). Trans coming out narratives and trajectories of transsexuality are so culturally pervasive patients know exactly the performative confession they ought to give in order to convince their medical audience to interpret the truth of gender dysphoria. In regurgitating medical discourses for the purpose of gaining access to transition technologies, gender nonconformists creatively resist discursive medical apparatuses through the practice of subversion.

Empirical research shows that trans persons practice *assujettissement* to problematize medicalization and the natural ordering of the species, conducting heterogeneous transitions and practices of sexuality. If it can be agreed that the mechanics behind biopower employ anatomopolitical tactics to assimilate bodies into a normative sex/gender/sexuality social system, and that sex reassignment techniques were developed to normalize gender-variant bodies, then recent studies show that trans people live outside these medical discourses. That is, *assujettissement* illustrates how subjects use technologies of the self to re-imagine medicalization and a new organization of the human species body. There are many dominant assumptions about gender-variant bodies and sexuality circulating the medical treatment of gender dysphoria. In particular, the idea of medically transitioning sexes often mistakenly signifies genital reassignment (Scheim & Bauer, 2014). At the same time, SRS practices (such as vaginoplasty or phalloplasty) surgically design bodies to fulfil the anatomical requirements necessary to participate in heterosexual penetrative sexual acts. But instead, trans men and trans women report changes in sexual identity and desires after gender reassignment which include same-sex practices (Bauer et al., 2013; Schleifer 2006). Similarly, a qualitative study of trans persons and their partners show much sexual diversity within the sample in that the majority of participants identify as bisexual (Sanger, 2008). And most of the 433 gender nonconforming individuals who took part in a trans health study in Ontario reveal non-linear transitions with little medical intervention: an estimated 23 percent of trans-identified individuals were living aligned with their internal gender identity with no medical assistance at all; and just 15 percent of trans women had completed vaginoplasty, and only 0.4 percent of trans men accessed phalloplasty (Scheim & Bauer, 2014). These data were retrieved from the Canadian province of Ontario, which does have provincially funded SRS, so it seems that financial barriers were not the primary reason for low SRS numbers in the sample. An additional report from this study shows that 63.3 percent of transmen have sex with men or identify as gay, or bisexual (Bauer et al. 2013). And this is precisely why procedures used to transition sexes are not often used in the way biomedical institutions may have intended, in terms of offering a cure. Although pscyhomedical discourses resolve that sex reassignment is a cure for gender dysphoria, many trans people do not have linear transition trajectories from one sex to another, or end up as practicing heterosexuals. These empirical data highlight that, in fact, many trans people resist the anatomopolitical ordering of sex/gender/sexuality. From this discussion on resistance it is evident that despite being subjected and caught up in the psychomedical institution's apparatuses of biopower, gender-variant individuals are neither duped nor docile. There is an astute awareness and subversion of these mechanisms that are intended to regulate, discipline, and normalize in order to maintain social order and propagate the human population.

Within this critical investigation I have applied Foucault's theory of biopower in order to deconstruct the pervasive medicalization of gender variance which has discursively hailed psychosexualized trans subjects. Earlier it was argued that trans intelligibility is hinged upon normative narratives of transsexuality stylized within a motif of confessing to doctors that one's psychological gender identity is misaligned with one's anatomical sex, which is followed by a gender dysphoria diagnosis. In this way, gender-variant individuals are embedded with psychomedicalized subjectivity when presenting for care in medical institutions. Through this discussion of the processes whereby gender variance has become medicalized, it has been suggested that anatomopolitical and biopolitical matrices of hegemonic powers are insistent on disciplining and regulating non-normative bodies for the purpose of maintaining a naturalized sex/gender/sexuality systemic ordering for human population growth. Bodies that transgress this system present a threat to species propagation, and are therefore coaxed into a normative dualistic system of male/female to maintain social order. At the same time, although trans individuals are indeed subjectified through medical discourses, institutions, and sex reassignment techniques, much subversion of power occurs. Through the arts of existence and *assujettissement*, gender nonconforming and trans persons resist apparatuses of biopower through embodied practices of heterogeneous genders and sexualities, and non-linear transition trajectories, which disrupt the sex/gender/sexuality system of human social order.

References

Bauer, G. R., Redman, N., Bradley, K., & Scheim. A. I. (2013). Sexual health of trans men who are gay, bisexual, or who have sex with men: Results from Ontario, Canada. *International Journal of Transgenderism*, 14(2), 66–74.

Butler, J. (2001). Doing justice to someone: Sex reassignment and allegories of transsexuality. *GLQ: A Journal of Lesbian and Gay Studies*, 7(4), 621–636.

Butler, J. (2004). *Undoing gender*. New York: Routledge.

Creighton, S., & Minto, C. (2000). Managing intersex. *BMJ*, 323(7326), 1264–1265.

Davy, Z., & Steinbock. E. (2012). 'Sexing up' bodily aesthetics: Notes towards theorizing trans sexuality. In S. Hines & Y. Taylor (Eds.), *Sexualities: Past reflections and future directions. Genders and Sexualities in the Social Sciences* (pp. 266–85). Basingstoke: Palgrave Macmillan.

Diamond, M., & Sigmundson, K. H. (1997) Sex reassignment at birth: Long-term review and clinical implications. *Archive of Pediatric Adolescent Medicine*, 151(3), 298–304.

Drummond, K. D., Bradley, S. J., Peterson-Badali, M., & Zucker, K. J. (2008). A follow-up study of girls with gender identity disorder. *Developmental Psychology*, 44(1), 34–45.

Elliot, P. (2010). *Debates in transgender, queer, and feminist theory: Contested sites*. Burlington, VT: Ashgate.

Fassinger, R. E. & Arseneau, J. R. (2007). 'I'd rather get wet than be under that umbrella': Differentiating the experiences and identities of lesbian, gay, bisexual, and transgender people. In K. J. Beischke, R. M. Perez, & K. A. DeBord (Eds.), *Handbook of Counselling and Psychotherapy with Lesbian, Gay, Bisexual, and Transgender Clients* (pp. 19–49). Washington, DC: American Psychological Association.

Foucault, M. (1979). *The history of sexuality: An introduction.* (R. Hurley, Trans.) New York: Random House.

Foucault, M. (1982). The subject and power. *Critical Inquiry,* 8(4), 777–795.

Foucault, M. (1984). *The history of sexuality, volume 2: The use of pleasure.* (R. Hurley, Trans.) Harmondsworth: Penguin.

Foucault, M. (1989). *The birth of the clinic.* New York: Routledge.

Foucault, M. (1998). *Ethics, subjectivity, and truth: The essential works of Michel Foucault, 1954–1984.* P. Rabinow (Ed.). (R. Hurley et al., Trans.) New York: The New Press.

Foucault, M. (2003). *Psychiatric power: Lectures at the Collège de France, 1973–1974.* J. Lagrange (Ed.). (G. Burchell, Trans.) New York: Picador.

Foucault, M. (2004). *The birth of biopolitics: Lectures at the Collège de France, 1978–1979.* M. Senellart (Ed.). (G. Burchell, Trans.) New York: Picador.

Giami, A. & Beaubatie, E. (2014). Gender identification and sex reassignment surgery in the trans population: A survey study in France. *Archives of Sexual Behaviour,* 43(8), 1491–1501.

Harrer, S. (2005). The theme of subjectivity in Foucault's lecture series *l'hermeneutique du sujet. Foucault Studies,* 2, 75–96.

Heyes, C. J. (2006). Foucault goes to weight watchers. *Hypatia,* 21(2), 126–149.

Hodge, J. (2010). Sex reassignment surgery in Canada. [Gender Focus Blog]. Retrieved From: www.gender-focus.com/2010/11/23/sex-reassignment-surgery-in-canada/

Johnson, A. H. (2015). Normative accountability. How the medical model influences transgender identities and experiences. *Sociology Compass,* 9(9), 803–813.

Karkazis, K. (2008). *Fixing sex: Intersex, medical authority, and lived experience.* Durham, NC: Duke University Press.

Levitt, H. M., & Ippolito, M. R. (2014). Being transgender: Navigating minority stressors and developing authentic self-presentation. *Psychology of Women Quarterly,* 38(1), 46–64.

Majowski, A. (2014). Chosen family provides support for the LGBTQ community. *The Calgary Journal.* Retrieved from: http://calgaryjournal.ca/index.php/family-life/1011-chosen-families-provide-support-for-the-lgbtq-community

Meyerowitz, J. (2004). *How sex changed: A history of transsexuality in the United States.* Cambridge, MA: Harvard University Press.

Milchman, A., & Rosenberg, A. (2007). The aesthetic and ascetic dimensions of an ethics of self-fashioning: Nietzsche and Foucault. *Parrhesia,* 2, 44–65.

Monstrey, S. J., Ceulemans, P., & Hoebeke, P. (2011). Sex reassignment surgery in the female-to-male transsexual. *Seminars in plastic surgery,* 25(3), 229–244.

Queers United. (2010). Open forum: (LGBTI) the intersexual intersection?. [Queers United Blog]. Retrieved from: http://queersunited.blogspot.ca/2010/01/open-forum-lgbti-intersexual.html

Rabinow, P. & Rose, N. (2006). Biopower today. *BioSocieties,* 1, 195–217.

Reicherzer, S. (2008). Evolving language and understanding in the historical development of the gender identity disorder diagnosis. *Journal of LGBT Issues in Counseling,* 24(4), 326–347.

Repo, J. (2013). The biopolitical birth of gender: Social control, hermaphroditism, and the new sexual apparatus. *Alternatives: Global, Local, Political,* 38(3), 228–244.

Sanger, T. (2008). Trans governmentality: The production and regulation of gendered subjectivities. *Journal of Gender Studies*, 17(1), 41–53.

Scheim, A. I., & Bauer, G. R. (2014). Sex and gender diversity among transgender persons in Ontario, Canada: Results from a respondent-driven sampling survey. *Journal of Sex Research*, 52(1), 1–14.

Schleifer, D. (2006). Make me feel mighty real: Gay female-to-male transgenderists negotiating sex, gender, and sexuality. *Sexualities*, 9, 57–75.

Sullivan, N. (2007). *A critical introduction to queer theory*. New York: New York University Press.

Tando, D. (2011). Gender identity vs. sexual orientation. [Gender Blog]. Retrieved from: http://darlenetandogenderblog.com/2011/11/05/gender-identity-vs-sexual-orientation/

Toscano, M. E. & Maynard, E. (2014). Understanding the link: "Homosexuality," gender identity, and the DSM. *Journal of LGBT Issues in Counseling*, 8, 248–263.

Vipond, E. (2015). Resisting transnormativity: Challenging the medicalization and regulation of trans bodies. *Theory in Action*, 8(2), 21–44.

Walters, W. (2012). *Governmentality: Critical encounters*. New York: Routledge.

15

THE PROFESSIONAL RECOURSE TO THE ADOLESCENT BODY

The bathroom wars and the limit of thinking in education

Aziz Guzel

In 2015 the judge presiding over high school student Gavin Grimm's lawsuit stated, "I have no problem with transgender. I have a lot of problems with sex" (Holden, 2015, para. 7). As media reports spread the story of the lawsuit Grimm opened against the school board to gain access to the boys' restroom no one reading the news could have anticipated the catalyzing series of events known as the bathroom debates that would erupt only a year later in North Carolina.

The events began with the refusal of Grimm's request for access to the boys' restroom in his school and was made manifest in a trial that bore witness to the judge's statement, "I have chosen to dismiss Title IX. I decided that before we started." Grimm's case precipitated a series of events that can be thought as emblematic for the ways that adolescent sexuality is posed in educational frameworks. First detected in the words, "I have no problem with transgender, I have a lot of problems with sex," we come to understand in subsequent statements from Judge Robert Doumar that Grimm's appeal cannot be considered because it presents a troubling demand, as it disrupts the consensual reality, upsetting the established order of institutional life. And yet, the verdict "I have chosen to dismiss Title IX. I decided that before we started" conveys what might happen when the notion of sexuality no longer makes sense to us (para. 3).

Sexuality brings together a wide range of assumptions, preferences, and idealizations about what sexuality, adolescence, and education should be and what should be done to secure the adolescent's and society's developmental trajectories accordingly. The following question structures my discussion: what clue might the institutional drift to idealization that recurrently lays emphasis on order, certainty, and borders give to thinking about these frameworks given that frameworks concerned with adolescent development have repeatedly emphasized the value of uncertainty in development? This brings me to a larger question about adolescent education that I consider through a simple paradox which I will approach by way of two cases: If questions around adolescent development are already understood to be laced with a kind of pedagogical imagination that is closely tied to idealizations of learning, sexuality, and growth and these are understood to determine transitions such as that from childhood to adulthood, or from an immature sexuality which is then replaced by a mature sexuality to be sustained, how do we interpret the suspension of the established order which prevailed in Gavin Grimm's case?

Judge Doumar's statements can be also be read as ways of attempting to reassure us that an order is made possible by maintaining a separation between transgender and sex. There, in that separation, the text of sexual difference appears certain and puts at our disposal that which seems to be in danger with a transgender student's access to the bathroom. These statements also remind us how the adolescent too easily presses pedagogical frameworks and other organizational compositions to their limits.

The judge's statements are ingrained idealizations that create a "we" by virtue of their commitment to the realities that make institutions possible. And by its natural consequence the assumption is that if only we could be realistic about our sexuality and consent to the reality of adolescent development and the regulations necessary to avoiding "the problem" Judge Doumar understood to reside with sex. This chapter reopens this logic. My inquiry centers on the paradox of this logic. I explore the ways how adolescent sexuality came to be an externally observed, treated, and measured object, and consider the question of why adolescent sexuality—despite counterarguments (Bartlett et al., 2000; Wren et al., 2002) that have increasingly proven these approaches to be based in statistically poor and recurrently failing constructions—has come to be handled as a self-contained phenomenon.

To do that, I pursue two lines of inquiry. Firstly I consider educational, clinical, administrative, and consequently legal responses to Gavin Grimm's request to access the boys' washroom in his high school. Here I explore the logic of delinking embedded in the recourses to the non-relational adolescent body made through institutional responses. Delinking, here, signifies the institutional responses grounded in biomedical approaches that propose a split between adolescence and adulthood, development and stagnancy, and order and disorder.

Secondly this chapter turns to the question why the biomedical approach has sustained its persuasiveness despite expanding fracture between the progress of biomedicalization in research and its repeating failure to be adapted for the research in diagnostics and clinical practice (Cuthbert & Insel, 2013; Vanheule, 2014). Here I explore the history of gender dysphoria in DSM to shed light on what Lisa Appignanesi (2007) writes of as the "subtle interplay between cultural perspectives and what is also a shifting biological reality" (p. 5).

The mechanism of delinking in responses grounded in biomedical realities is personalized in ways that can be illustrated through cases, and this brings me to the method of exemplary cases conceptualized by John Forrester (2016). Forrester treats the case study "as a way of thinking" and emphasizes the internal mechanism—of thought—embedded in cases. In *Thinking in Cases* Forrester suggests, in conversation with Kuhn's ideas on the exemplar, that studying successful examples of practice provides us with the opportunity to see what binds a professional community together and study of it offers a glimpse of the "group's unproblematic conduct of research" (Kuhn, 1977, p. 318–319 as cited in Forrester, 2016, p. 7).

For the sake of clarity, I wish to note that the DSM here is understood primarily as a textbook for its capacity to provide us with the opportunity to see what binds a professional community together and study of it offers a glimpse of the "group's unproblematic conduct of research." The DSM, among its controversial aspects, is a textbook and it carries the limitation that any other textbook carries. The significance of textbooks don't stem from their representational capacity but rather the capacity to highlight the "research activity itself" (1). Kuhn (2012) once famously pointed out that making generalizations about a professional activity only on the basis of textbooks is analogous to learning about a "national culture drawn from a tourist brochure or a language text" (1). Textbooks host the logic of the profession and, as Forrester succinctly explains, the argumentation through which one internalizes the profession. Forrester explains it succinctly:

> Through internalization of ways of carrying on whereby the would-be scientists know how to recognize a problem that is feasible and how to convert that problem into analogue of ones already solved, he or she acquires the tacit knowledge involved in bridging that gap between the paradigm and the unknown object of research.
>
> *p. 8*

I work from Forrester's conceptualization of the case study as a methodology. This approach brings together cases that could be qualified as exemplars of the prevalent approach to adolescent experience. Forrester's methodology offers a new orientation to adolescent sexuality and the intersubjective experience of responding through sustaining a discussion where the interplay of discourses embedded in the question of care. As it can be observed in law, clinic's relation to specificity of each person is what "grants the word 'clinical' its meaning" (p. 128). This chapter is informed by Gozlan's (2014) conceptualization of the figure of transgender that "invites us to consider gender as a problem of thinking and of resistance to stability and time," that "rattles the very idea of origin by opening the question of desire and its effervescent nature" (p. xii).

Avoiding experience: opening arguments on delinking

Gavin Grimm's case began in his sophomore year when he informed the school administration about his transition and requested access to the washroom corresponding with his identity, supported by a doctor who provided diagnosis of gender dysphoria. Grimm's request was answered with approval by the school administration until some seven weeks later when an anonymous complaint was logged regarding Grimm's use of the washroom. The complaint quickly made its way to the Gloucester County School Board, "which placed Grimm at the top of its meeting agenda" (Riley 2016, para. 13). Grimm's request was subsequently interpreted as inappropriate and his access to the boys' washroom was barred with a 6–1 vote. The board deemed that an "alternate, private facility"—a unisex washroom—would be the appropriate response (para. 14). The school was pressed to furnish an additional washroom and so hastily overhauled an unused janitor's closet for Grimm and any other transgender students to access. Given a dark and closeted space, Grimm instead made use of the washroom in the nurse's station while he followed up his request with the courts.

Grimm would take this decision to the District Court that witnessed the federal judge's puzzling responses and which serves here as an example par excellence for thinking about the underlying mechanism of care in responses to adolescents. This means of handling adolescent development only generates solutions by renouncing that which links (delinking) and thus reinforcing a culture corroborated by the avoidance of experience. In fact, in the responses to Grimm we find an entire series of renounced links: Besides renouncing the relationship between sex and transgender, Judge Doumar, by the same logic, overruled the plea for Grimm's case to be considered under Title IX. The therapist, too, can be implicated in the logic of delinking, as when Grimm came out as transgender, the therapist avoided the nature of experience by saying, "You don't have to explain yourself," and, "I get it" (para. 44). The court, school, and clinic each, in turn, moved with motions that dismissed Grimm's complaint by way of a logic that refuses integration.

What are the renounced links in these responses? We can speculate that what is meant by the therapist's response is that Gavin's experience of transitioning is irrelevant to the experience of therapy, seemingly made apparent in the inability to sustain a conversation about Gavin's experience. The response issued by the court judge carries a similar quality when ruling the appeal cannot be considered under Title IX of the Education Amendments of 1972 which guarantee, "No person in the United States shall, on the basis of sex, be excluded from participation in, be denied the benefits of, or be subjected to discrimination under any education program or activity receiving federal financial assistance" (United States Department of Labor, para. 1) The judge said little about the grounds on which the decision was based, and still his puzzling response provides enough material to speculate on why transgender is seen as irrelevant to sex.

When we search into these situations and ask where it could be possible to ask after that which rendered Gavin's request and consequent appeal unthinkable, we find that any consideration of what might be educational in Grimm's request was yielded to the legal framework. Each framework deferred, as if in a search of a new situation. The legal and educational collapsed on one another. And in the therapist's case what is clinical was collapsed with parental concerns. Extending beyond the webs of the school, family and clinic with their preoccupations with developmental trajectories—the legal framework was not immune to this single-minded approach that saw gender and sex collapsed together.

What is common in each context is the privileging of one framework over another made on grounds of objectivity—a kind of objectivity that enabled the therapist, the school board, and the judge to avoid thinking with the significance of experience. Analyst Oren Gozlan (2015) writes that the "profession's demand of objectivity translates into the psychological numbing of the clinician as a defense mechanism against becoming response- able" (p. 174). The insistence of certainty over the meaning of human experience for Gozlan is the only possible by way of situating oneself as the responder, outside of experience. The judge's response, then, might make us wonder what it means to presume to guarantee a split between experience and responding through the claims made possible by objectivity.

We can now begin thinking about the underlying logic of delinking, seen in the renounced links between Grimm's demand and the educational, clinical, administrative and legal responsibilities to respond to his demand. In each response there is a lack of care for Grimm's experience and strikingly there doesn't seem to be any concern for the need to engage the nature of Grimm's response in order to formulate a response to his request. To explore how these responses laced with as-if responses present themselves simply as expectations for the ways we should approach adolescents, we need to understand how the logic of delinking has become internalized.

Has sexuality anything to do with education?

How can we understand the resistance to sexuality and limits of thinking embedded in the responses to Grimm? In each response there is an assumption that sexuality (through claims about adolescence, bodies, and parenting) is situated as a purely biological phenomenon, as self-evident empirical knowledge that can be seen in the routine backslide to moralism, and as biologism that tenders proof that sexuality has nothing to do with a profession's ethical responsibilities in working with adolescents. In his 1996 paper "Has sexuality anything to do with psychoanalysis?" Andre Green reminds us that our interpretation of sexuality has drifted towards compartmentalization and notes the significance that sexuality brings to clinical frameworks: "[sexuality] is no longer considered to be a major factor in child development . . . It is as if sexuality were now considered a topic of specialised significance, a limited area of the internal world among other such" (p. 871).

What Green is attentive to is the way the absence of sexuality in clinical frameworks resembles the early confusion about genitality and sexuality. With an eye to the horizons of interpretation, Green raises a lucid question that can take on the different orientations of the clinical framework by pressing the problem; what if sexuality is ignored and limited to the manifest level? Ian Parker (2011) raises a similar concern in his book *Lacanian Psychoanalysis*. Parker observes that in the clinic the role of sexuality is either avoided or obscured through what he calls "pious appeals to sweet reason, dissolving sex into attachment in 'relationships'" (p. 16).

Education has inherited the fundamental tenets of the clinical imagination since the very beginning of its institutionalization when, as early as the 1900s, adolescent sexuality became central to frameworks concerned with the education of adolescents (Hall, 1908; Perito 2008). It is possible to read this history of the institutionalization of adolescent education as burdened by formulating the questions that sexuality poses to adolescent education, which in most cases took the form of renouncing the relationship. The question of sexuality propelled the field of adolescent education towards a form of hygienism laced with moralistic and essentialist ideas (Alexander, 1998). What might it mean to search for an engagement with adolescent sexuality that doesn't jump to conclusions about sexuality, adolescence, education, and society?

To consider this, I begin by taking the very absence of relevance between phenomena that are already understood to be irrelevant. In the case of adult and adolescent experiences, and sexuality and education, can the very absence of links be understood as what Corfield and Leader (2008) describe as the sway of a very "strong defence mechanism at play" (p. 13)? If we echo Corfield and Leader it is possible to speculate that the very absence of an interpretive link between sexuality in adolescent education and sexuality in adolescent development is the link.

In the biomedical model, by which I mean the rapid expansion of discourses stemming from the 1980 paradigmatic shift that took place with the introduction of the DSM III, we find adolescent sexuality as a self-contained phenomenon (American Psychiatric Association, 1980). With this paradigmatic shift the medical discourse on adolescent sexuality gained the status of an untouchable cultural authority, primarily won through its statistical construction. The observation was increasingly made that the biomedical discourse tended to regurgitate conventional morality under the auspices of data, reliability, and objectivity.

To invoke Adam Phillips (1999), we could say that whether or not we read into clinical literature to find those bits concerned with adolescent sexuality, clinical literature reads us. We can see this in another of Judge Doumar's reactions to Grimm's case where he resolved the situation through a recourse to "mental disorder" (Holden, 2015, para. 1). This exploration, therefore, asks why among all other explanations of adolescent sexuality the fragmented description of the biomedical formulation stuck to the clinical, educational, and legal imagination.

The logic of diagnosis or the story of gender dysphoria

Debates about gender dysphoria cannot be understood separately from the histories of professionalization and institutionalization in the treatment of mental health, access to medical care, political activism, and the construction of the "normal" adolescent alongside other factors of cultural anxiety (Sedgwick, 1991; Corbett, 1997; Bryant, 2006; Stryker, 2008; Rose, 2016). Some 35 years after the major shift marked by the third revision of the DSM, Robert Spitzer and Kenneth Zucker (2005), held to be among the chief architects of modern classifications of mental disorders, commented on their motivation for introducing the entity of Gender Identity Disorder of Childhood Diagnosis into the DSM III despite insufficient data. The justifications for why GIDC was introduced take us to the heart of the matter regarding idealization:

We argue that GIDC was included as a psychiatric diagnosis because it met the generally accepted criteria used by the framers of DSM-III for inclusion (for example, clinical utility, acceptability to clinicians of various theoretical persuasions, and an empirical database to propose explicit diagnostic criteria that could be tested for reliability and validity). In this respect, the entry of GIDC into the psychiatric nomenclature was guided by the reliance on "expert consensus" (research clinicians)—the same mechanism that led to the introduction of many new psychiatric diagnoses, including those for which systematic field trials were not available when the DSM-III was published (31).

The emphasis placed on clinical utility and expert consensus by Spitzer and Kenneth is a useful start. What is this clinical utility? And how else can we understand the motive to introduce a psychiatric category before there is enough data? It is worth noting that introducing a new diagnostic entity without achieving a statistically sound structure is an ongoing problem for the adolescent clinic (Perring & Wells, 2014). It is crucial to ask why diagnosis is too often believed to have a privileged relationship to truth even when it recurrently fails to be translated into research in diagnostics and psychotherapy (Cuthbert & Insel, 2013). If a biomedical solution seems to be insufficient on its own terms, what kind of solution does it offer?

This new utility based model is a response to the crisis stemming from the ever-expanding critiques of earlier editions of the DSM which have regarded mental health professions to be unscientific and judged their methods to be too vague. From that long list we could pull a few key names of those who, albeit in different contexts, challenged early institutional attempts to standardize the clinic: Rosenhan (1973), Rawnsley (1967), and the US–UK Diagnostic Project (Cooper, 1972). With reference to the blurred lines between sanity and insanity and normal and pathological proposed by the DSM I and II, critics concentrated on the impossibility of adhering to such categories. These studies cast grave suspicion on the nature of diagnosis. Statistically speaking what was challenged can be translated as findings of poor reliability and validity in the development of diagnostic classifications.

The foremost solution generated by the DSM taskforce chose this problem as the major expression of crisis and concentrated upon the question of the inter-rater agreement. A statistical analysis called kappa statistic was used to measure the likelihood of random clinicians arriving at the same diagnosis. The DSM III task force calculated the kappa co-efficiency of existing categories in the DSM and this enabled them evaluate "agreement between judges, but [also] incorporat[e] a correction for agreement based on mere chance" (Vanheule, 2014, p. 14).

The insistent discourse of reliability lies here. Reliability is high when the kappa coefficient number is high, between .70 and .90. Having a high kappa coefficient can be understood as delivering a more concretely structured entity. The reliable classification of psychopathology was arrived at through this solution because it was seen to provide ways "disorders can be studied independently of the particularities of people's lives and thus merely require correct classification" (Vanheule, 2014, p. 32). On a technical note, there is no strict consensus or standard as to what kappa coefficient is required for making a diagnostic category. The kappa coefficient has remained largely unchanged while the checklist model has established itself in the cultural arena as the chief framework (Vanhuele, 2014). The change is the "threshold for which they were being interpreted" (p. 15).

Institutional efforts to address questions regarding gender variant children began prior to the publication of the DSM III, with a special focus on gender variant boys; these normative approaches mainly formulated how to detect and treat gender variant children (Green, 1967; Green & Money 1960, 1961). With normative visions of the development of boys and girls in mind, the DSM III hastily introduced the category of Gender Identity Disorder following the studies carried out by sexologists Richard Green and John Money. In these studies we find gender variance is identified as a great risk and therefore in need of treatment (Bryant, 2006).

The urgency in these studies was one the chief reasons why just a handful of case studies was considered sufficient to draw conclusions and confidence for handling the complexity of the experience of gender. Some of the studies were carried out through discourses that determined the *real* of sexuality based on birth assignment and external observation that paved the way for "behavioral modification" (Rekers, 1977). Rekers proposed notions of atypical gender development and psychosocial adjustment to transform whatever was ,held to be typical (Rekers, 1977). The early imaginary on which the DSM III based its conceptualization of GIDC, pulled from methods such as those of Rekers who "used classic reinforcement techniques to extinguish feminine behaviors and replace them with masculine ones" (Bryant 2006, p. 28).

The baseline for what was perceived to be atypical changed constantly, to the point that parents and teachers were drawn into the behavioral program to ensure the time "feminine boys" spent with their sisters was reduced to zero or near zero in order to eliminate feminine content. These efforts still amounted to statistical failure where field studies did not support the assumptions proposed in the DSM III and consequently were dropped.

What was being done through these studies can be understood as a reification of sexuality by treating it as a result of some sort of mistake. And yet, the basic mismatch presented by the nature of sexuality resists this reification. The translation of sexuality through the concretization of knowledge embedded in causal accounts relieves us from the work of choice and interpretation by assuming to provide the "real" of sexuality as self-contained. In the article "To what extent is personal therapeutic experience and external validation essential in therapeutic training?" Corfield and Leader (2008) points to this basic mismatch:

> The footage of a crying baby shown to an audience told it was a boy took it as transparent that 'he' was angry, yet when the baby was described as a 'she' this 'anger' became 'sadness'. What we see thus depends on our expectations and what we are taught to look for. One hundred years of history and philosophy of science and sociology have shown us that the criteria of empirical verification are never uncomplicated.
>
> *p. 389*

Consequences of statistically constructed conceptions of adolescent sexuality and associated practices (misdiagnosis, overdiagnosis, low reliability, etc.), which rely solely on external validation, have been widely documented and they can be read as what Jacqueline Rose (2011) calls the "return of the referent," with the qualification of "the referent as a problem, not as a given" (p. 224). As a failed category gender identity disorder returns us to the fantasy of absolute sexual difference which shook the clinical field with its insistence on stabilizing the picture of development by trying to create a conversation in which what a boy looks like and should look like are formulated in the same question. For Corbett (1997) this is the picture of gender that is equated with health.

It may suffice to say that attempts to emulate the biomedical approach didn't necessarily stem from discovering "an underlying biomedical reality that could be linked to the behaviours" (Vanheule, 2014, p. 21). Rather, the profession was guided by a radical and highly persuasive epistemology of the construction of suffering based on a method that seemed to offer a shortcut around the problems of meaning, interpretation, relationality, and the question of suffering accessed via coordinates to the promises of utility, consensus, objectivity, and cure.

Operationalizing suffering and stabilizing symptoms

To solve the manifold crisis undergone in clinical frameworks involved generating an immediate solution for the question of inconsistency with new techniques of evaluation applied through the kappa efficiency. This sweeping technique had broad impact. One of the consequences of this shift was an inevitable decline in the centrality of interpretation that streamed through the operational method and the subsequent gradual reduction of the diagnostic method to identifying predetermined behavioral signs. A diagnosis (signified) was imagined to be an ensemble of symptoms (sign), always to be observable without interference. The insistence that diagnosis become more like a sign requires us to consider the logic of the construction of the sign as an object.

The construction of the sign as an object dates back to the works of the American physicist Percy W. Bridgman. Bridgman argued that concepts are always understood in terms of a set of preconceived properties which cannot be found in nature. When we think of something like a fast car, we understand that to be fast is to be in relation to other determinants. "A concept is only fixed," write Parnas and Bovet (2015), "when the operations by which it is determined are fixed" (p. 191). However singular and independent they might seem, concepts built and depend on this radically relational quality. For Bridgman, concepts, whatever else they are, "are synonymous with the corresponding set of operations" (Bridgman, 1927, p. 5 as cited in Kendler & Parnas 2015, p. 191). Trouble begins for a term when operational logic is assimilated by behavioral approaches to solve and master the problem of meaning.

For Bridgman what was operational about the concept of operationalism was the act of observation by which one was able to pin down the constituents of a concept.

Hempel, for his part, unhinged operationalism from the act of observation by proposing the operational definition be innovated through a new method of determining objective criteria, putting forward "the idea of unity of science and (ultimately) a *nomological regulation* of scientific concepts (i.e., the use of concepts becoming anchored by their role in the laws of nature)" (Parnas & Bovet, 2014, p. 193).

At work here is a shift to a model of conceptualization that can be qualified as externalization as a project. Externalization intensifies the tail-chasing wordplay of the diagnostic method, egging on the race to match signs and symptoms. Lost in this chase is the subject living with the symptoms and left to make sense of the diagnosis. If subjectivity has become a scholarly bugaboo, by provoking anxiety and inflicting irregularity and incoherence, at what cost? Experience is reduced to narrowly defined signs. And, Parnas and Bovet (2014), "theoretically speaking," elaborate how

> a psychiatric symptom is not a well-demarcated thing-like object, but rather a certain configuration that involves the flow of phenomenal consciousness, with its intentional contents and forms (structures). The symptoms are certain wholes of interpenetrating experiences, beliefs, expressions, and actions, all of them permeated by the patient's dispositions and by biographical (and not just biological) detail. The symptom individuates itself in the synchronic and diachronic *contexts* along all these dimensions, which combine into specific meaning-wholes. In short, a symptom/ sign is not an entity "in itself"—easily or arbitrarily isolated out of the ongoing flow of consciousness, and described independently of its context.
>
> *p. 204*

While thinking about a subjective experience through well-defined, compartmentalized signs made to generate evidence, what is overlooked in this vocabulary is that subjectivity and the significance of one's relation to a sign/symptom has increasingly became a monstrous vocation in scholarly, cultural, educational, clinical, and political contexts. The exclusion of experience might lead to statistically infallible entities, yet it strips the investigation of its two constitutive dimensions— two dimensions that are constitutive of the human subject—history and relationality.

Some thoughts on a signifying frame for thinking about adolescent sexuality

Judge Doumar's persisting certainty has a link, I suggest, with the clinical disavowal of subjectivity maintained through compartmentalization. Just as the judge insists that transgender has nothing to do with sex, the clinical imagination—along with other frameworks of adolescence—has long maintained a practice of multilayered splitting through reductive biological thinking. Sexuality has paradoxically been situated in both the realm of biology and as irrelevant to adolescent development. Adolescence is then situated apart from adulthood, and by charging signs with particular meanings to compensate for the "inchoateness of experience," experience too is situated apart from the work of interpretation, its meaning and handed over to the external realm of validation (Gozlan, 2014, p. 181). Thus it is that we arrive at that mechanism of splitting that I find to be at the heart of the trouble surrounding attempts to stabilize adolescent sexuality.

There is an immediate susceptibility as soon as one reads the institutional responses to adolescent sexuality as a form of defense against the emotional experience of working with adolescence and sexuality. This susceptibility ushers institutional frameworks back to patrol the creep across those shifting borders between normality and pathology and the adolescent and adult. Borders, Corbett (2001) notes, "need constant patrol" (p. 13). And we find the crossing is strongly defended in the school board's solution to provide further compartmentalization to the bathroom with the addition of a new buffer zone.

Adolescent sexuality, read through Gavin Grimm's case, brings to the fore the manifold crises in clinical, political, legal, and educational frameworks. It presents us the prevailing ideality on sexuality that is unhinged from the complexity of growing up. To bar the complexity of adolescent sexuality in the confinements of selectively constructed operational logic provides what Gozlan calls "illusionary reassurances"; as we saw in the revision efforts applied to gender dysphoria, this also compels institutional frameworks to cling to the fantasies of operationalism that lead to the failure to formulate an ethical encounter with difference (Gozlan, 2015, p. 182). Still, thinking about the questions that Grimm's case poses for educational and legal frameworks, we can also take note of what Gozlan calls the "aesthetic shift" in thinking about sexuality—sexuality as "always transformative and in transit" (p. 1). Grimm's case and the history of gender dysphoria, then, gives us access to "the unrepresentable tension that the gender binary both enacts and veils" (p. 1).

In "Questions of ethics and aesthetics for a profession in crisis," Gozlan (2015) suggests that the instrumentalization of mental health has resulted in the lack of a framework and signifying chain that would contain the responder. According to this claim, we could consider the series of events precipitated by Gavin Grimm's demand for access to the bathroom as symptomatic of the larger crisis in educational frameworks. And indeed, parallel with early scholarship on the questions of gender, gender-variant children and adolescents have been used in the clinical framework "in response to their own existing professional concerns and crises" (Bryant, 2006). Colette Soler (2000) describes this as imposing a standard solution and rejecting all other solutions as atypical or pathological. "Providing semblances capable of ordering the relation between sexes", Colette adds, "tells us what we should do as men or a women" (p. 40).

Reactions following Gavin Grimm's request to access the boy's washroom and debates over gender identity disorder elucidate the subtle—and not so subtle—flights to idealized constructions of development, sexuality, and learning. Attempting to create all-encompassing constructions of development and adolescent sexuality, then, can appear as a way of easing the tension adolescent sexuality underscores in taken for granted ideas about the adolescent–adult relationship, sexuality, and development. And rather than confining sexuality to the realm of biologically grounded genitality and "degrading [its] significance as known and certain," Grimm's case refuses these confines and insists upon the gendered bodily presence of sexuality in the world (Gozlan 2014, p. 4).

Just as the impossibility of eradicating the tension sexuality creates cannot be foreclosed by the idealization of gender (Butler, 1993; Dimen & Goldner, 2010; Gozlan, 2014), the question of adolescent sexuality requires an approach that can enter into conversation with the complexity of sexuality in a way that does not simply foreclose through forms of segregation. Our project will be to treat the question of adolescent sexuality as a question of the sign with unassigned meaning, as an indicator that "sexuality is always in excess of the signifier" (Gozlan, 2014, p. 12). This very failure to acknowledge the excess of sexuality we witness in various responses to adolescent sexuality, be it a diagnostic entity or a decision made by a school board, can appear as a significant example of what Gozlan discusses as the projection of lack.

References

Alexander, R. (1998). *The girl problem: Female sexual delinquency in New York, 1900–1930*. Ithaca, NY: Cornell University Press.
American Psychiatric Association. (2013). *Diagnostic and statistical manual of mental disorders* (5th ed.). Arlington, VA: American Psychiatric Publishing.
Appignanesi, L. (2007). *Mad, bad and sad*. London: Virago.
Bartlett, N. H., Vasey, P. L., & Bukowski, W. M. (2000). Is gender identity disorder in children a mental disorder? *Sex Roles*, 43(11–12), 753–785.
Bryant, K. (2006). Making gender identity disorder of childhood: Historical lessons for contemporary debates. *Sexuality Research and Social Policy*, 3(3), 23–39. http://dx.doi.org/10.1525/srsp.2006.3.3.23
Butler, J. (1993). *Bodies that matter: On the discursive limits of "sex"*. New York: Routledge.
Corbett, K. (1997). It is time to distinguish gender from health: Reflections on Lothstein's "Pantyhose fetishism and self cohesion: A paraphilic so." *Gender and Psychoanalysis*, 2(2), 259–271.
Corbett, K. (2001). Faggot = loser. *Studies in Gender and Sexuality*, 2(1), 3–28.
Corfield, D., & Leader, D. (2008). *Why do people get ill? Exploring the mind–body connection*. London: Penguin.
Cuthbert, B., & Insel, T. (2013). Toward the future of psychiatric diagnosis: The seven pillars of RDoC. *BMC Medicine*, 11(1). http://dx.doi.org/10.1186/1741-7015-11-126
Forrester, J. (2016). *Thinking in cases* (1st ed.). Cambridge: Polity Press.
Goldner, V., & Dimen, M. (2010). *Gender in psychoanalytic space: Between clinic and culture*. New York: Other Press.
Gozlan, O. (2014). *Transsexuality and the art of transitioning: A Lacanian approach*. Abingdon: Routledge.
Gozlan, O. (2015) Trauma and evil: Questions of ethics and aesthetics for a profession in crisis. In Jon Mills & Ron Naso (Eds.) *Humanizing evil: Psychoanalytic, philosophical and clinical perspectives* (pp. 171–188). New York: Routledge.

Green, A. (1996). Has sexuality anything to do with psychoanalysis? *The International Journal of Psycho-Analysis*, 76(5), 871–883.
Hall, G. S. (1908). *Youth: Its education, regimen, and hygiene*. New York: D. Appleton & Co.
Holden, D. (2015). Judge throws out key argument in transgender student restroom case. *Buzzfeed*. Retrieved 9 April 2017, from: www.buzzfeed.com/dominicholden/judge-throws-out-key-argument-in-transgender-student-restroo?utm_term=.hakLOjPg1#.byyQMlaB0
Kendler, K. S., & Parnas, J. (Eds.). (2015). *Philosophical issues in psychiatry: Explanation, phenomenology, and nosology*. Baltimore, MD: Johns Hopkins University Press.
Kuhn, T. (2012). *The Structure of Scientific Revolutions: 50th Anniversary Edition*. Chicago: The University of Chicago Press.
Money, J., & Green, R. (1960). Incongruous gender role: Nongenital manifestations in prepubertal boys. *The journal of nervous and mental disease*, 131(2), 160–168.
Parker, I. (2011). *Lacanian psychoanalysis: Revolutions in subjectivity*. Hove: Routledge.
Parnas, J., & Bovet, P. (2015) Psychiatry made easy: Operation(al)ism and some of its consequences. In Parnas, J. & Kendler, K. (Eds.), *Philosophical issues in psychiatry III: The nature and sources of historical change* (pp. 190–212). Oxford: Oxford University Press.
Perito, J. E. (2008). *Adolescent sexuality: Too much too soon*. Danvers, MA: American Book Publishing.
Phillips, A. (1999). *Darwin's worms*. London: Faber & Faber.
Rekers, G. (1977). Atypical gender development and psychosocial adjustment. *Journal of Applied Behavior Analysis*, 10(3), 559–571. http://dx.doi.org/10.1901/jaba.1977.10-559
Riley, J. (2016). Gavin's Story: Gavin Grimm is the new face of the transgender movement. *Metro Weekly*. Retrieved August 25, 2017, from: www.metroweekly.com/2016/05/gavin-grimm-story/
Rose, J. (2016). LRB · Jacqueline Rose · who do you think you are? *Trans narratives*. Retrieved September 18, 2016, from: www.lrb.co.uk/v38/n09/jacqueline-rose/who-do-you-think-you-are
Rose, J., & Clemens, J. (2011). The Jacqueline Rose Reader (1st ed.). Durham, NC: Duke University Press.
Rosenhan, D. (1973). On being sane in insane places. *Science*, 179, 250–258
Salecl, R. (2000). *Sexuation: SIC 3*. Durham, NC: Duke University Press.
Sedgwick, E. (1991). How to bring your kids up gay. *Social Text*, (29), 18–27. http://dx.doi.org/10.2307/466296
Soler, S. (2000) The curse on sex. In R. Salecl (Ed.) *Sexuation: Sic 3* (Vol. 3) (pp. 39–57). Durham, NC: Duke University Press.
Spitzer, R., & Zucker, K. (2005). Was the gender identity disorder of childhood diagnosis introduced into DSM-III as a backdoor maneuver to replace homosexuality? A historical note. *Journal of Sex & Marital Therapy*, 31(1), 31–42.
Stryker, S. (2008). *Transgender history*. Berkeley, CA: Seal Press.
Symington, J., & Symington, N. (1996). *The clinical thinking of Wilfred Bion* (1st ed.). London: Routledge.
Title IX, Education Amendments of 1972. *Dol.gov*. Retrieved April 9, 2017, from www.dol.gov/oasam/regs/statutes/titleix.htm
Vanheule, S. (2014). *Diagnosis and the DSM: A critical review*. Basingstoke: Palgrave Macmillan.
Wells, L., & Perring, C. (2014). Diagnostic dilemmas in child and adolescent psychiatry: Philosophical Perspectives. Oxford: Oxford University Press.
Wren, B., Griffin, C., & Wilson, I. (2002). The validity of the diagnosis of gender identity disorder (child and adolescent criteria). *Clinical Child Psychology Psychiatry*, 7(3), 335-351.

INDEX

Abourahme, Nasser 62
Abraham, Karl 77
accepting approach 118; *see also* affirmative approach
accepting parental approach 124–5
acculturation 53, 146, 151
Adam and Eve 39
Adler, Alfred 77
adolescent body: avoiding experience: opening arguments on delinking 210–12; has sexuality anything to do with education? 212–13; the logic of diagnosis or the theory of gender dysphoria 213–16; operationalizing suffering and stabilizing symptoms 216–17; some thoughts on a signifying frame for thinking about adolescent sexuality 217–18
adolescent education, and the established order 208–9
aesthetic play 53
aesthetic shift 218
aesthetic, the 49, 56, 98
affirmative approach 118, 120, 126 n20
Agassi, Andre 185
Akin (Chase) 48–58; defense narratives in 55–6; theme of transitions 51–5
ambivalence over 54–5
Ambrosio, Giovanna 83
American Psychiatric Association 105, 132
American Psychological Association 105
Amsterdam Center of Expertise on Gender Dysphoria, VU Medical Center 104

anatomopolitics 196–7, 204, 205
anecdotes, rejection of 17
anti-psychiatry 171
Appignanesi, Lisa 209
Arbus, Diane 17
Argentieri, Simona 91
art therapy 152
assigned sex/gender, use of term 116, 117
Association for the Advancement of Psychotherapy 80
assujettissement 202–3
authenticity 5, 7
Ayatollah Khomeini 158

Baker, Sean S., *Tangerine* 67–8
Barbin, Herculine 178 n8; *Middlesex* (with Eugenides) 172, 173
Bastian, Michelle 64–6
Bataille, George 20
beauty 6–7
behavior modification 103
behavior modification program, UCLA 102–3
behavioral intervention 200
behaviorist model 81
Benjamin, Harry 2, 79–81, 85, 201; *Transsexualism and Transvestitism as Psycho-Somatic and Somato-Psychic Syndromes* 190 n1
Berlin Psychoanalytic Society 77
Bettcher, Talia Mae 183–4, 185
Binnie, Imogen, *Nevada* 59, 65–6, 69

biological sex, and psychological gender 200
biomedical approach 209, 213
biomythograph 173, 178 n9
Bion, W. R. 45–6; caesura 38; container/contained interaction 39–40
biopolitics 196–7, 205
biopower: anatomopolitics, biopolitics, and the deployment of (hetero)sexuality 196–7; confession as technical strategy of 199; Foucault's theory of 194–207; knowledge production and the subjectification of patients 197–8; psychiatric questioning, confessions, and psychosexual deviance 198–9; resisting medical discourse: trans subjects and *assujettissement* 202–3; sex-reassignment techniques and the invention of gender identity 199–200; and sexual apparatus 200
bisexuality 204
Boellstroff, Tom 68, 69
border youth: an intersectional approach to gender-fluidity 152–6; invisibilization 147–8, 150; oppression of 147; psychological research with 149–51; therapeutic guidelines: models of identification and grassroots mental healthcare initiatives 151–2; use of term 147
Bornstein, Kate 84
Bovet, P. 216, 217
Boyerin, Daniel 172
Bradley, Susan 103
Bridgman, Percy W. 216
Britton, Robert 39
Brocéliande, Ludiane de 115
Bullough, V. 78
bullying 107, 120, 121, 155
Butler, Judith 24–5, 178 n11, 179 n11, 197, 199

caesura 38–42, 45, 46
Canada 66; access to transition 181, 204; indigenous peoples 156 n2; gender research 103, 105, 146, 149–51; settler-colonial whiteness 184, 191 n8; see also border youth
Canadian Constitution 156 n2
Canetti, Elias, *Crowds and Power* 171
capitalism 188, 189, 191 n10
Carlson, Shanna 82–3, 95, 191 n9
Carson, Anne 56
Castoriadis, Piera Cornelius 19
castration 3–4, 84, 173, 176

castration anxiety 78
castration complex 76
Caujolle, Christian 17
Cauldwell, David 78–9; *Psychopathia Transexualis* 78
Cavanagh, Sheila 191 n9
Center for Alcoholism and Mental Health (CAMH), Toronto 103, 105
Chiland, Collete 83
Child and Adolescent Center 108
child and mother, imaginary space between 49–50
child development: Oedipal stage 93; and sexuality 212; uncertainty in 208; see also development theory
childhood 119–20; and professionals 123–5
children: best interests of 104, 120–1, 124, 125; gender communications 110–12; knowledge of own sex/gender 113, 118; rejection of genitalia 120; self-referencing 120
children's rights-oriented approach 124, 125
chosen family 201
chrononormativity (Freeman) 65
Clare, Eli 184, 188
clothes 123
clothing 119, 124, 126 n14
Coffman, Chris 99
cognitive constriction 104
Cohen-Kettenis, Peggy 104
Coldwell, David Oliver 2
coming out 121, 126 n22, 204
community-based model 156
conceptualization, model of 217
confession 197, 198–9, 199, 202, 204, 205
container/contained interaction 39–40
conversion 60–1
Corbett, K. 216, 218
Corfield, D. 213, 215
counter-transference 63, 83
Cox, Laverne 191 n3
creativity 49, 56–7
critical disability theory 188, 191 n10
cross-dressing 77–8, 152; see also transvestitism/transvestites

Dan/Dania 42–6
Davenport, Lindsay 185
Davidman, Sara 17
De Certeau, M. 172
Dean, T. 76, 84
death 75, 85
deception 62
Deleuze, Gilles 171

delinking 209, 210–12
delivery, and therapists 211
depression 120
Descartes, René 25
desire of the Other (Lacan) 90, 92, 94, 96, 99, 171
development theory 106–7, 109; *see also* child development
diagnosis, logic of 213–16
Diagnostic and Statistical Manual for Mental Disorders (*DSM*) 2, 6, 108, 133, 177, 184, 188, 209, 210, 214; clinical language 183, 191 n5; homosexuality removed from 199
Diagnostic and Statistical Manual for Mental Disorders, third edition (*DSM* III) 213–15
Diagnostic and Statistical Manual for Mental Disorders, fourth edition (*DSM* IV) 132
Diagnostic and Statistical Manual for Mental Disorders, fifth edition (*DSM* V) 89, 145
Diamond, M. 112
different transformations 45–6
dissociative detachment 37, 42
doorkeeper(s) *see* gatekeeping
Dor, Joël 91
double temporal logic (Bastian) 64
Doumar, Robert 208, 209, 211, 213, 217
drive 77
Dumaresq, Michelle 191 n3
Dyer, Hannah 55

ecological interventions 103
Eigen, Michael 83
Ekins R. 79
Elba, Lili 8
Elliot, Patricia 176, 191 n9; *Lacanian Analysis and Transsexuality: Take 2* 178 n4
Ellis, Havelock 77, 79, 80
embodied autobiography 185–6
emergent mode 39–40
empathy, and therapy 139–40
Engdahl, Ulrica 182
epistemology 98, 145–6, 216
Eros 7, 23, 24
eroticism (Bataille) 20
eschewing or avoiding approach 119
ethics 105, 123, 124, 202, 212, 218
Eugenides, Jeffrey, *Middlesex* (with Barbin) 172, 173
Eve 39; creation of 36, 37

family 103; chosen 201; consultation 107–8; importance and power of 200–1;

see also mother; parents; paternal metaphor
family system re-structuring 103
family violence 54
female-to-male (FTM) 82, 161, 162
feminism 63–4
feminization 80, 93, 94, 186, 203; Schreber 93–4, 170, 171, 172, 173, 175, 177
fetishism 42–6, 78
Fink, Bruce 92
Fiorini, Glocer 4
First Nations 156 n2
Flechsig, Dr. 171
Forensic Medicine Organization (FMO) 159
forms of address 122
Forrester, John: *Thinking in Cases* 209–10
Foucault, Michel 171, 194; *Abnormal* 197; arts of existence 202; *The Birth of the Clinic* 200; on the body 15; *History of Sexuality* 76, 178 n8, 196; *Psychiatric Power* 196, 197, 201; *Society Must Be Defended* 178 n3; techniques of the self 202; theory of biopower 194–207; *Use of Pleasure* 202
Freeman, Christine 65
Freeman, Elizabeth 64
Freud, Sigmund 4, 52, 172, 177; anatomy and destiny 75; *Beyond the Pleasure Principle* 85; "Hysterical fantasies and their relation to bisexuality" 77; libido theory 171; notion of Eros 7; Oedipus Complex 76, 85, 171, 178 n11; *Psycho-Analytic Notes on an Autobiographical Account of a Case of Paranoia* 169; pulsional theory 21–2, 23; on Schreber 170–1, 172, 173, 177; seduction theory 174; theory of; hysteria 57 n2; theory of sexuality 58 n4; theory of the unconscious 57 n2; *Three Essays on the Theory of Sexuality* 77; the uncanny 20; "working through" 53
fugue state 66

gatekeeping 50, 132, 133, 134, 138, 139, 184
gay *see* homosexuality
gaze, the: microscopic 8; mimetic quality 17
Geller, Jay 172
gender: as agentic project 155; definition of 48; fetishization of 4; fills space of lack 56; fluid nature of 60; and health 216; natal sex as determinant of 187; non-binary 23–5; notion of 4–5;

performative power of 16–17; resolves sexual difference 54; selecting 186–7; as unfolding process 106–7; use of term 2–3

gender affirmative model 106–13; basic therapeutic tenet 108–9; and children's knowledge of gender identity 113; evidence-based outcomes 112; final task: dispelling myths 112–13; goals 107; learning to read a child's gender communications 110–12; major mental health treatment models 102–10; premises 106, 108; procedure 109–10; reality of 113; reason for treatment 108; role of mental health professionals 108; rubber-stamping 112; surgery 112; translation tools 112

gender binary, and wrong-body narrative 184–5

gender certitude 187, 190

gender communications: children 110–12; listening 111; translation tools 111–12

gender crossing: danger 45; pathology versus growth 41; as psychotic-fetishistic expression 42–6; saturated crossing 40–2; two types of 36–7

gender dichotomy 36, 38, 38–9, 44, 45

gender dysphoria 108, 132, 210; diagnosis 198–9, 205; in *DSM* 89, 209; history of 218; as measurable condition 181; theory of 213–16

gender excess 37, 40

gender-fluid/ity: and ghetto-like mentality 150; intersectional approach to 152–6; use of term 148–9

gender harassment 155

gender identity 52; belief in 200; children's knowledge of 113; invention of 199–200; and the penis 81; and sex-reassignment techniques 199–200; and sexuality 195

Gender Identity Center, UCLA 81

Gender Identity Disorder (GID) 132, 182, 199, 215–16

Gender Identity Disorder of Childhood Diagnosis (GIDC) 213–14, 215

gender mobility *see* gender crossing

gender non-conformity, use of term 1–2, 3, 195

gender novel 172–3

gender passing, as protective/defense mechanism 154, 212

gender presentation, as priority 153–5

gender roles 81, 200

gender space 39, 40

gender terrorism 84

gender variance: discipline and normalization 199–200; use of term 195

gender web 110–11

genitalia 112; rejection of 120, 126 n17

Gerdes, Kendall 16–17

Geyskens, Tomas 97

Gherovicci, Patricia 55, 90, 93, 95, 96, 173, 175, 176, 183; *Please Select Your Gender* 57 n2, 172

Gloucester County School Board 210–11

GnRH agonists 104

Godsey, Keelin 191 n3

Goffman, E. 133

golden ticket therapy: collaborative process 139–40; historical construction of disorder 131–3; managing stigma within the confines of pathology 133; manipulation: it was on *my* timeline *135*, 137–40; methodology 134; resistance: we're not crazy *135*, 140–3; strategies for managing stigma: submission, manipulation, and resistance 134–43, *135*; submission: doing what needs to be done 134–6, *135*; good enough mother 50

Gozlan, Oren 24, 45, 48, 52–3, 55, 56, 95, 173, 210, 212, 218, 219; "Questions of ethics and aesthetics for a profession in crisis" 218; *Transsexuality and the Art of Transition: A Lacanian Approach* 172, 186–7

Green, Andre, "Has sexuality anything to do with psychoanalysis?" 212

Green, James 184

Green, Richard 79, 102–3, 215

Greyson, John, *Murder in Passing* 59, 66

Grimm, Gavin 208, 209, 210–12, 213, 218–19

Guattari, Félix 171

Guernica Magazine 191 n11

Gutheil, Emil 78

Hadelman-Julius, E. 79

Halberstam, Jack 64

Hamburger, C. 80

Harrer, S. 202

Harris, Adrienne 46

Harry Benjamin Standards of Care 201

Hasselblad Center 17

Hausman, B. 81

health/healthiness 188; and gender 216; and homosexuality 177

Hempel, C. 217

hermaphrodite, use of term 195

Heyes, C. J. 203

Hidalgo, M. A. 106, 118
Hingis, Martina 185
Hirschfeld, Magnus 2, 77–8, 78–9; coined term "transvestite" 77; *Transvestites: The Erotic Drive to Cross-Dress* 77, 190 n1
homosexuality 78, 81, 174, 204; and health 177; Iran 160, 163; minoritizing positions on 58 n4; and pathology 183; removed from *DSM* 199; repressed/suppressed 171, 172, 173, 177; and rights 77; and sex-reassignment surgery 160–1
hormone therapy 44, 61, 62, 63, 65, 69, 79, 80–1, 85, 89, 90, 91, 103, 104, 106, 113, 122, 132, 135, 136, 140–1, 142, 159, 182, 184, 185, 187–8, 189, 194, 203
hospital, as curing machine 201
Hunter, Richard 171, 172, 173, 177, 178 n4
hysteria 95, 198; Freud's theory of 57 n2

identity: ideality of 6; theories of 57 n3; *see also* gender identity
image: of the double 19; and lack 23; mirror 19–20; as stolen 17
Imaginary, the 92–3, 97; through Lacanian angle 15–35
imperialism 57 n3
in-voice 175–6
Indian Act (Canada) 156 n2
Indigenous, use of term 156 n1
inter-disciplinary therapy 46–7
inter-rater agreement 214
interactive subjectivity 17
International Classification of Diseases (ICD) 160, 163
intersectional approach to gender-fluidity 152–6
intersex 117, 125 n8, 172, 191 n3, 194, 195, 200–2; activism 203; children 200, 201, 203; use of term 195
Intersex & Transgender Luxembourg asbl 121
invisibility 188
Iran *see* transgenderism in Iran
Irving, Dan 189

Jenner, Caitlyn 59, 60–1, 191 n3
Jorgensen, Christine 2, 8, 80, 190 n3
jouissance 91, 94, 95, 172
Joyce, James 85, 94
Joynt, Chase 48–59
judgment 69, 82
Jung, Carl Gustave 77, 170

Jupiter Ascending (Wachowski and Wachowski) 67, 68–9

Kafka, Franz 50
kappa statistic 214–15
Kendler, K. 216
King, D. 79
Kinsey, A. 81
kinship 178 n11
Klein, Melanie 39, 58 n5
Knape, Gunilla 16
knowledge, production of 197–8
Krafft-Ebing, Richard von 77, 79; *Psychopathia Sexualis* 78, 190 n1
Krauss, Friedrich S. 78
Kristenson, Örjan 16, 21
Kristeva, Julia 17
Kuhn, Thomas 209–10

Lacan, Jacques 23, 52, 53, 83, 89, 173; aporia of sexual difference 90; *The Clinic of Transference* 18–19; desire of the Other 90, 92, 94, 96, 99, 171; image of the double 19; the Imaginary 15–35, 92–3, 97; mirror as constitutive of the body 25; the Name of the Father 93–4, 94; penis/phallus identification 84, 86 n3; "pronominal embodiment" 97–8; *The Psychoses* 91; on psychosis 90, 91–2; the Real 45, 52, 84–5, 86 n3, 92–3, 96, 97–8, 176; on Schreber 170, 171; the semblant 20–1; the Symbolic 92, 93, 94, 97, 98; *On Transference* 19; "transsexualist jouissance" 91
Lacanian psychoanalysis 82–3, 85, 89, 172, 176, 178 n11; *see also* Gherovicci, Patricia; Millot, Catherine
lack 45, 56, 219; and image 23
Lane, C. 76
language 97–8, 190 n2, 201; *DSM* 183, 191 n5; and psychosis 91–2, 93; of wrongness 188
Laplanche, J, 174
Latino gender fluid youth, mental healthcare and 145–57
Laurent, Eric 91
Leader, D. 213, 215
Lévi-Strauss, Claude 178 n11
libidinal body 176
libido 21
libido theory (Freud) 171
life chances 188, 189, 191 n11
listen and act model *see* gender affirmation model
listening, as translation tool 111, 112

livability 85, 185–6
live in your own skin model 103–4, 105, 106, 109, 111, 113
Lorde, Audre, *Zami: A new spelling of my name* 178 n9
Lothstein, Leslie 79, 83
love 54
Lyotard, Jean-François 21, 23, 172

MacAlpine, Ida 171, 172, 173, 177, 178 n4
male-to-female (MTF) 82, 84, 161, 162
malignant containment 40
Martin, G. 176
maternal body 6–7
Maupassant, Guy de 19
Mauresmo, Amelie 185
McDougall, Joyce 24
medical care 189
medical certificate 159, 185; collaborative process 139–40; *see also* golden ticket therapy
medical discourse 213; resisting 202–3; and rights movements 201–2
medical intervention 105; and analytical work 97; diagnosis 118–19; *see also* hormone therapy; psychotherapy; sex-reassignment surgery; therapy
medical research 194–5
Meltzer, D. 6
mental health: instrumentalization of 218; and Latino gender-fluid youth 145–57
mental healthcare initiatives 151–2
mental healthcare services, barriers to access 147–8, 150, 154
mental illness 7–8, 203
mental space, lyrical dimension of 39–40
Meyerowitz, Joanne 79, 81, 184
microscopic gaze 8
Milchman, A. 202
Millot, Catherine 84, 85, 173, 177; "horsexe" 170; *Horsexe* 84, 89, 94–9, 172
Milner, Marion 56–7
Mind the Gap 108
mindful present 62, 63, 68
mirror image 19–20, 25
mirroring, as translation tool 111–12, 112
misgendering 111–12
models of identification 151–2
modernity 57 n3
Moebius strip 19
Molkara, Ms. 158
Money, John 79, 81, 200, 201, 215
Morel, Geneviève 98; *Sexual Ambiguities* 91
Morgan, Diane 173

mother: and child imaginary 49–50; role of 82
Munchhausen by proxy syndrome 120
Muñoz, José Esteban 67
mutilation 43, 44–5, 46

Name of the Father (Lacan) 93–4, 94
names 97–8, 120, 121, 122, 124, 190 n2
Nancy, Jean-Luc 22, 23
narrative, and the libidinal body 176
natal sex 98; as determinant of gender 187; working through 190
National Post 103
neoliberalism 184, 188–9, 191 n10; use of term 191 n6
neurosis 90, 92, 94, 98–9, 198
New Lacanian School, France 91
Niederland, W. 171
non-compliance 56, 57 n3
non-verbal communication 119
normalizing approach 118, 119

object a 19–20
object relations theory 52
Oedipus Complex (Freud) 76, 85, 171, 178 n11
OISE 146
Olson, K. R. 118
Other/Otherness 93, 94, 95; identification with 98–9; perfect union with 95–6
other room/this room 39
Otte, George 175–6
outing 121, 126 n24
outsidesex 84, 85, 95
Oversey, Lionel 82

Paniagua, F. 155
paraphilia 78
parasitical relations 40–1
parenthood 119–20
parents: accepting parental approach 124–5; got child's sex wrong 112; and third party hostility 120; *see also* family; mother; paternal metaphor
Parker, Ian, *Lacanian Psychoanalysis* 212
Parnas, J. 216, 217
past, rejecting 41
Pasteur, Louis 198
paternal metaphor 90, 93, 94, 179 n11
pathologization, critique of 188
pathology 6, 51–2, 57 n2, 75–6, 79, 118; versus growth 41; history of 131–3; and homosexuality 183; and social context 107; and stigma 133

patients: declaration of mental illness 198–9; subjectification of 197–8; *see also* strategies for managing stigma: submission, manipulation, and resistance
pedagogues 124
penis envy 76
penis, the: confused with phallus 84, 86 n3, 97, 98; and gender identity 81; *see also* phallus, the
Person, Ethel Spector 82
phallus, imaginary identification with 84
phallus, the 4, 86 n3, 95: confused with penis 84, 97, 98; and the Imaginary 93; maternal 78; *see also* penis, the
phantasm 21
phantasy 58 n5
Phelan, Tom 191 n3
Phillips, Adam 213
Phillips, Rasheedah 69
photographic truth 22
photography: and outgoing transformations 25; *see also Place Blanche* (Strömholm); Strömholm, Christer
pictogram 19
Place Blanche (Strömholm) 18
play 119, 123, 126 n14; and psychoanalysis 50; and self-discovery 50; as translation tool 112
Plett, Casey 172–3
Pontalis, Jean-Bertrand 24
primal longings 50
projective transformations 46
"pronominal embodiment" (Lacan) 97–8
pronouns 60, 61, 63, 97–8, 107, 124, 154
Prosser, Jay 85, 148, 149, 169, 176, 183, 184, 185; *Second Skins: The body narratives of transsexuality* 60
protest 57 n3
psychiatric questioning 198–9
psychoanalysis 41, 48, 52, 57 n2, 75–6, 191 n9; cross-dressing 77–8; paraphilia 78; perspectives on identity 57 n3; and play 50; *psychopathia transexualis* 78–9; transgender and psychosis 82–5; transsexualism 79–82; and wrong-body narrative (WBN) 182
psychoanalytic work: the Name of the Father 93–4; what did Lacan say about psychosis? 91–2
psychoanalytical work, *Horsexe* 94–9
psychological gender, and biological sex 200
psychological research, with border youth 149–51

psychological sex, as learned 200
psychology, decolonizing 145–7
psychopathia transexualis 78–9
psychosexual deviance 198–9
psychosis 42–6, 82–5, 92, 98; Lacan on 90, 91–2; and language 91–2, 93
psychosocial stress 123, 124
psychotherapy 41, 122, 125; children and youth 111; cleft-lip and cleft tongue 42–6; oppressive 145–57
Puar, Jasbir 188
puberty 44, 105–6, 109, 112, 117, 122, 124
puberty blockers 103–4, 105, 106, 113, 122, 124
public interest 181, 190 n3
pulsional theory (Freud) 21–2, 23
push-toward Woman (Lacan) 89, 90, 92, 93, 94, 172

queer affect 53
queer coincidental time 68
queer theory 58 n4, 178 n11; and temporality 64
Quinodoz, Danielle 41, 42, 83

Rabinow, P. 196, 199
Rank, Otto 39
re-transition 124
Real jouissance 93
Real, the (Lacan) 45, 52, 84–5, 86 n3, 92–3, 96, 97–8, 176
referrals 102
Rekers, G. 215
religious conversion, compared with sex transition 51
reparation 53, 55
Repo, J. 200, 201
reproduction 197, 202, 205
"return of the referent" (Rose) 216
Reucher, Tom 126 n13
Richards, Renée 186
Rickman, John 7
rights movements: children 124, 125; homosexuals 77; and medical discourse 201–2
rigid motion gender crossing 46
rigid motion transformations 45–6
role models 151–2
Rose, Jacqueline, "return of the referent" 216
Rose, N. 196, 199
Rosenberg, A. 202
Rosenhan, D. 214
Russell, H. 105

Index

SAIL IN (Support | Acceptance | Information | Learning) 121
Saketopoulou, Avgi 189, 190, 191 n9; "Mourning the body as bedrock: Developmental considerations in treating transsexual patients analytically" 187
Salah, Trish 51; *Writing Times* 178 n7
Salamon, Gayle 85; *Assuming a Body: Transgender and the Rhetoric of Materiality* 82
Sander, Gilman 172
Santner, Eric 171, 174, 175; *My Own Private Germany: Daniel Paul Schreber's Secret History of Modernity* 178 n7
saturated crossing 40–2
saturated gender dichotomy 38–9, 41, 46
Sawyer, Diane 60, 61
Schatzman, M. 171
Schilt, Kristen 62
school 121–2, 124; Iran 162
Schreber, Daniel Paul 91, 92, 93–4, 173; as abject 172; as abused 171; as anti-Oedipal 171; as anti-Semitic 71–2; "bellowing miracle" 176; birds 174–5; "cross sexed wish" 170; as fascist 171; feminization of 93–4, 170, 171, 172, 173, 175, 177; Freud on 170–1, 172, 173, 177; *Great Thoughts of A Nerve Patient* 170–1; Lacan on 170, 171; *Memoirs of My Nervous Illness* 169–70, 172, 174–5, 176; as Oedipal 170; Order of the World 171, 174; persecutory transference 171; "a return to" 169–80; as transsexual 172; Schreber-in-Freud 171–2
Schreber, Moritz 171
scientific discursivity 197
Sedgwick, Eve 58 n4
self-constitution 202, 203
semblant, the (Lacan) 20–1
settlement 153–4
sex-reassignment surgery 41, 42, 44–5, 46, 52, 56, 79, 80, 81, 84, 85, 90, 91, 96, 97, 99 n2, 103, 104, 112, 135, 136, 140–1, 142, 182, 184, 185, 187–8, 189, 194, 199–200, 203, 204; and homosexuals 160–1; incompleteness of 188, 189–90; Iran 159–60, 161–2
sex-transition, compared with religious conversion 51
Sexology 78
sexual apparatus, a biopolitical tool of biopower 200
sexual difference 8
sexual force, and *object a* 20

sexual trauma 51
sexual violence 51
sexuality 58 n4; and adolescent development 218; aesthetic shift in thinking about 218; assumptions about 208; and biological sex 196–7; and biology 218; and child development 212; discourses of, within history of madness 199; and education 212–13; excess of 219; Freud's theory of 58 n4; and gender identity 195; and power 196; reification of 215; study of, and wrong-body narrative 183
sexuality: adolescent, signifying frame for 217–18
shame 105
sharing time (Bastian) 64–5
Shepherdson, Charles 84, 98
sign, as an object 216–17
sinthome 53–4, 172, 178 n4
social justice approach 156
social transition 120–2
social work 124
Soler, Colette 218
Spade, Dan 191 n11
Spitzer, Robert 213–14
splitting 44, 45, 217–18
Standards of Care for Gender Identity Disorders 132
Standards of Care (SOC) 132
Stein, Ruth 83
Steinach, Eugen 79, 85
Stekel, Wilhelm 77, 78; *Sexual Aberrations: The Phenomenon of Fetishism in Relation to Sex* 78
stereotypes 118
Stewart, Suzanne 146
stigma 188: Iran 161, 162–4; management among trans men 131–43; and pathology 133
Stokes, Adam 18
Stoller, Robert 79, 81–2
Stone, Sandy 184
strategic existentialism 5
Strömholm, Christer 15–35; construction of the subject 21–2; sameness 22
Stryker, Susan 1, 24, 79, 178 n3, 190 n1
subjugation 202
Suchet, Melanie 97
suffering, operationalizing 216–17
suicidiality 120
Sullivan, Nikki 18
Sunden, Jenny 61
Symbolic, the (Lacan) 92, 93, 94, 97, 98
symptoms, stabilizing 216–17

Tabare 151, 152, 154
taking (my) time: "classic" trans temporalities 60–1; conclusion: present dangers, present hopes 69–70; disrupting the progress 61–4; hung up out of fugue states 64–6; seizing time 66–9
Tangerine (Baker) 67–8
Tehran Psychiatric Institute 159, 161, 162
Thanatos 23, 24
The Skin I Live In (Almodovar) 161
The Transgender Studies Reader 190 n1
therapist: delinking 211; disapproving 140; flexibility of 138–9; meaning attached to term 155–6
therapy: as a barrier 138; and biographical information 136–7; collaborative letter-writing process 139–40; criticizing psychological diagnoses 140–1; and empathy 139–40; emphasizing transgender diversity 141; ending 142; ending relationships with disapproving therapists 140; fixed timeline for 139; and flexibility of therapist 138–9; includes constructions of strategic narratives 136–7; inter-disciplinary 46–7; and loss of agency 135–6, 138; power dynamics of 139; power imbalances 147; power imbalances of 138; supportive and elective 141–2; as temporary means to an end 136; trans-disciplinary 46
Thurer, Shari 83
Tipton, Billy 190 n3
Tiresian poetics 169
Title IX, Education Amendment 208, 211
toys 119, 123, 126 n14
transgender, use of term 8
trans: as birth defect 188; depathologization 183, 188; and disability 188, 191 n10; pathologization of 184; use of term 178 n2, 181, 190 n2; *see also* transgender; transsexuality
trans*, use of term 178 n2
trans-affirmative practice 191 n9
trans-disciplinary therapy 46
trans genre 169, 173
trans identities, politicization of 63–4
Trans-Kinder-Netz 121, 126 n11, 126 n12
trans-normativity 181, 184
Trans Pulse Survey 90
transformations in hallucinosis 46
transformations in K 46
transgender: and psychosis 82–5; queering of 203; use of term 1–2, 3, 34 n1, 57 n1, 99 n1, 143 n1, 178 n2

transgender performativity 15–16
transgenderism: and pathology 84; use of term 47 n1, 158
transgenderism in Iran: effects of legal favoritism toward transsexuality 160–1; epidemiology of transsexuality and sex-reassignment outcomes 161–2; overview of current situation 158–60; stigma 161, 162–4; transition, use of term 191 n6
transition and childhood: childhood and parenthood 119–20; professionals and childhood: considering whose needs 123–5; questioning medical interventions 115–16; social transition: what?—when?—who has to decide? 120–2; terminology, definitions, and concepts 116–19
transitional space (Winnicott) 22
transphobic social world 184–5
transsexual, use of term 8, 143 n1, 178 n2
transsexual embodiment 97
transsexual temporality 52, 60–1, 62–3, 64
transsexualism 79–82; biological aspect of 80–1; as experiment 81, 82; palliative treatment 82; replaced with Gender Identity Disorder (GID 132
transsexuality 57 n3, 78; among both sexes 161–2; "born this way" 45; caesura or cut? 38–42, 45, 46; definition of 48, 49, 57 n2; epidemiology of 161–2; favoritism toward 160–1; first use of word 78; kinship to trauma 53; as palliative 82, 90, 92, 94, 96, 97; and pathology 6, 94; and psychosis 89–91; as social construct 52; trajectories of 204; use of term 1–2, 3, 47 n1, 57 n1, 158, 173
transvestitism/transvestites 80, 81, 82; as asexual 78; and paraphilia 78; queering of 203; use of term 8, 77, 78, 173; *see also* cross-dressing; Strömholm, Christer
trust 155
20/20 60

Ulrichs, Karl Heinrich 80, 183
uncanny, the (Freud) 20
unconscious, Freud's theory of 57 n2
United Nations' Convention on the Rights of the Child 119, 120–1, 124
unmetabolized affect 53
Urbild-ideal (Lacan) 19
US–UK Diagnostic Project 214
utility based model 214

Van Haut, Phillipe 96–7
Vanheule, S. 216
Vanity Fair 60
verbal hallucinations 91, 92
Vu agency 17

Wachowski, L. and Wachowski, L. 67
wait and see approach 118–19; *see also* watchful waiting model
Wallace, R. 105
Walters, W. 196
watchful waiting model 104–6, 109
Westbrook, Laurel 62
Whittle, Stephen 1, 79, 83, 190 n1
Wiedner, Kati 126 n11
Williams, M. H. 6
Winnicott, D. W. 7–8, 39, 49, 52, 53, 56; good enough mother 50; play 50; transitional space 22
Woolf, Virginia, *Orlando* 36–8, 42

working through 53
World Professional Association for Transgender Health (WPATH) 105, 132; *see also* WPATH SOC
WPATH SOC 132, 134–5, 136, 137, 138, 140, 141, 142–3
wrong body: notion of 182; trapped in 203; *see also* wrong-body narrative (WBN)
wrong-body narrative (WBN) 181; de-pathologization 183; development and proliferation of 182; and gender binary 184–5; notion of "wrong body" 182; producing a wrong body 183–90; and psychoanalysis 182; and study of sexuality 183; and trans-cis dichotomy 186–7; two key functions of 185
wrongness, language of 188

Zeitschfrit für Sexualwissencraft 77
Zucker, Kenneth 103, 213–14